# Programming for Game Design

## A Hands-On Guide with Godot

Wallace Wang
Tonnetta Walcott

Apress®

*Programming for Game Design: A Hands-On Guide with Godot*

Wallace Wang
San Diego, CA, USA

Tonnetta Walcott
El Cajon, CA, USA

ISBN-13 (pbk): 979-8-8688-0189-1
https://doi.org/10.1007/979-8-8688-0190-7

ISBN-13 (electronic): 979-8-8688-0190-7

Managing Director, Apress Media LLC: Welmoed Spahr
Acquisitions Editor: Miriam Haidara
Development Editor: James Markham
Editorial Assistant: Jessica Vakili

Cover designed by eStudioCalamar
Cover image designed by Freepik (www.freepik.com)

Distributed to the book trade worldwide by Springer Science+Business Media New York, 1 New York Plaza, Suite 4600, New York, NY 10004-1562, USA. Phone 1-800-SPRINGER, fax (201) 348-4505, e-mail orders-ny@springer-sbm.com, or visit www.springeronline.com. Apress Media, LLC is a California LLC and the sole member (owner) is Springer Science + Business Media Finance Inc (SSBM Finance Inc). SSBM Finance Inc is a **Delaware** corporation.

For information on translations, please e-mail booktranslations@springernature.com; for reprint, paperback, or audio rights, please e-mail bookpermissions@springernature.com.

Apress titles may be purchased in bulk for academic, corporate, or promotional use. eBook versions and licenses are also available for most titles. For more information, reference our Print and eBook Bulk Sales web page at http://www.apress.com/bulk-sales.

Any source code or other supplementary material referenced by the author in this book is available to readers on GitHub. For more detailed information, please visit https://www.apress.com/gp/services/source-code.

Paper in this product is recyclable

# Table of Contents

# About the Authors

**Wallace Wang** has been writing computer books for over 30 years, including *Steal This Computer Book, Microsoft Office for Dummies, Beginning Programming for Dummies, Beginning iPhone Development with SwiftUI*, and *The Structure of Game Design*, to name just a few. He created the board game "Orbit War" for Steve Jackson Games, which simulated satellite warfare in the near future. He also writes screenplays and won first place in Scriptapalooza's 2023 screenwriting competition.

**Tonnetta Walcott** is a writer, podcaster, gamer, and programmer who is passionate about video games and technology. She graduated from San Diego State University with a bachelor's in English and has a certificate in computer programming. After being offered an internship at Sony Online Entertainment, Tonnetta learned computer programming (C++ and Java), web development, and game design using the Unity and Godot game engines. Tonnetta has programmed a simulation to chess, Battleship, and a matching concentration game and is currently working on a game called NinChibi, where tiny chibi ninjas play tag in single-player and multiplayer modes. The NinChibi game is built with the Godot game engine.

# About the Technical Reviewer

**Massimo Nardone** has more than 27 years of experience in security, web/mobile development, and cloud and IT architecture. His true IT passions are security and Android. He has been programming and teaching how to program with Android, Perl, PHP, Java, VB, Python, C/C++, and MySQL for more than 27 years. He holds a Master of Science degree in Computing Science from the University of Salerno, Italy. He has worked as chief information security officer (CISO), software engineer, chief security architect, security executive, and OT/IoT/IIoT security leader and architect for many years.

# CHAPTER 1

# Why Learn Programming with the Godot Game Engine?

Many people want to learn programming because the idea of creating a program can be fun and exciting. Although programming is a skill that anyone can learn, far too many beginner programming books and courses forget about making programming fun right from the start.

Programming appeals to people because they want to create projects that are interesting and show off their programming skills. Unfortunately, the time for novices to gain the necessary skills to achieve their dreams can take way too long. The end result is that too many programming students give up because they fail to see how the skills that they gradually learn can be useful in achieving the dreams that they want to achieve.

It doesn't have to be that way. Persistency and patience are key. Programming is about trial and error; however, it comes with the reward of successfully completing a task.

© Wallace Wang, Tonnetta Walcott 2024
W. Wang and T. Walcott, *Programming for Game Design*,
https://doi.org/10.1007/979-8-8688-0190-7_1

That's why this book is different. All beginning programming books and courses must start with the basics. Unfortunately, those basics provide minimal feedback to make programming interesting. That's why this book teaches the principles of programming using the Godot game engine. Besides Unity and Unreal Engine, Godot is a top upcoming game engine used to make mobile games, PC games, and any type of video game overall.

Learning to program through a game engine can offer greater motivation. Rather than learn programming in isolation, it's far better to use a student's interest and familiarity with video games to learn the basics of programming while also learning how video games work. By visually seeing, changing, and controlling simple video game elements using their fledging programming skills, beginners can get instant feedback in a meaningful way. This can help motivate students to keep learning more.

While there are plenty of game engines students can use, the Godot game engine is unique for several reasons. First, the Godot game engine runs on the three major operating systems for personal computers: Windows, macOS, and Linux. That means the Godot game engine is accessible to the greatest number of students than most other game engines.

Second, the Godot game engine is open source and completely free. There are no licensing fees or restrictions for anyone to use the Godot game engine. This makes Godot available to everyone.

Third, and most importantly, the Godot game engine is far smaller than most of the major game engines on the market today. The Godot game engine can run just fine on older and slower computers with minimal storage that cannot run many other game engines. This makes the Godot game engine especially suitable for most people who do not have access to the latest, fastest, or most expensive computers on the market that most other game engines require before you can use them. Godot also excels in building 2D platforms and has recently been updated to also support 3D games.

Because the Godot game engine is free, runs on all the major platforms (Windows, macOS, and Linux), and runs on older, slower computers, the Godot game engine offers a perfect introduction to both programming and video game development.

You won't learn how to develop the next massively multiplayer AAA game title from this book, but you will learn programming principles and basics in a fun and engaging manner. Although Godot uses its own proprietary programming language called GDScript, it's based on Python and C. That means learning GDScript will prepare students to learn other programming languages in the future.

So if you're interested in both programming and video games, this book is for you. We'll start with the basics of a video game, then focus on programming principles common in all programming languages. Finally, we'll focus on the specifics to making 2D video games. By the time you complete this book, you should have a solid understanding of programming principles and video game development.

This book will make programming fun by teaching video game design in an accessible, fun, and interesting step-by-step manner. When you finish this book, you'll be well on your way to creating more sophisticated programs and more complex video games. This book can help open the doors to the fun and excitement of programming and video game development. After this book, the entire world of programming and video game development will be open to you no matter what programming language or game engine you choose next.

As the Chinese proverb states, "A journey of a thousand miles begins with a single step." Let this book be your first step and you'll find that programming can be just as fun and exciting as you always thought it should be.

# CHAPTER 2

# Getting to Know Godot

The best way to learn any new skill is to start practicing it and not be afraid of making a mistake. To learn programming, you need to spend time practicing on your computer, so before you go any further, download and install the Godot game engine (`https://godotengine.org`) on your computer. Once you've installed Godot, you won't need to install any other programs to write programs in Godot. Remember, practicing takes time and patience in order to be good at something. Learning Godot is a fresh start!

The main steps to using Godot involve creating, editing, and running a project. A project represents a complete video game. Each time you want to create a different video game, you'll need to create a separate project. Godot isolates projects by storing them in different folders. The more projects that you create, the more you'll understand the mechanisms of Godot. Still, it would be wise to focus on one project at a time to avoid overload.

Although projects represent a complete video game, you may want to create projects to test out different ideas. For example, you might want to create a project to test out a combat system and another project to test out an inventory system. Separate projects let you experiment with different ideas in isolation, making them easier and faster to test without worrying about integrating with the rest of an existing project.

© Wallace Wang, Tonnetta Walcott 2024
W. Wang and T. Walcott, *Programming for Game Design*,
https://doi.org/10.1007/979-8-8688-0190-7_2

While you can create as many projects as you wish, you'll most likely spend the bulk of your time editing an existing project rather than creating new projects. Editing a project involves several tasks. The first way to edit any project is to add assets such as graphic items to represent players, obstacles, or background images. The best part of the project is that you can be as creative as you want with your assets to your game. There are different ways to create or obtain assets with enough research, so you don't have to make everything yourself.

Once you've added assets to a project, a second way to edit a project is to modify the assets such as defining their position on the game field, their size, their orientation, and their appearance. Assets have both a physical appearance and a spatial location that you can define. Take as much time as you need to modify and position your assets in order to build a fun, playable, and functional game.

The appearance and position of assets create a static image. To make a project interactive, you'll need to write scripts that define how an asset should behave when your project runs. A script is a code or program that gives instructions to make assets function in a certain way. You will learn more about scripts later on throughout this book. For example, a cartoon car might need to avoid running into trees, telephone poles, and other cars. If that should happen, then the cartoon car needs to change its appearance to show the results of the crash. In addition, the cartoon car should also behave differently after it's been damaged.

In Godot, such scripts are written in a proprietary language called GDScript, which resembles the Python programming language. Scripts let assets in a project respond to user control through a keyboard or touch screen and interact with other game assets.

A cartoon spaceship might fire lasers that can destroy asteroids in the way. This might require a script to control and fire lasers from the spaceship and another script for the asteroid to detect when it's been hit by a laser. Essentially, scripts make assets interactive and controllable by the user.

Editing a project lets you change the way the project looks and behaves. To test if your project looks and works the way you want, you'll need to run the project periodically. These three steps (creating a project, editing a project, and running a project) define the main actions you'll take while using Godot.

# Creating and Opening a Godot Project

When you use a word processor, you create an empty document that you can fill with words that you can rearrange and format to change its appearance. Likewise, when you use a game engine like Godot, you create a bare-bones video game that you can fill with graphics and audio that you can rearrange and modify to change their appearance.

Before you can use Godot, you must first know how to create a Godot project. Every Godot project must be stored in a folder. To avoid mixing Godot files with any existing files, it's best to create a new, empty folder to hold your Godot project.

To create a new Godot project, follow these steps:

1.  Start Godot. Godot displays a Project Manager window. The Project Manager window lists any previously opened Godot projects as well as gives you options to create a new project as shown in Figure 2-1.

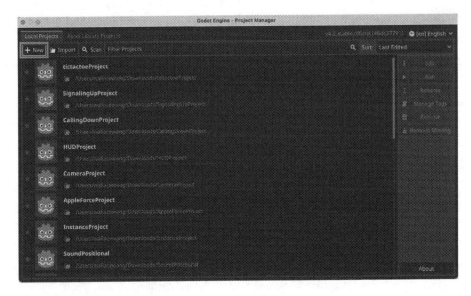

**Figure 2-1.** *The Project Manager window*

2.  Click New in the upper left corner. A Create New
    Project dialog box appears as shown in Figure 2-2.
    Godot requires that you create a new folder for each
    project.

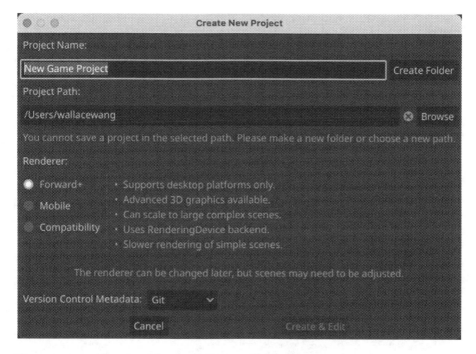

*Figure 2-2.* The Create New Project dialog box

3.  Click the Browse button in the Project Path. A dialog box appears, showing all the folders available.

4.  Click a folder where you want to store your Godot project and click Select Current Folder.

5.  Click the Project Name text field and type a folder name to store your project. (The default folder/ project name is New Game Project.)

6.  Click the Create Folder button.

7.  (Optional) Click the Option button to choose a renderer version. For this project, it doesn't matter which renderer option you choose.

9

8.  Click the Create & Edit button. Godot creates
    an empty project in the folder that you selected
    in step 4.

Once you've created at least one Godot project, you can open
that project at a later time. To open an existing Godot project, follow
these steps:

1.  Start Godot. Godot displays a Project Manager
    window (see Figure 2-1).

2.  Click the Import button. An Import Existing Project
    dialog box appears as shown in Figure 2-3.

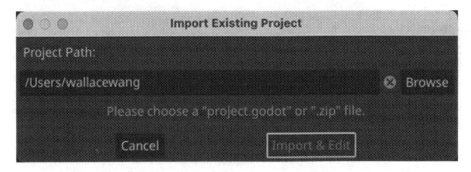

*Figure 2-3.* *The Import Existing Project dialog box*

3.  Click the Browse button. A Directories & Files dialog
    box appears as shown in Figure 2-4.

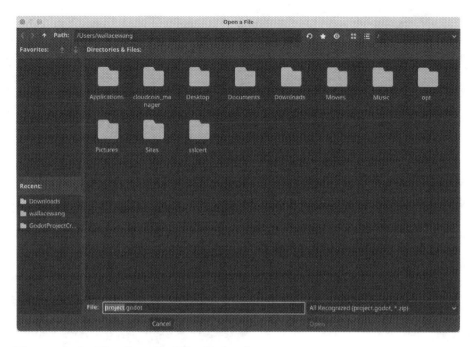

***Figure 2-4.*** *The Open a File dialog box*

4.  Double-click the folder that contains the Godot
    project file that you want to load. (You may need to
    repeat this process until you find the project.godot
    file that you want to load as shown in Figure 2-5.)

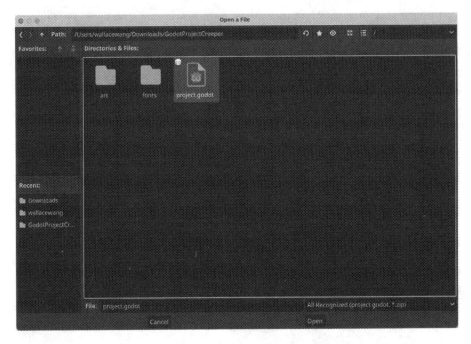

***Figure 2-5.*** *Look for the project.godot file stored in your Godot project folder*

5.    Click the project.godot file and then click the Open button. Godot loads your chosen project.

If you had created or opened a project recently, the name of your project may appear in the Project Manager window (see Figure 2-1). In that case, you can skip all of the preceding steps and simply double-click the Godot project you want to open that appears in the Project Manager window.

# Creating a Scene and Nodes

Whether you create a new project or open an existing project, you'll see the Godot editor window where you can add, delete, and modify the different parts of your project. The main window in the center of the screen, called the viewport, is where you can create and modify data.

The viewport can display two types of project data:

- Graphic elements that define the visual appearance of a scene (2D or 3D)

- GDScript code that defines how to respond to an action such as the user pressing a key or the objects colliding (Script)

In Godot, a project consists of one or more scenes. One scene might define a game level or playing field, a second scene might define the player in the level or playing field, and a third scene might define a weapon that the player can hold. Godot stores scenes in files that end with the .tscn file extension as shown in Figure 2-6.

***Figure 2-6.*** *Every Godot scene gets stored in a file with the .tscn file extension*

A single scene consists of one or more nodes where nodes provide additional features for customizing the appearance or behavior of a scene. One node might define an area to detect collisions, while another node might define the graphic images to display on the screen as shown in Figure 2-7.

*Figure 2-7.* *A scene can consist of multiple nodes*

To design the visual appearance of your Godot project, you'll need
to create one or more scenes and then customize each scene with one or
more nodes.

To see how to create a scene and add a node, follow these steps:

1.  Create a new Godot project and give it a descriptive
    name. Until you add a scene, Godot displays a menu
    of the different types of scenes you can add as the
    initial or root node as shown in Figure 2-8.

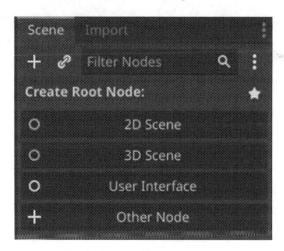

*Figure 2-8.* *Choosing an initial scene for a project*

2.   Click Other Node. A Create New Node window
     appears as shown in Figure 2-9.

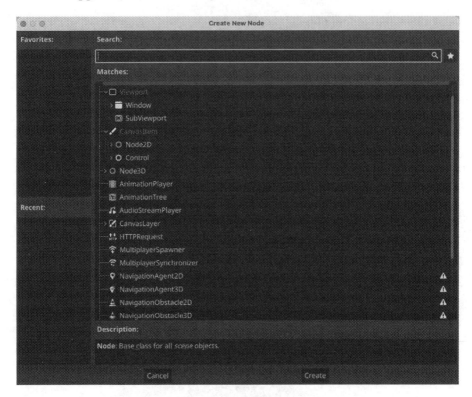

***Figure 2-9.*** *The Create New Node window*

3.   Click the Search text field at the top of the Create
     New Node window and type ***node***. The Create New
     Node window only displays those options that
     contain the word "node" as shown in Figure 2-10.

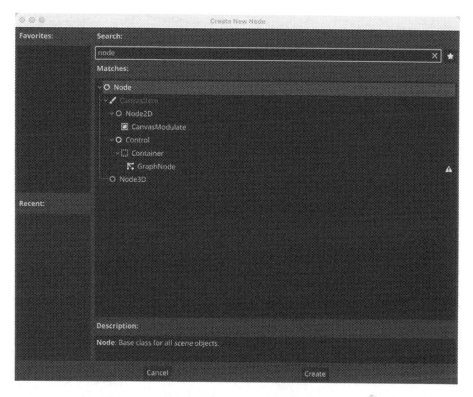

***Figure 2-10.*** *Typing in the Search text field filters out the list of options*

4. Click Node2D and click the Create button. Godot displays the Node2D in the Scene dock, a cross representing the Node2D in the viewport, and all the different properties you can change in the Node2D in the Inspector pane as shown in Figure 2-11.

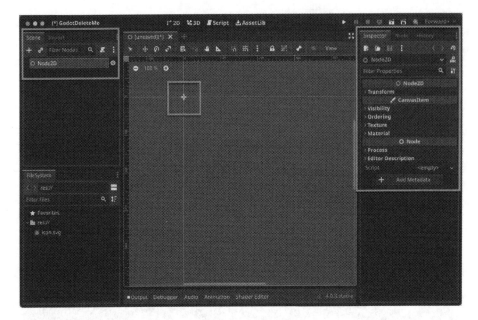

**Figure 2-11.** *The Node2D in the Godot editor*

5.  Click the Node2D in the Scene dock to select it. To
    display a graphic image on the Node2D, we need
    to attach another node, called a child node, to
    the Node2D.

6.  Attach a child node to the Node2D using one of the
    following methods as shown in Figure 2-12:

    •  Click the Add Child Node icon that appears as
       a + icon.

    •  Press Ctrl+A (Windows/Linux) or Command+A
       (Macintosh).

    •  Right-click, and when a pop-up menu appears,
       choose Add Child Node.

Another Create New Node window appears (see Figure 2-9).

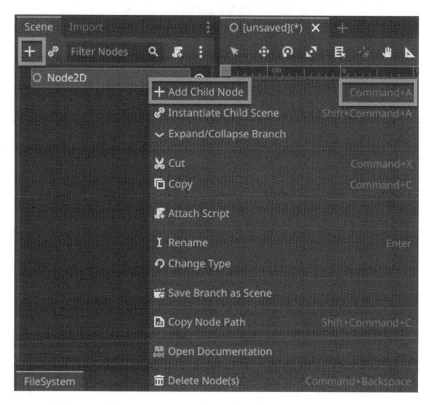

***Figure 2-12.*** *Adding a child node*

7. Click the Search text field at the top of the Create New Node window and type **sprite**.

8. Click Sprite2D and click the Create button. The Scene dock displays the Sprite2D node as a child attached to Node2D as shown in Figure 2-13.

***Figure 2-13.*** *The Sprite2D child node attached to Node2D*

9. Click Sprite2D in the Scene dock to select it. Notice that the Inspector dock now displays properties you can modify.

10. Click <empty> in the Texture property in the Inspector dock. A pop-up menu appears as shown in Figure 2-14.

*Figure 2-14. The Texture pop-up menu in the Inspector dock*

11.   Choose Load or Quick Load. A dialog box appears as shown in Figure 2-15.

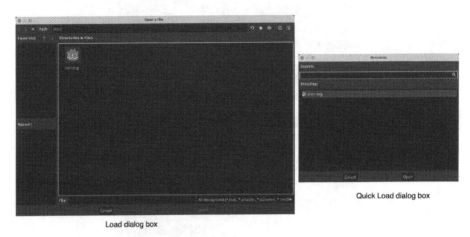

Load dialog box

Quick Load dialog box

***Figure 2-15.***   *The Load and Quick Load dialog boxes*

12.   Click icon.svg and click Open. Godot displays the icon.svg graphic image in the viewport as shown in Figure 2-16.

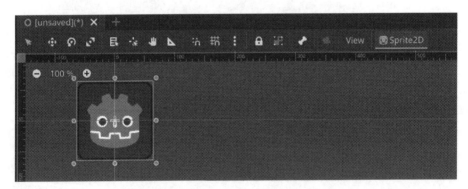

***Figure 2-16.***   *The icon.svg graphic file displayed in the viewport*

13. Choose Scene ➤ Save Scene or choose Ctrl+S
    (Windows/Linux) or Command+S (Macintosh).
    A Save Scene As dialog box appears. The default
    name is node_2d.tscn, but you can give it a more
    descriptive name if you wish.

14. Click Save. Godot saves your changes to the
    project. It's generally a good idea to save your scene
    periodically to avoid losing data if your computer
    crashes.

At this point, we've created a scene (Node2D). Since the Node2D
doesn't look like anything, we attached a child node to it (Sprite2D). Using
this Sprite2D node, we could then display a graphic image through the
Sprite2D's Texture property to load the icon.svg file.

# Viewing and Modifying a Scene

After creating a scene, attaching child nodes, and modifying the different
properties of these nodes, you can test what the scene looks when it's
actually running. To run a project, follow these steps:

1. Click the Run icon at the top of the screen as shown
   in Figure 2-17. The first time you run a project, it
   may ask you to define the main scene, which is the
   first scene to appear.

*Figure 2-17.* *The Run icon*

23

2.  (Optional) If a dialog box appears, asking for you to choose a main scene, click the Select Current button to use the currently open scene. When a project runs, it appears in a (DEBUG) window. Notice that the image, stored in the Sprite2D node, appears partially cut off in the upper left corner of the window as shown in Figure 2-18.

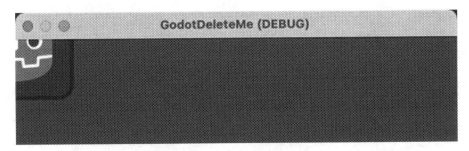

*Figure 2-18.*   *The icon.svg image appears partially cut off*

3.  Click the close icon in the (DEBUG) window to stop running the project.

You may wonder why the graphic image appears partially cut off in the upper left corner of the (DEBUG) window. That's because the upper left corner is the default position every time you create a node. To see how to view the contents of a scene, follow these steps:

1.  Click the Node2D in the Scene dock to select it. Notice that the icon.svg graphic image appears at the origin of an x axis (red horizontal line) and y axis (green vertical line) as shown in Figure 2-19.

Move    Rotate    Scale

Distraction Free Mode icon

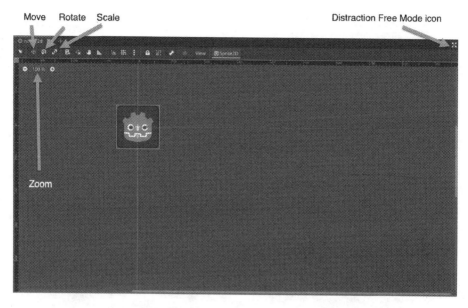

Zoom

***Figure 2-19.*** *Displaying the Node2D in the viewport*

2. Click the Distraction Free Mode icon in the upper
   right corner of the viewport window twice. This icon
   toggles between expanding the viewport window
   to fill the entire screen or shrinking it down to also
   display the Scene, FileSystem, and Inspector docks
   on the left and right side of the screen.

3. Click the – and + Zoom icons in the upper left corner
   of the viewport window. The – icon decreases the
   magnification of the viewport window, while the +
   icon increases magnification.

4.  Click the – Zoom icon until the magnification displays 50%. At 50% magnification, Godot displays a faint outline that defines the size of the project window as shown in Figure 2-20. Notice that 50% magnification makes it easy to see the entire project window boundary and how the icon.svg appears cut off in the upper left corner of the window when you run the project.

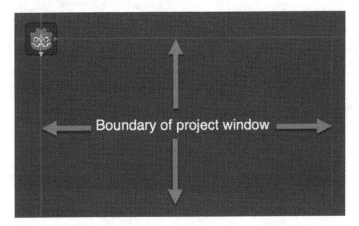

*Figure 2-20.*  *At 50% magnification, the viewport displays the faint outline of the project window*

5.  Choose Project ➤ Project Setting. A Project Settings window appears.

6.  Click Window under the Display category. Notice that you can now change the Viewport Width and Height as shown in Figure 2-21.

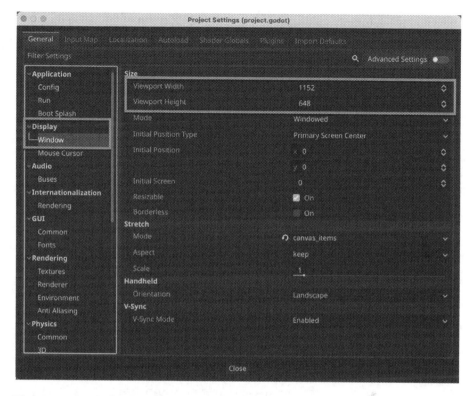

***Figure 2-21.*** *The Project Settings window lets you change the size of the window when your project runs*

7. (Optional) Change the Viewport Width and Viewport Height values.

8. Click the Close button. The Project Settings window goes away. Let's move the position of Node2D so it doesn't appear in the upper left corner of the window.

9. Click the Node2D in the Scene dock to select it.

10. Click the Move icon (see Figure 2-19). Godot displays a right-pointing arrow (red) and a downward-pointing arrow (green) as shown in Figure 2-22.

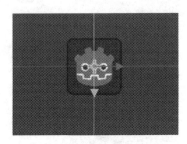

***Figure 2-22.*** *The Move icon displays an x axis and y axis arrow on the selected node*

11. Drag the red and green arrows to position the Node2D in the middle of the window outline.

12. Click the Run icon. The (DEBUG) window appears, but notice that the icon.svg image now appears near the middle of the window where you dragged the Node2D.

13. Click the close icon of the (DEBUG) window to stop running the project.

# Rotating and Scaling a Node

By using the Move icon, you can change a node's position from the upper left corner of the project window (where it got partially cut off) to the middle of the project window. In addition to the Move icon, you can also use the Rotate and Scale icons to modify the appearance of the Node2D.

The Rotate icon lets you rotate a node in different positions, while the Scale icon lets you shrink or enlarge an icon. To see how to use the Rotate and Scale icons, follow these steps:

1. Click the Node2D in the Scene dock to select it.

2. Click the Rotate icon near the top of the viewport.

3. Move the mouse pointer over the icon.svg image and drag the mouse clockwise and counterclockwise to rotate the image.

4. Press Ctrl+Z (Windows/Linux) or Command+Z (Macintosh) to undo any rotation you added to the image.

5. Click the Scale icon near the top of the viewport. A red line and square (x axis) and green line and square (y axis) appears on the selected node as shown in Figure 2-23.

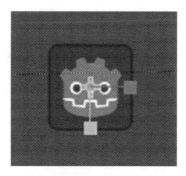

***Figure 2-23.*** *The Scale lines and squares*

6. Drag the red square right and left. Notice that this expands and shrinks the width of the selected image.

7. Press Ctrl+Z (Windows/Linux) or Command+Z (Macintosh) to undo any scaling you added along the x axis to the image.

8. Drag the green square up and down. Notice that this expands and shrinks the height of the selected image.

9. Press Ctrl+Z (Windows/Linux) or Command+Z (Macintosh) to undo any scaling you added along the y axis to the image.

10. Hold down the Shift key and drag either the red or green square. Notice that when you hold down the Shift key, both the width and the height of the image expand or shrink at the same time.

11. Press Ctrl+Z (Windows/Linux) or Command+Z (Macintosh) to undo any scaling.

When you want to keep the proportion of the width and the height constant, hold down the Shift key before dragging one of the scaling squares. By using the Rotate and Scale icons, you can modify the appearance of an image displayed in the viewport.

# Summary

You should store every Godot project in a separate folder. That will keep files from one project from accidentally interfering with files used in a different project. While each project creates a complete video game, don't be afraid to create projects to test ideas out or to learn different features of Godot.

A Godot project consists of one or more scenes where a scene can represent a playing field, a single object, or parts of an object such as the separate tires of a cartoon car. Scenes define what users see when they run your project.

Scenes are made up of one or more nodes. Nodes contain properties that you can modify in the Inspector dock. You may need to add multiple nodes to include all the features you need for a particular object in your project. A common node for displaying graphics is the Sprite2D node. There are many types of nodes to work with, so do not be afraid to test out different nodes that you may find suitable for your project.

Once you've created a scene, you can arrange objects in that scene using the Move, Rotate, or Scale icons. The Move icon lets you place an object on the screen. The Rotate icon lets you change the angle of an object so that it appears tilted or on its side. The Scale icon lets you change the height and width of an object.

The main steps to using Godot are creating and opening projects. Once you open a project, you can edit it by adding, deleting, and changing scenes through nodes that add additional features. Modifying a project defines what users will see when your project runs.

# CHAPTER 3

# Writing Scripts

When you create a project with at least one scene that displays graphic images on the screen, that scene will appear static no matter what the user does. To make a project interactive, you need to write scripts that respond when something happens to a specific node. Two common ways to make a project interactive are to let the user control an object in a project and to let the computer change the appearance of a project when collisions occur between objects.

Scripts are essentially mini-programs written in one of two programming languages:

1. C#

2. GDScript

C# is a programming language developed by Microsoft and heavily used to create Windows programs. Because C# is so popular, many game engines have adopted the language as well including Unity and Godot.

One problem with C# is that it was designed as a general purpose, safer version of the C++ programming language. As a result, C# was never designed for creating video games. Because of this, the developers of Godot have created a proprietary language called GDScript, specifically designed for creating games.

Although you can create a Godot project using both C# and GDScript, it's far more common to use one language. For the purposes of this book, all script examples will focus on GDScript. One difference between C# and GDScript is the way they define blocks of code.

© Wallace Wang, Tonnetta Walcott 2024
W. Wang and T. Walcott, *Programming for Game Design*,
https://doi.org/10.1007/979-8-8688-0190-7_3

In C#, you use curly brackets to define the start and ending of a block of code such as follows:

```
if x > y
  {
      print("X is bigger than Y");
  }
```

In GDScript, you use a colon followed by indentation to define the start and ending of a block of code such as follows:

```
if x > y:
      print("X is bigger than Y")
```

A second difference between C# and GDScript is that C# requires a semicolon (;) at the end of each statement, while GDScript does not. Also, there is a difference when declaring variables. In C#, for example, you may use "String" or "int" to establish a variable. For example, "String car; or int car = 2." With GDScript, variables are established by simply stating "var" then the name of the variable such as "var health = 100" or "var car." There are many types of variables that can be defined when working with GDScript that one will learn later the further they work with Godot. Because of these differences, GDScript code can often be shorter and easier to write than equivalent C# code. If you're familiar with the Python programming language, you'll find GDScript very similar.

Because GDScript is simpler to write, this book will focus on GDScript exclusively. Once you get familiar with GDScript, you should have little trouble learning another programming language. Programming in general is universal.

# Creating a Script

When you create a Godot project, you need to create scenes and build those scenes using nodes. Nodes are the basic building blocks used to define a scene. You will add nodes as soon as you open up a scene. To make a scene responsive, you need to attach scripts to nodes that make up your scene. A node does not need a script, but if you do attach a script, you may only attach one script to one node.

To attach a script to a node, you must select a node and then attach a script to that selected node. Godot stores scripts in files that end with the .gd file extension.

To see how to attach a script to a node, follow these steps:

1.  Make sure you have opened the Godot project that you created from Chapter 2. This project should display the icon.svg image in a window.

2.  Click the Sprite2D node in the Scene dock.

3.  Attach a script to the Sprite2D node in one of the following ways as shown in Figure 3-1:

    •   Click the script icon.

    •   Right-click the Sprite2D node, and when a pop-up menu appears, choose Attach Script.

    An Attach Node Script dialog box appears as shown in Figure 3-2.

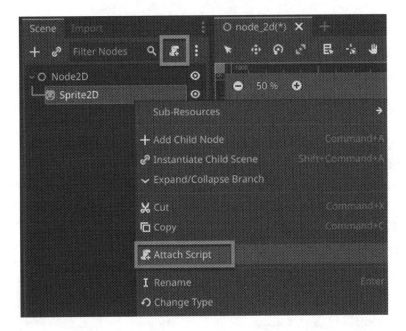

***Figure 3-1.*** *Attaching a script to a node*

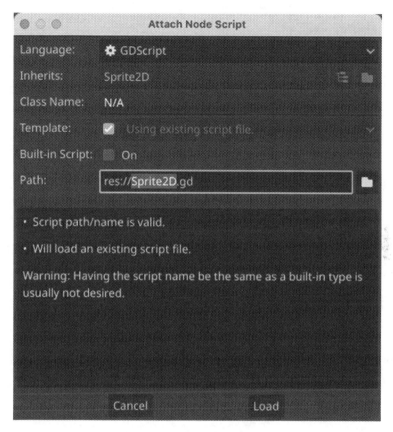

*Figure 3-2.* *The Attach Node Script window*

4. (Optional) Type a descriptive name for your script
   in the Path text field. By default, Godot names your
   script using the name of the node that it's attached
   to such as Sprite2D.

5. Click the Load button to attach the script to the
   node. Initially, every script will be empty except
   for some functions that will contain "pass," which
   means they don't do anything until you add your
   own code in them.

# Writing a Script

Once you've created a script that's attached to a node, you can then write GDScript code to make that script work. Every script file contains one or more functions where each function runs when a certain event occurs.

To see how a script works in a Godot project, follow these steps:

1. Make sure you have created and attached a script to the Sprite2D node. A script icon appears to the right of a node in the Scene dock to show that a script is attached to that node as shown in Figure 3-3.

***Figure 3-3.*** *A script icon identifies nodes that have a script attached*

2. Click the script icon that appears to the right of the node in the Scene dock. The viewport displays the contents of the attached script. Notice that within the viewport, Godot displays a separate menu bar that contains commands just for editing code as shown in Figure 3-4.

***Figure 3-4.*** *The GDScript menu bar for editing code*

3.  Edit the script as follows:

```
extends Sprite2D
func _ready():
        print("Ready function here")

func _init():
        print("Init function here")
```

Both the ready() and the init() functions will run exactly once when the project runs.

4.  Click the Run icon. Godot displays the icon.svg graphic in the window.

5.  Click the close icon in the Godot window to make it go away. The Godot editor window appears. Notice that an Output pane appears at the bottom of the screen and displays "Init function here" followed by "Ready function here" as shown in Figure 3-5.

***Figure 3-5.*** *All print commands display text in the Output pane when a project runs*

Notice that even though the ready() function appears first in the script, the init() function actually runs first, and then the ready() function runs second. The order you store functions in a script doesn't matter. Functions only run when certain events occur. In this case, the init() function runs first, and then the ready() function runs next, but both only run exactly once.

The init() and ready() functions are useful for performing tasks when a scene runs such as initializing a game by resetting the score to zero. Godot offers several built-in functions that run when certain events occur. One of the most common functions you'll often use when creating video games is the process(delta) function.

The process(delta) function runs continuously instead of just once like the init() and ready() functions. This function can be useful for performing repetitive tasks such as checking if the user presses a key or clicks the mouse.

To see how the process(delta) function works, follow these steps:

1. Click the script icon next to Sprite2D in the Scene dock. Godot displays the script in the viewport window.

2. Edit the script as follows:

```
extends Sprite2D
var speed = 2
func _process(delta):
        rotation += speed * delta
```

The second line declares a variable called "speed" and stores the number 2 in that variable. Then the third line defines the process(delta) function. Indented underneath that function is the code rotation += speed * delta.

The rotation variable defines the rotation of the Sprite2D, which will rotate the icon.svg graphic. The += symbols mean that the rotation variable constantly adds a new value to the existing value. That makes the icon.svg graphic image rotate constantly in a clockwise direction.

The speed * delta code multiples the value stored in the "speed" variable (2) with the value stored in "delta," which is the time that has elapsed since the previous frame. Remember, video games display graphics like movies, measured in frames per second, so the "delta" value, multiplied by the "speed" variable, calculates a numeric value to rotate the icon.svg graphic at a constant rate.

3. Click the Run icon. The (DEBUG) window appears. Notice that the icon.svg graphic rotates at a constant speed in a clockwise direction.

4. Click the close icon of the (DEBUG) window.

Notice that the process(delta) function runs the rotation += speed * delta code continuously, which makes the icon.svg graphic rotate. What if you delete the process(delta) function and replace it with the ready() function like this:

```
extends Sprite2D
var speed = 2
func _ready():
        rotation += speed
```

Since the ready() function only runs once, the preceding code would rotate the icon.svg just once and stop. By understanding when certain functions run, you can put code in the right functions to make your project interactive.

# Viewing the GDScript Documentation

The key to writing scripts is knowing which functions are available (such as ready() or process(delta)) and then writing code within each function. To help you learn which functions are available and what they do, you need to read the GDScript documentation.

The upper right corner of the viewport displays two icons where you can view documentation as shown in Figure 3-6.

***Figure 3-6.*** *Documentation icons appear in the upper right corner of the viewport*

The Online Docs icon opens your default browser to view the documentation stored on the Godot website (`https://docs.godotengine. org`). You can also access this online documentation by choosing Help ➤ Online Documentation from the Godot menu bar.

The Search Help icon opens a Search Help window to help you view the different properties and methods available for each type of node as shown in Figure 3-7. A property is a predefined variable for storing data, and a method is a predefined function for performing a specific task.

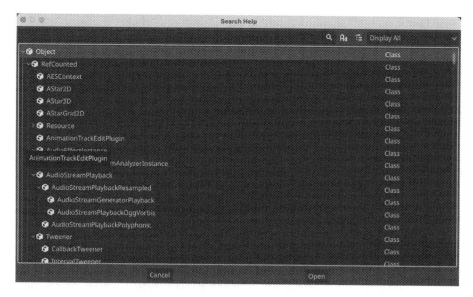

***Figure 3-7.*** *The Search Help window*

To see how to use the Search Help window, follow these steps:

1. Click the script icon next to Sprite2D in the Scene dock. Godot displays the script in the viewport window.

2. Click Search Help in the upper right corner of the viewport (or choose Help ➤ Search Help from the main Godot menu bar). The Search Help window appears (see Figure 3-7). One way to use the Search Help window is to scroll and click the topics you want to view. A faster way is to type in part or all of a topic you want to view

3. Click the Search text field at the top of the Search Help window and type "sprite." The Search Help window now shows only information that matches the word "sprite" as shown in Figure 3-8.

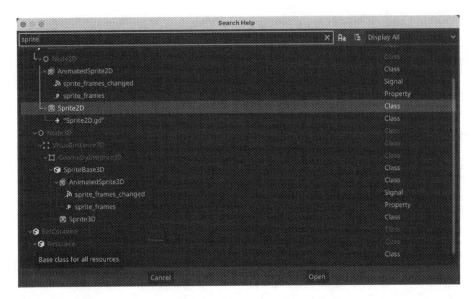

**Figure 3-8.** *Searching for specific topics in the Search Help window*

4.  Click Sprite2D and click the Open button. The
    viewport window now displays help related to the
    Sprite2D node as shown in Figure 3-9. Notice that
    the Sprite2D documentation file now appears in the
    left pane of the viewport. This lets you quickly view
    the information at a later time.

*Figure 3-9.* *Information about the Sprite2D node*

5.  Click any underlined link such as <u>texture</u> to view
    more information. The viewport displays your
    chosen information.

6.  Click the Back arrow in the upper right corner of the
    viewport window to go back to the Sprite2D page.
    The Back/Forward arrows in the upper right corner
    act like the Back/Forward arrows in a browser to let
    you go back and forth between previously viewed
    information.

7.  (Optional) Right-click the Sprite2D documentation
    file that appears in the left pane, and when a pop-up
    menu appears, choose Close to remove this file from
    the left pane as shown in Figure 3-10.

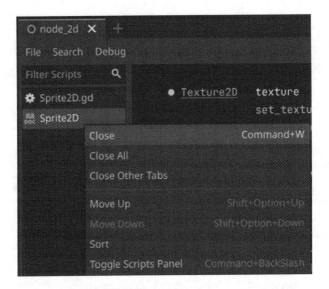

*Figure 3-10.* *The Close command will remove a documentation file from the left pane*

Rather than type in a term in the Search text field of the Search Help window, another option is to move the cursor in a GDScript command that you want more information about. Then choose Search ➤ Contextual Help as shown in Figure 3-11.

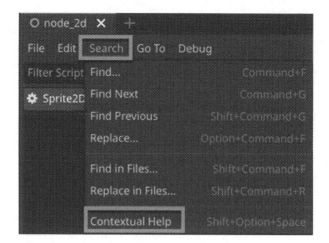

**Figure 3-11.** *The Search menu displays the Contextual Help command*

To see how to use Contextual Help, follow these steps:

1. Click the script icon next to Sprite2D in the Scene dock. Godot displays the script in the viewport window.

2. Edit the script file to look like this:

```
extends Sprite2D
var speed = 2
func _process(delta):
      rotation += speed * delta
```

Notice that Godot color codes certain words. This color coding can help you identify when you've typed certain GDScript commands correctly (or incorrectly).

3.  Move the cursor inside the term "_process," which should appear in light blue to let you know it represents a GDScript command.

4.  Choose Search ➤ Contextual Help. The Search Help window appears. Notice that Godot displays "_process" in the Search text field at the top of the Search Help window automatically, so you don't have to type it in yourself.

5.  Click the Open button. Godot displays help for your chosen GDScript command.

At this point, you most likely won't understand all the information displayed in the documentation. Just be aware that you can search for documentation within the Search Help window or on the documentation web pages of the Godot website.

Oftentimes you may know what you want to do but have no idea how to do it. That's why Godot offers a special Questions and Answers web page that you can access by choosing Help ➤ Questions and Answers.

This Questions and Answers page, as shown in Figure 3-12, lists common problems that people run into while using Godot. By accessing this page, you can find answers to common problems and even contribute your own answers to problems that others might have.

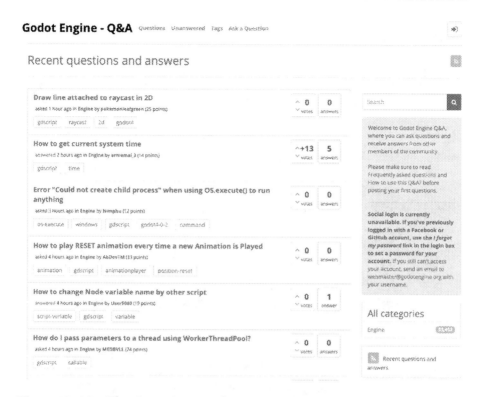

**Figure 3-12.** *The Questions and Answers page*

One fast way to get help on specific Godot keywords and predefined functions is to hold down the Ctrl (Windows/Linux) or Command (Macintosh) key and then move the mouse pointer over a Godot keyword or function. If Godot recognizes a keyword or function, it will appear underlined as shown in Figure 3-13.

49

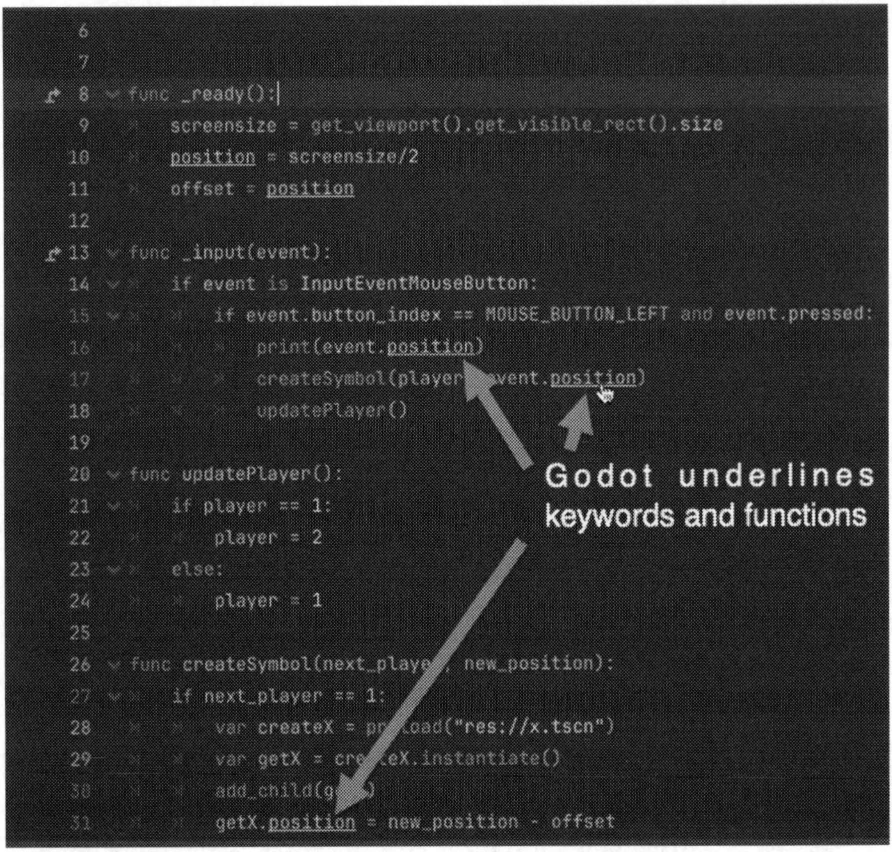

```
   6
   7
 8   func _ready():|
   9       screensize = get_viewport().get_visible_rect().size
  10       position = screensize/2
  11       offset = position
  12
 13   func _input(event):
  14     if event is InputEventMouseButton:
  15       if event.button_index == MOUSE_BUTTON_LEFT and event.pressed:
  16         print(event.position)
  17         createSymbol(player, event.position)
  18         updatePlayer()
  19
  20   func updatePlayer():
  21     if player == 1:
  22       player = 2
  23     else:
  24       player = 1
  25
  26   func createSymbol(next_player, new_position):
  27     if next_player == 1:
  28       var createX = preload("res://x.tscn")
  29       var getX = createX.instantiate()
  30       add_child(getX)
  31       getX.position = new_position - offset
```

**Godot  underlines**
**keywords and functions**

*Figure 3-13.* *Godot underlines keywords and functions when holding down the Ctrl/Command key*

Clicking an underlined keyword or function then displays help as shown in Figure 3-14. By holding down the Ctrl/Command key and moving the mouse pointer over different parts of your GDScript code, you can let Godot identify keywords and functions.

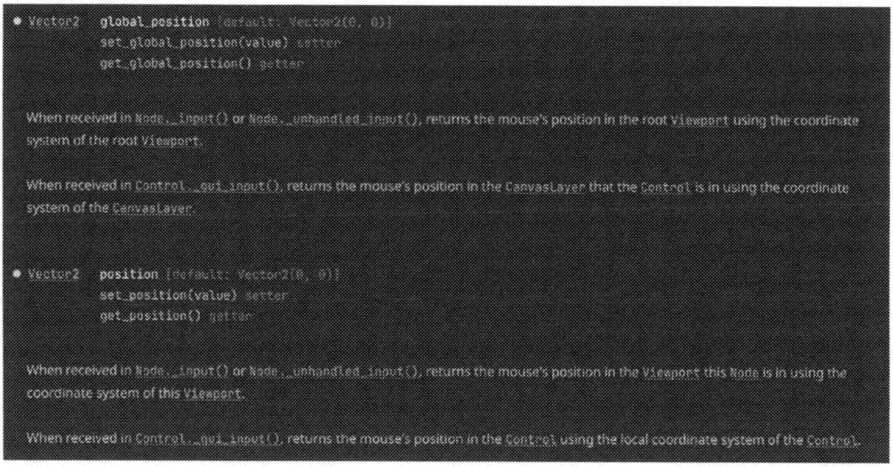

*Figure 3-14.*  *Godot underlines keywords and functions when holding down the Ctrl/Command key*

# Summary

This chapter introduced you to the basics of attaching a script to a node and then writing GDScript code to respond to some event. You can only attach one script to a node at a time. Scripts consist of one or more functions that respond to specific events. The init() and ready() functions run exactly once when the project starts. The process(delta) function runs continuously. By storing GDScript code in functions, you can make a project interactive.

Since you can't memorize all possible commands available, Godot provides help that you can access at any time. If you get stuck trying to solve a particular problem, Godot offers a questions and answers section where you can post a question and offer solutions to other people's problems.

When you create a video game in Godot, you use nodes to define the visual part of your game. Then you use the GDScript language to write scripts to make those nodes respond to specific events. The GDScript programming language is optimized to help you create projects using Godot.

Now that you have a brief idea how scripts work, the next step is to start learning basic programming principles so you can learn to control different game objects on the screen.

# CHAPTER 4

# Storing Data in Variables

The whole purpose of programming is to solve problems. To solve any problem, you need to know the facts of the problem so you can figure out how to use those facts to solve that problem. In computer programming, facts represent data and the steps needed to solve a problem are called algorithms. Computer programming and problem-solving are essential to creating video games in Godot.

Suppose you wanted to convert a temperature from Celsius to Fahrenheit. First, you need to know the temperature in Celsius, so let's assume it's 20 $^0$C. Once you know the temperature in Celsius, you can use the following formula to convert that Celsius temperature to its equivalent Fahrenheit temperature:

Fahrenheit temperature = (Celsius temperature * 9/5) + 32

In this problem, the known data is the Celsius temperature (20 $^0$C), and the algorithm is the conversion formula. To convert 20 $^0$C to Fahrenheit, you can just plug in 20 $^0$C into the conversion formula like this:

Fahrenheit temperature = (20 $^0$C * 9/5) + 32

Fahrenheit temperature = (180/5) + 32

Fahrenheit temperature = (36) + 32

Fahrenheit temperature = 68

© Wallace Wang, Tonnetta Walcott 2024
W. Wang and T. Walcott, *Programming for Game Design*,
https://doi.org/10.1007/979-8-8688-0190-7_4

Problem-solving involves listing out the facts of the problem and then making step-by-step instructions to find an answer. Once you know how to solve a problem, the next step is to tell a computer how to solve that problem by converting your instructions using a programming language. In computer programming, a computer program is just that: a list of instructions to perform certain tasks to solve a problem.

To store facts about a problem, programming languages temporarily hold data in memory. To make it easy to retrieve data later, these memory locations are given descriptive names and called "variables."

# Creating a Variable

Until you create (also called "declaring") a variable, you can't store any data in your program. It is important to name and declare all variables within a program; otherwise an error will occur, and the program may not run. The two steps to creating or declaring a variable are

- Use the "var" keyword to tell Godot you want to create a variable.

- Define a unique name for your variable.

In Godot, the GDScript language creates variables by using a keyword called "var," which is short for "variable." Immediately following this, "var" keyword must be the name of your variable.

Variables get their name because the data they hold can vary at any given time. One moment a variable might hold the number 4 and the next it might hold the number -73. Some examples of creating variables in GDScript include the following:

```
var x
var age
var first_name
var   lastName
```

You can give a variable any name you wish, but it's best to use descriptive names to make your code easier to understand. In the preceding examples, a variable named "age" would likely contain a number such as 37 or 24, while another variable named "first_name" would likely contain text such as "John" or "Mary."

Variable names can be as short as a single character ("x") or consist of multiple words smashed together. When combining multiple words to make a variable name, Godot uses a convention known as "snake case" where individual words are written in all lowercase and separated by an underscore:

```
var snake_case_variable_name
```

When you create a variable, it initially has no value. If you try to use that variable without a value stored in it, then your program will likely crash. So when creating a variable by giving it a name, it's common to also store a value in that variable at the same time like this:

```
var age = 46
```

Assigning an initial value to a variable prevents you from trying to use a variable when it doesn't contain anything. Trying to use a variable that doesn't contain a value will simply crash your project when you try to run it.

To see the dangers of declaring a variable without giving it a value, follow these steps:

1. Make sure you have created a Godot project that consists of a Node2D with a Sprite2D child node.

2. Make sure the Sprite2D node displays the icon.svg graphic in its Texture property. Position the Sprite2D node so that it appears in the middle of the window.

3. Edit the script attached to the Sprite2D node and
   edit it as follows:

```
extends Sprite2D
var age

func _process(delta):
        print(age)
```

With this script, we're declaring a variable called
"age," but it does not contain a value. Then within
the process(delta) function, we try to print the value
of the age variable. Since this age variable does not
contain a value, Godot will simply print <null>.

4. Click the Run icon at the top of the window. The
   Godot window briefly appears, then disappears
   when your project crashes.

The general rule is that whenever you create a variable, never use it
until you actually store a value in that variable.

## Storing and Retrieving Values in a Variable

When you create a variable, it's usually best to store a value in that variable
right away such as follows:

```
var age = 0
```

GDScript stores (or assigns) a value to a variable using the equal sign.
Whatever appears on the right of the equal sign gets stored in the variable
name that appears to the left of the equal sign.

Although you can assign values to a variable as often as you want, a
variable can only hold one value at a time. Each time you store a new value
in a variable, it erases the currently stored value. The following code stores

three different values in the same variable, but by the end, only the last value remains in the variable:

```
var age = 0
age = -15
age = 25
age = 137
```

The first line in the preceding code creates a variable called "age" and stores an initial value of 0. The second line replaces the value of 0 with -15. The third line replaces the value of -15 with 25. Finally, the last line replaces the value of 25 with 137.

To retrieve the value stored in a variable, just use the variable name. The simplest way to do that in GDScript is to use the print statement to print the data out like this:

```
print(age)
```

This print command tells Godot to retrieve the value stored in the "age" variable and print it out. To see how to store values in a variable and retrieve those values, follow these steps:

1. Make sure you have a Godot project that consists of a Node2D and a child node Sprite2D that displays the icon.svg image in a window.

2. Click the Sprite2D node in the Scene dock.

3. Edit the script attached to the Sprite2D node as follows:

```
extends Sprite2D
var age = 0
func _init():
        print("First value = ", age)
        age = -15
```

```
print("Second value = ", age)
age = 25
print("Third value = ", age)
age = 137
print("Last value = ", age)
```

Notice that we created the "age" variable and gave it an initial value of 0. Then we used the init() function, which only runs once. Inside this init() function, we print the value stored in age (0), store -15 in the "age" variable and print it out again, store 25 in the "age" variable and print it out, then store 137 in the "age" variable before printing it out. Also note how the print command works. We can define multiple items to print by separating them with a comma.

4. Click the Run icon at the top of the window. The Godot project window appears.

5. Click the close icon of the project window to make it go away. Notice that the Output pane at the bottom of the Godot window displays the results of the print command like this:

First value = 0
Second value = -15
Third value = 25
Last value = 137

Experiment with storing different values in the "age" variable to see how you can store different values in a variable, but each time you store a new value, it deletes the currently stored value in that variable.

# Understanding Data Types

A variable can hold different types of data, but the most common types of data are numbers and text. Numbers can be whole numbers (9, -37, 71) or decimal numbers (-0.36, 24.6, 172.38). Text is called "strings" and represents anything that appears within double quotation marks such as "Hello," "This is a string," or "1239.45." In Godot, a string or number may be used to track objects, nodes, and sprites in the game such as the player, the player's health, enemies, and the enemies' health.

Each time you create a variable, that variable can hold any type of data. One moment it might store a whole number, the next it might store text, and the next it might store a decimal number.

To see how a variable can hold different types of data, follow these steps:

1. Make sure you have a Godot project that consists of a Node2D and a child node Sprite2D that displays the icon.svg image in a window.

2. Click the Sprite2D node in the Scene dock.

3. Edit the script attached to the Sprite2D node as follows:

```
extends Sprite2D
var age = 0
func _init():
      print("First value = ", age)
      age = "This is a string"
      print("Second value = ", age)
      age = 25.127
      print("Third value = ", age)
      age = 137
      print("Last value = ", age)
```

4.  Click the Run icon at the top of the window. The
    Godot project window appears.

5.  Click the close icon of the project window to make
    it go away. The Output pane at the bottom of the
    Godot window displays the results of the print
    command like this:

First value = 0
Second value = This is a string
Third value = 25.127
Last value = 137

Notice that the "age" variable initially contains a whole number (0),
then stores text ("This is a string"). Then it stores a decimal number
(25.127), and finally, it stores a whole number again (137).

Letting a variable contain all types of data (whole numbers, text, or
decimal numbers) can be convenient, but sometimes you may want to
restrict a variable to hold only certain types of data. For example, if you
create a variable to store someone's name, you don't want that variable to
hold non-text data such as -45.2 or 83 since a number wouldn't make any
sense for someone's name.

To restrict a variable to hold only one type of data, you need to
understand the different data types available as follows:

- Whole numbers (int)

- Decimal numbers (float)

- Text (String)

GDScript calls whole numbers "int" (short for integer) and decimal
numbers as "float" (short for floating-point numbers). Text is called
"String" for text string. To restrict a variable to contain only one specific
type of data, you need to follow the variable name with a colon and the
data type you want to use such as follows:

```
var age: int
var weight: float
var name: String
```

The first line creates a variable called "age" and specifies that it can only hold integers (int). The second line creates a variable called "weight" and specifies that it can only hold decimal numbers (float). The third line creates a variable called "name" and specifies that it can only hold text strings. Notice that all the data types (int and float) use lowercase letters but String starts with an uppercase letter.

To see how declaring a specific data type works when creating a variable, follow these steps:

1. Make sure you have a Godot project that consists of a Node2D and a child node Sprite2D that displays the icon.svg image in a window.

2. Click the Sprite2D node in the Scene dock.

3. Edit the script attached to the Sprite2D node as follows:

```
extends Sprite2D
var age: int = 0
func _init():
        print("First value = ", age)
        age = "This is a string"
        print("Second value = ", age)
        age = 25.127
        print("Third value = ", age)
        age = 137
        print("Last value = ", age)
```

Notice that Godot won't even let you run this program because it's trying to store a text string ("This is a string") into the age variable as shown in Figure 4-1.

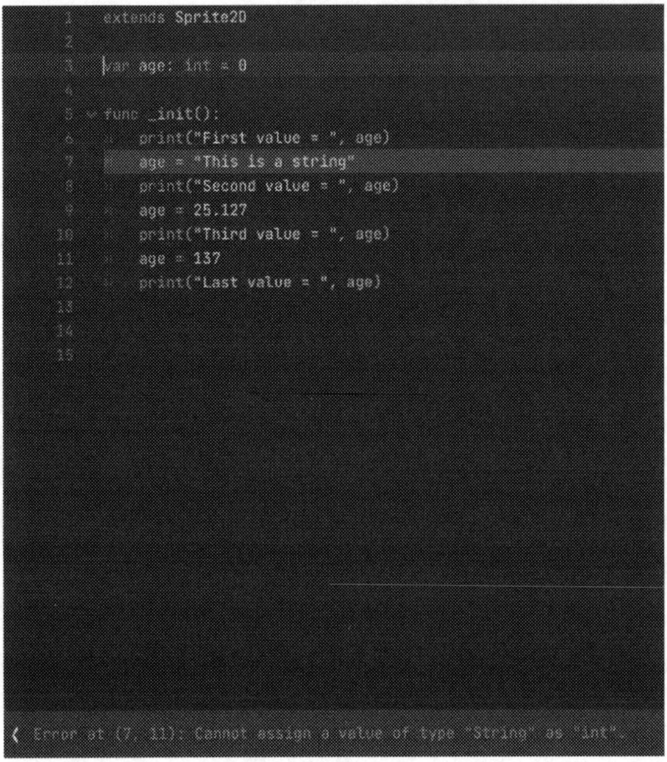

```
1    extends Sprite2D
2
3    var age: int = 0
4
5  ~ func _init():
6        print("First value = ", age)
7        age = "This is a string"
8        print("Second value = ", age)
9        age = 25.127
10       print("Third value = ", age)
11       age = 137
12       print("Last value = ", age)
13
14
15
```

‹ Error at (7, 11): Cannot assign a value of type "String" as "int".

***Figure 4-1.*** *Godot warns you when a variable tries to store a data type it's not designed to hold*

To avoid problems in your code, it's a good idea to assign initial values to your variables when you create those variables. This prevents problems trying to use a variable before it has a value in it.

A second way to avoid problems is to define variables to hold specific data types. This helps ensure that your code doesn't try to store the wrong type of data in a variable, such as a number into a variable meant to hold names.

GDScript offers two ways to define specific data types for a variable. One way is to define the variable name followed by a colon and the data type it can hold like this:

```
var legs: int = 4
var height: float = 18.25
var first_name: String = "John"
```

A second way to declare a variable and define its data type at the same time looks like this:

```
var legs := 4
var height := 18.25
var first_name := "John"
```

These two variable declarations are equivalent. The combination := symbols assign a value to a variable, and then based on the data type of that value, Godot infers the data type. So the number 4 is an integer, which means GDScript infers that the "legs" variable must be an int data type.

Likewise, 18.25 is a decimal number, so GDScript infers that the "height" variable must be a float data type. The name "John" is a string, so GDScript infers that the "first_name" variable is a String data type.

To see how data types work, follow these steps:

1. Make sure you have a Godot project that consists of a Node2D and a child node Sprite2D that displays the icon.svg image in a window.

2. Click the Sprite2D node in the Scene dock.

3. Edit the script attached to the Sprite2D node as follows:

```
extends Sprite2D
var age := 0
var weight := 102.03
```

```
var first_name := "John"
func _init():
        print("Age = ", age)
        print("Weight = ", weight)
        print("Name = ", first_name)
```

4.  Click the Run icon at the top of the window. Godot displays your project (DEBUG) window.

5.  Click the close icon of the (DEBUG) window.

Notice that the Output pane at the bottom of the Godot window displays the print command's output:

Age = 0

Weight = 102.03

Name = John

For clarity and readability, it's often better to specify the data type when declaring a variable like this:

```
var amount: float = 1258.47
```

For typing efficiency, many programmers prefer the shorter version of declaring a variable and inferring the data type like this:

```
var amount := 1258.47
```

Programming is often a trade-off between greater clarity (and more typing) vs. greater efficiency due to less typing (but more potential for confusion). In general, it's better to make sure your program works first before worrying about making it run more efficiently. Efficiency means nothing if your program doesn't work.

Making code clear and understandable is crucial because most programs are modified over time to add new features or eliminate problems (known as "bugs"). If a program is hard to read and understand, it won't be easy to fix or modify in the future, so strive for clarity as much as possible.

# Understanding Variable Scope

Variables are meant to store data that can be used and retrieved at a later time. However, one problem with variables is that any part of a program can potentially store new data in a variable. In a small program, it's easy to see what parts of a program might store new data in a variable that could change its contents. However, in a large program consisting of thousands of lines of code, finding what part of a program may be storing incorrect data in a variable can be nearly impossible.

For that reason, programming languages limit the visibility or "scope" of a variable. The smaller the variable scope, the fewer places where code might change a variable by mistake. The two main options for variable scope are called

- Global

- Local

The scope of a variable depends on where you create a variable. If you declare a variable outside of every function, it's a global variable that can be accessed by any function. If you declare a variable inside of a function, it's a local variable that can be accessed only within that function. Figure 4-2 shows that a global variable, declared outside of all functions, can be accessed by all functions while a local variable, declared inside of a function, can only be accessed within that function.

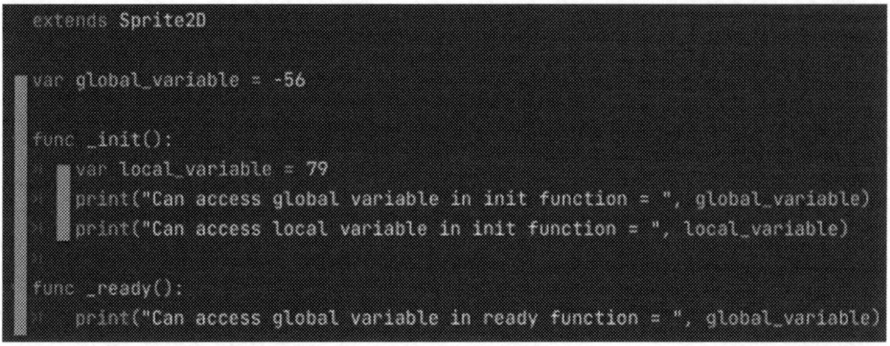

***Figure 4-2.*** *Local variables can only be accessed within a function, while global variables can be accessed anywhere*

To see the difference between local and global variables, follow these steps:

1.  Make sure you have a Godot project that consists of a Node2D and a child node Sprite2D that displays the icon.svg image in a window.

2.  Click the Sprite2D node in the Scene dock.

3.  Edit the script attached to the Sprite2D node as follows:

```
extends Sprite2D
var global_variable = -56
func _init():
        var local_variable = 79
        print("Can access global variable in init
        function = ", global_variable)
        print("Can access local variable in init
        function = ", local_variable)
```

```
func _ready():
    print("Can access global variable in ready
    function = ", global_variable)
```

4.  Click the Run icon at the top of the window. Godot displays the (DEBUG) window.

5.  Click the close icon on the (DEBUG) window to make it go away. Notice that the Output pane at the bottom of the window displays the following:

    Can access global variable in init function = -56

    Can access local variable in init function = 79

    Can access global variable in ready function = -56

Because the global variable is declared outside of both functions, it's actually accessible to both functions. However, the local variable is only declared inside the init() function, which means it cannot be accessed within any other part of the program such as the ready() function. If the ready() function tries to access the local variable (declared inside the init() function), Godot will display an error message, warning you that this is not possible as shown in Figure 4-3.

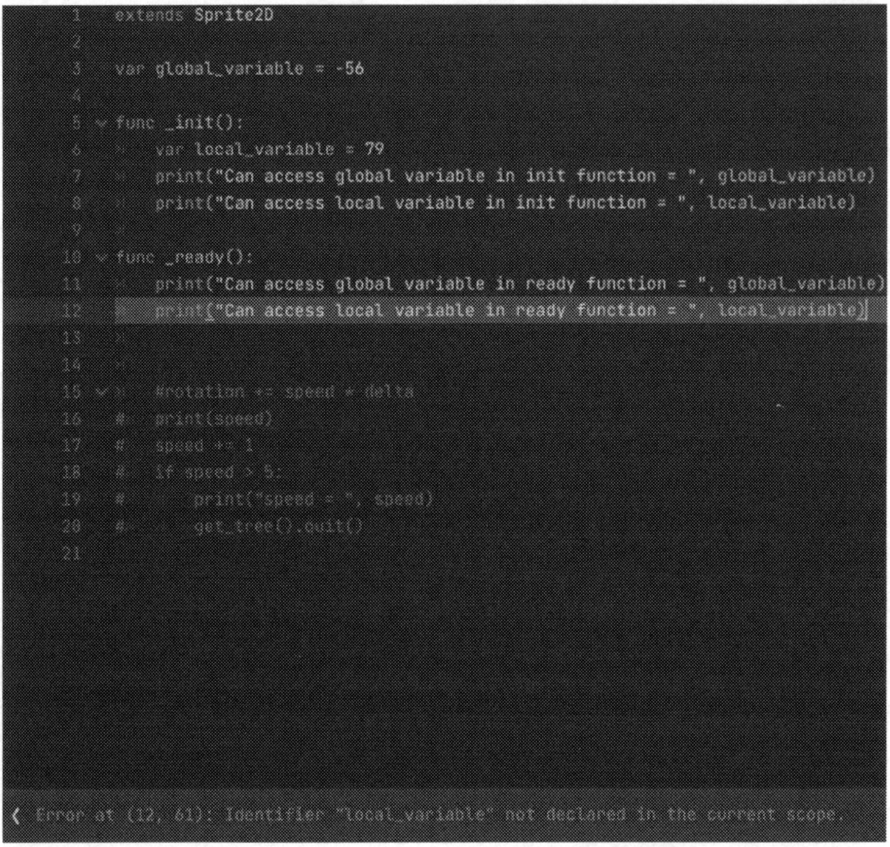

```
1    extends Sprite2D
2
3    var global_variable = -56
4
5  ∨ func _init():
6        var local_variable = 79
7        print("Can access global variable in init function = ", global_variable)
8        print("Can access local variable in init function = ", local_variable)
9
10 ∨ func _ready():
11        print("Can access global variable in ready function = ", global_variable)
12        print("Can access local variable in ready function = ", local_variable)
13
14
15 ∨     #rotation += speed * delta
16   #    print(speed)
17   #    speed += 1
18   #    if speed > 5:
19   #        print("speed = ", speed)
20   #        get_tree().quit()
21
```

< Error at (12, 61): Identifier "local_variable" not declared in the current scope.

***Figure 4-3.*** *The ready() function cannot access the local_variable declared inside the init() function*

When naming variables, give each variable a descriptive, unique name. In other words, you can't declare the same variable name like this:

```
var x: int = -3
var x: int = 41
```

If you try to give two variables the exact same name, Godot won't run your program and will display an error message as shown in Figure 4-4.

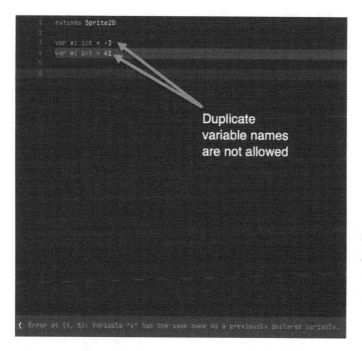

***Figure 4-4.*** *You cannot give two variables the same name in the same scope*

However, Godot will allow two variables to have identical names if those two variables have different scopes such as one variable declared as a global variable and the second variable declared as a local variable like this:

```
extends Sprite2D
var x: int = -3

func _init():
    var x: int = 41
    print(x)
```

In this example, the first x variable is declared as a global variable with a value of -3. Then the second x variable is declared as a local variable within the init() function. Since the print(x) statement occurs within the init() function, it looks for the x value declared as a local variable. Thus, this program would print the value of 41 (and not -3).

Although using duplicate variable names can be allowed if one variable is a global variable and the second variable is a local variable, notice how the duplicate variable names can make the code harder to understand. For that reason, it's always best to avoid using duplicate variable names even if it may be technically allowed.

In general, it's usually best to create local variables to limit the code that can access and change that variable. Global variables can be convenient, but it can be difficult to know which part of a program might be accessing and changing a variable, especially if changing a global variable's value causes a problem.

# Constants and Enumerations

A variable can store one chunk of data at a time, but when you store new data in a variable, that new data overwrites any data already stored in that variable. Rather than use a variable, you could use a fixed value such as 0.08, but using fixed values (called literals) in code can be confusing since it's not clear what that value represents.

To solve this problem of using fixed values but giving them a descriptive name, you can use constants. A constant looks like a variable except you can only store data in it once. Unlike a variable that can store new data over and over again, once a constant gets a value, it can never change its value again. That ensures that a constant's value will always be predictable.

To create a constant, use the "const" keyword followed by a descriptive name and assign an initial value like this:

const sales_tax = 0.08

This stores a value of 0.08 in a constant named "sales_tax." Now instead of using the value of 0.08 throughout a program, you can just use the constant "sales_tax" to represent 0.08. Not only is "sales_tax" more descriptive of what 0.08 represents, but if you need to change its value, you just need to change the constant value once, and any code that uses that constant value will use the updated value.

One limitation of constants is that they can only hold one value. To get around this limitation, GDScript also lets you create enumerations, which let you define a list of valid options. If you're creating a racing video game, you might have three types of vehicles: cars, trucks, and motorcycles.

An enumeration lets you define these valid options in a list in two different ways. In the first way, you store everything on a single line like this:

```
enum Vehicles {CAR, TRUCK, MOTORCYCLE}
```

This uses the "enum" keyword to define an enumeration, which is followed by the actual name of the enumeration such as Vehicles. Within curly brackets are the valid options, which are typically listed in uppercase to make them easier to recognize as part of an enumeration. A second way to declare an enumeration takes up multiple lines to make it clearer what all the options in the enumeration might be like this:

```
enum Obstacles {
    ROCK,
    SIGN,
    POTHOLE
}
```

71

An enumeration essentially acts like a data type, which means you can assign an enumeration option to a variable like this:

```
var player: Vehicles = Vehicles.CAR
```

The preceding code declares a variable called "player" that can only hold data types defined by the Vehicles enumeration. Then it assigns that data, which is defined by the enumeration name (Vehicles) followed by a period and the actual enumeration option such as CAR.

As a shortcut, you could also declare the preceding variable without defining the data type like this:

```
var player = Vehicles.CAR
```

The options listed in an enumeration actually represent integer values where the first item in the list is 0, the second is 1, the third is 2, and so on. You can even assign any integer value to the options in an enumeration by defining it within the enumeration declaration like this:

```
enum Obstacles {
      ROCK,
      SIGN = 45,
      POTHOLE
}
```

To see how to use constants and enumerations, follow these steps:

1.  Make sure you have a Godot project that consists of a Node2D and a child node Sprite2D that displays the icon.svg image in a window.

2.  Click the Sprite2D node in the Scene dock.

3.  Edit the script attached to the Sprite2D node as follows:

```
extends Sprite2D
const hard = 3
enum Vehicles {CAR = 78, TRUCK, MOTORCYCLE}
enum Obstacles {
        ROCK,
        SIGN,
        POTHOLE = 64
}

func _ready():
        var player = Vehicles.CAR
        var enemy = Obstacles.POTHOLE
        print("Player value = ", player)
        print("Enemy value = ", enemy)
        print("Number of obstacles = ", hard * 2)
```

4.  Click the Run icon at the top of the window. Godot displays the (DEBUG) window.

5.  Click the close icon on the (DEBUG) window to make it go away. Notice that the Output pane at the bottom of the window displays the following:

```
Player value = 78
Enemy value = 64
Number of obstacles = 6
```

Notice that the two enumerations define a unique integer value for CAR and POTHOLE. That means Vehicle.CAR actually represents the integer 78 and Obstacles.POTHOLE actually represents the integer 64. Assign the "player" variable to Vehicles.TRUCK and the "enemy" variable to Obstacles.SIGN, and both of their values will be 1 since they appear as the second item listed in the enumeration.

Experiment with changing the "hard" constant value to a different number, and you'll see that the code uses this new value. By using constants and enumerations, you can make code more descriptive and understandable.

# Comments

Descriptive names for variables, constants, and enumerations can make your code easier to understand, but sometimes you may need to add more explanation. To make sure anyone looking at your code can understand how your program works, GDScript lets you type comments directly into your code.

A comment lets you add explanatory text, either on a separate line or sharing the same line as code. To create a comment, type the # symbol like this:

# This is a comment

Anything that appears to the right of the # symbol will be ignored by the computer. That way you can type explanations in your code to explain who wrote the code, when it was last modified, what assumptions the code expects, what it's doing, and why. The more comments you add to your code, the easier it will be for you or someone else to understand your code, so they can fix problems later or add new features.

Longer programs often result in "spaghetti code" making it hard to process and containing more errors. Therefore, it is best to make the program simple to follow and use comments to explain how a program works. Comments are grayed out. They do not compile when running the program but are simply used to help clarify what a program is doing and how it works.

To see how comments look within code, follow these steps:

1. Make sure you have a Godot project that consists of a Node2D and a child node Sprite2D that displays the icon.svg image in a window.

2. Click the Sprite2D node in the Scene dock.

3. Edit the script attached to the Sprite2D node as follows:

```
extends Sprite2D
# This is a comment that appears on a separate line
func _ready():
        print("Hello, world!")  # This is a comment that
        appears to the right of valid code
```

4. Click the Run icon at the top of the window. Godot displays the (DEBUG) window.

5. Click the close icon on the (DEBUG) window to make it go away. Notice that the Output pane at the bottom of the window displays "Hello, world!" Also notice that the comments don't affect the code in any way and exist solely for humans to read while the computer completely ignores them.

A fast way to comment out (or remove comments) on multiple lines of code is to select multiple lines of code and then press Ctrl/Command+K.

# Exercise: Seeing Variables Change

Once you have written some GDScript code to create and use a variable, it's time to visually demonstrate how variables work by using the values of variables to change the position of an image on the screen. The most common way to access variables is to modify the GDScript code and run your project again. However, a more convenient way to access and change variables is to make those variables appear in the Inspector dock. That way you can type in a different value and see how that changed value affects the appearance of a project.

In GDScript, you can display a variable on the Inspector dock by adding an @export in front of the variable declaration like this:

```
@export var x_position: int = 0
```

In the preceding example, the variable is called "x_position"; it's declared to hold only integer (int) data types, and its initial value is set to 0. (Defining the data type is optional.) When you add @export in front of a variable, it becomes accessible within the Inspector dock as shown in Figure 4-5.

***Figure 4-5.*** *An @export variable appears in the Inspector dock*

To see how @export variables work within a Godot project, follow these steps:

1. Create a new Godot project. By default, the FileSystem dock includes the icon.svg image.

2. Click Other Node in the Scene dock. A Create New Node dialog box appears.

3. Click the Search text field and type **node2d**. The Create New Node dialog box displays Node2D as shown in Figure 4-6.

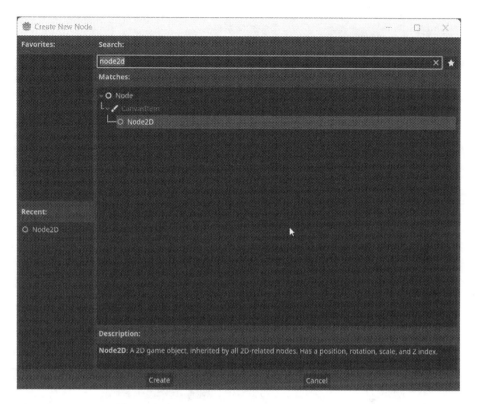

***Figure 4-6.*** *Finding the Node2D node in the Create New Node dialog box*

4. Click the Create button. Godot displays the Node2D in the Scene dock.

5. Click the + (Attach Child Node icon) as shown in Figure 4-7. The Create New Node dialog box appears again.

Attach Child
Node icon

*Figure 4-7.* *The Attach Child Node icon in the Scene dock*

6.  Type **sprite2d**. The Create New Node dialog box displays Sprite2D.

7.  Click Sprite2D and click the Create button. Godot displays the Sprite2D as a child of the Node2D in the Scene dock.

8.  Click Sprite2D in the Scene dock and then click the Inspector tab in the Inspector dock on the far right side of the screen.

9.  Drag the icon.svg file from the FileSystem dock into the <empty> Texture field in the Inspector dock as shown in Figure 4-8. The icon.svg image now appears in the viewport.

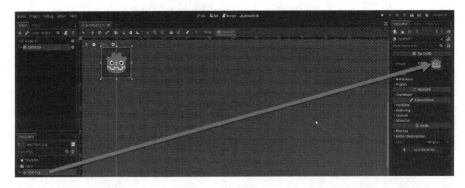

*Figure 4-8.* *The Texture property of the Sprite2D can display the icon.svg image*

10.  Click Node2D in the Scene dock.

11.  Click the Attach Script icon, or right-click Node2D
     and choose Attach Script from the pop-up menu as
     shown in Figure 4-9. An Attach Node Script dialog
     box appears.

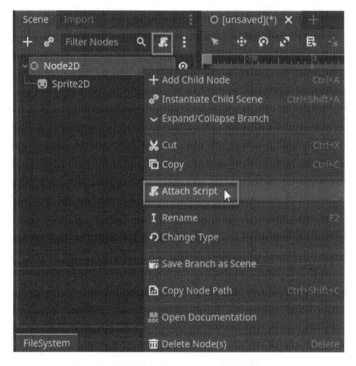

***Figure 4-9.*** *The Attach Script icon in the Scene dock*

12.  Click the Create button to create a script.

13.  Edit the script as follows:

```
extends Node2D
@export var x_position: int = 0
@export var y_position: int = 0
```

```
func _process(delta):
    $Sprite2D.position.x = x_position
    $Sprite2D.position.y = y_position
```

The function (func) _process(delta) runs repetitively and assigns the x and y position of the Sprite2D node to the x_position and y_position variables. Initially, both variables are set to 0 within the GDScript code, but these initial values will be changed by whatever value you type into the Inspector dock for the x_position and y_position variables. Because the Sprite2D node displays the icon.svg image, changing the position of the Sprite2D node changes the position of the icon.svg on the screen.

14. Choose Scene ➤ Save Scene. A Save Scene As dialog box appears.

15. Click Save.

16. Click the Node2D in the Scene dock. Notice that the two @export variables (x_position and y_position) now appear in the Inspector dock (see Figure 4-5).

17. Click the Run icon as shown in Figure 4-10. A dialog box appears, asking you to choose a main scene.

*Figure 4-10.* *The Run Project icon*

18.  Click Select Current. Notice that the (DEBUG) window displays the icon.svg image in the upper left corner of the window.

19.  Click the close icon on the (DEBUG) window.

20.  Click the X Position property in the Inspector dock and type 550. (Positive x values increase toward the right.)

21.  Click the Y Position property in the Inspector dock and type 250. (Positive y values increase downward.)

22.  Click the Run Project icon (see Figure 4-10). Notice that the icon now appears away from the left edge (x_position = 550) and down from the top edge (y_position = 250).

23.  Repeat steps 20–22 with different values for the X Position and Y Position variables. By typing in different values for each variable within the Inspector dock and running the project again, you can change the icon's x and y position within the (DEBUG) window.

In this simple exercise, you learned

- How to create a variable that appears in the Inspector dock (by using @export)

- How to display an image in a Sprite2D node (by dragging and dropping an image in the Texture property in the Inspector dock)

- How the Godot x and y axis work (positive x values increase to the right and positive y values increase downward) as shown in Figure 4-11

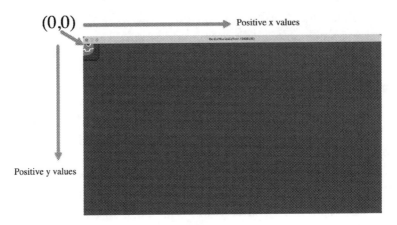

**Figure 4-11.** *The Godot x and y axis*

## Summary

To solve problems, you need to identify the facts of that problem (data). Then using those facts, you can create step-by-step instructions (algorithms) to find a solution. Finally, you need to translate the known facts and instructions into a programming language so a computer can solve that problem.

In programming, storing facts about a problem involves creating variables to hold and retrieve data. To create a variable, you must use the "var" keyword followed by a name for a variable. In GDScript, long names typically consist of multiple words separated by an underscore such as variable_name_here. Ideally, give each variable name a descriptive name.

A variable without a value may cause a program to crash, so it's best to give a variable an initial value. Since variables can hold any type of data, this can cause problems if you want a variable to only hold certain types of data such as numbers or text. For safety, variables can be defined to hold only certain types such as integers (int), decimal numbers (float), or text (String).

When creating variables, be aware of the scope. A global variable can be accessed anywhere in a program, while a local variable can only be accessed within that function. When naming variables, make sure you always give each variable a distinct name to avoid confusion.

Constants can only be assigned a value once and then can never change their value ever again. Enumerations let you define your own data types along with a list of valid options, which all represent integer values. The first option listed in an enumeration is considered 0, the second is considered 1, and so on, unless you explicitly define a different integer value for that particular option.

Ultimately, variables, constants, and enumerations are meant to give data descriptive names so your code will be easier to understand and modify in the future. By adding comments, you can add additional explanations about your code that can clarify how it works.

To make variables accessible within the Inspector dock, define them using the @export keyword. This will let you change variables by typing new values from the Inspector dock rather than editing GDScript code.

# CHAPTER 5

# Mathematical Operations

Nearly every nontrivial program needs to store data in variables. Once a program stores data, it needs to manipulate that data to create a useful result. Three ways to change data involve adding new data, deleting existing data, or modifying existing data.

For example, a word processor lets you delete words, add new words, or edit existing text. A spreadsheet lets you delete numbers, add new numbers, edit existing numbers, or perform calculations on numbers. A database lets you delete data, add new data, edit existing data, and search and sort the data. Manipulating data and calculating new results from existing data are two common ways programs use data to provide a useful function.

So two common types of data that most programs store and manipulate are

- Words (Strings)
- Numbers (integers and floating-point decimal numbers)

© Wallace Wang, Tonnetta Walcott 2024
W. Wang and T. Walcott, *Programming for Game Design*,
https://doi.org/10.1007/979-8-8688-0190-7_5

# Mathematical Operators

Every computer only understands binary numbers (0 and 1), so manipulating numeric data is a common task for computers. A video game, such as in Godot, needs to calculate where to move a player's character based on the player's movement of a joystick or mouse, while an accounting program needs to calculate financial formulas based on money. Since the most common ways to manipulate data involve numbers, every programming language offers mathematical operators such as the following:

- + (addition)
- - (subtraction)
- * (multiplication)
- / (division)
- % (modulo)
- ** (exponentiation)

The addition operator (+) adds two numbers together like this:

```
var x = 4
x = x + 6
```

The first line stores 4 in the "x" variable. The "4" that is stored is the declaration of an integer or int variable. The second line may look a bit odd since the "x" variable appears on both sides of the equal sign. This essentially means add 6 to the value stored in "x" (4) and calculate 10. Then store the value of 10 in the "x" variable, replacing (and erasing) whatever current value may be stored in the "x" variable. Whatever product comes after the "=" sign will usually be a String or integer of some kind.

Rather than list the "x" variable twice on both sides of the equal sign, GDScript offers a shortcut that looks like this:

x += 6

The += sign means "add 6 to the current value stored in x and store the total sum as the new value in x."

The subtraction operator (-), multiplication operator (*), and division operator (/) work the same way like this:

var x = 4

x = x – 6 (or x -= 6)

var y = 4

y = y * 6 (or y *= 6)

var z = 4

z = z / 6 (or z /= 6)

The modulo (%) operator divides two numbers and returns the remainder such as follows:

var a = 39

a = a % 5 (or a %= 5)

In this case, the % operator divides 39 by 5 which is 7 with a remainder of 4, so the % operator returns a value of 4.

The exponentiation (**) operator multiplies one number several times such as 2 ** 3, which means multiply 2 three times ( 2 * 2 * 2 = 8).

Besides adding two numbers together, the + operator can also be used to combine two strings together such as follows:

"John" + "Doe"

When using the + operator to combine two strings, make sure you put a space between the two strings or else the + operator will smash them together.

To see how to use these different operators, follow these steps:

1.  Make sure you have a Godot project that consists of a Node2D and a child node Sprite2D that displays the icon.svg image in a window.

2.  Click the Sprite2D node in the Scene dock.

3.  Edit the script attached to the Sprite2D node as follows:

```
extends Sprite2D
var x = 39
var y = 5
var first_name = "John "
var last_name = "Doe"

func _init():
        print("Addition = ", x + y)
        print("Subtraction = ", x - y)
        print("Multiplication = ", x * y)
        print("Division = ", x / y)
        print("Modulo = ", x % y)
        print("Exponentiation = , x ** 2)
        print("String concatenation = ", first_name +
        last_name)
```

4.  Click the Run icon at the top of the window. The (DEBUG) window appears.

5.  Click the close icon of the (DEBUG) window to make it go away. Notice that the Output pane at the bottom of the Godot window displays the results of mathematical operations as follows:

Addition = 44

Subtraction = 34

Multiplication = 195

Division = 7

Modulo = 4

Exponentiation = 1521

String concatenation = John Doe

# Creating Constants

When creating mathematical formulas, it's common to use variables and numbers such as this formula to calculate the circumference of a circle if you know the circle's diameter:

Circumference = 3.1415 * diameter

When code contains specific data such as numbers like 3.1415, these are called "literals." While there's nothing wrong with using specific data in a calculation, the meaning of that data may not be clear. To solve this problem, programming languages allow you to create something called "constants."

A constant looks like a variable because you can give it a descriptive name and assign it a value. The main difference is that you can store new values in a variable over and over again, but with a constant, you can only store a value in a constant exactly once.

As soon as you store a value in a constant, you can never change its value again. This makes constants perfect for storing data, such as specific numeric values, that your program may need to use multiple times. Because a constant can never change its value once it's assigned an initial value, you never have to worry that some part of your program may accidentally change the value of a constant, which is a problem you need to worry about with variables.

To create a constant, you need three parts:

- The "const" keyword

- The name of the constant

- A value stored in the constant

To create a constant to hold the value of pi, we could do the following:

```
const pi = 3.1415
```

For extra clarity, you can also define the data type of the constant like this:

```
const pi: float = 3.1415
```

To see how constants work, follow these steps:

1. Make sure you have a Godot project that consists of a Node2D and a child node Sprite2D that displays the icon.svg image in a window.

2. Click the Sprite2D node in the Scene dock.

3. Edit the script attached to the Sprite2D node as follows:

```
extends Sprite2D
var diameter: float = 3
var circumference: float = 0
```

```
const pi: float = 3.1415
func _init():
        circumference = pi * diameter
        print ("Circumference = ", circumference)
```

4.  Click the Run icon at the top of the window. The (DEBUG) window appears.

5.  Click the close icon of the (DEBUG) window to make it go away. Notice that the Output pane at the bottom of the Godot window displays the results of mathematical operations as follows:

```
Circumference = 9.4245
```

Notice that the pi constant makes it easy to understand what the number 3.1415 represents. By using descriptive constant names, literal values (such as ordinary numbers) can be easy to understand. Plus if you need to use the same value multiple times, you can just type the constant name instead of the actual value it represents.

Then if you need to change the value of a constant, you only need to change its value once (in the constant declaration). If you used literal values multiple times, you'd have to search and replace all literal values throughout your program.

# Understanding Precedence

When calculating simple formulas, you may only use one mathematical operator such as $4 + 57$ or $9.12 / 4.3$. However, if you create more complicated mathematical formulas that involve two or more operators, you may run into a problem on how the computer calculates an answer. Consider the following:

$$x = 5 + 3 * 2$$

Does the computer first add 5 + 3 (8) and then multiply it by 2 to get 16? Or does the computer first multiply 3 * 2 (6) and then add this to 5 to get 11?

The order that calculation occurs is known as precedence. Precedence defines which operators should be calculated first (higher precedence). The following shows the highest to lowest precedence in operators:

- ** (exponentiation)

- *, /, and % (multiplication, division, and modulo)

- + and – (addition and subtraction)

When two operators have equal precedence, the operator furthest to the left has higher precedence and gets calculated first.

Consider the following calculation: 2 ** 3 + 1 - 4 / 2

This is the way precedence determines how to calculate these operators:

- Calculate exponentiation first (2 ** 3 = 8).

- Calculate division next 4/2 = 2.

- Now the entire calculation looks like this: 8 + 1 – 2.

- Calculate addition next (8 + 1 = 9).

- Calculate subtraction last (9 – 2 = 7), so the final answer is 2 ** 3 + 1 - 4 / 2 = 7.

Because identifying precedence among multiple operators can be confusing, it's much better to use parentheses to define how to calculate operations. For example, consider the following calculation:

2 * 8 / 4

Since both multiplication (*) and division (/) have equal precedence, the operator that appears first (furthest left) calculates first. That means 2 * 8 = 256, then 256 / 4 to calculate 64.

However, if you use parentheses, you could change the way this calculation occurs like this:

$2 * (8 / 4)$

Now the parentheses tell the computer to calculate 8/4 first (2) and then multiply this value to get 2 ** 2 which is 4.

To see how precedence works, follow these steps:

1. Make sure you have a Godot project that consists of a Node2D and a child node Sprite2D that displays the icon.svg image in a window.

2. Click the Sprite2D node in the Scene dock.

3. Edit the script attached to the Sprite2D node as follows:

```
extends Sprite2D
func _init():
        var result1 = 2 ** 8 / 4
        var result2 = 2 ** (8 / 4)

        print (result1)
        print (result2)
```

4. Click the Run icon at the top of the window. The (DEBUG) window appears.

5. Click the close icon of the (DEBUG) window to make it go away. Notice that the Output pane at the bottom of the Godot window displays the results of mathematical operations as follows:

64

4

# Using Math Functions

By using mathematical operators (*, /, +, -), you can create any formula. However, some types of calculations are so common that you probably don't want to write your own code to calculate these results. That's why GDScript includes several built-in mathematical functions that you can use.

Some common mathematical functions include

- abs (absolute value)

- cos (cosine)

- log (logarithm)

- max (returns the maximum value from a list of numbers)

- min (returns the minimum value from a list of numbers)

- sin (sine)

- sqrt (square root)

- tan (tangent)

To see how these mathematical functions work, follow these steps:

1. Make sure you have a Godot project that consists of a Node2D and a child node Sprite2D that displays the icon.svg image in a window.

2. Click the Sprite2D node in the Scene dock.

3. Edit the script attached to the Sprite2D node as follows:

```
extends Sprite2D
func _init():
      print("Absolute value = ", abs(-248))
      print("Cosine = ", cos(1))
```

```
print("Logarithm = ", log(3))
print("Maximum = ", max(23, -5, 7))
print("Minimum = ", min(23, -5, 7))
print("Sine = ", sin(1))
print("Square root = ", sqrt(25))
print("Tangent = ", tan(1))
```

4.   Click the Run icon at the top of the window. The (DEBUG) window appears.

5.   Click the close icon of the (DEBUG) window to make it go away. Notice that the Output pane at the bottom of the Godot window displays the results of mathematical operations as follows:

Absolute value = 248

Cosine = 0.54030230586814

Logarithm = 1.09861228866811

Maximum = 23

Minimum = -5

Sine = 0.8414709848079

Square root = 5

Tangent = 1.5574077246549

By using built-in mathematical functions, you can calculate common formulas without having to write these formulas yourself. This makes calculating common formulas easy and more reliable.

# Creating Random Numbers

One unique feature of video games in particular is calculating random numbers. Surprisingly, there is no such thing as truly random numbers. That's because calculating random numbers does not give all possible numbers an equal chance of occurring.

In the real world, dice, cards, roulette wheels, and spinners have physical imperfections that make some numbers more likely to occur than others. Even if those odds may seem miniscule, they still exist. In the computer world, the way programs calculate random numbers also favors certain numbers over others.

The way random number algorithms work is that they require an initial seed value. This seed value determines which random numbers occur. However, if you give the same seed value to a random number algorithm, it will calculate the exact same list of random numbers in the exact same order.

So before calculating random numbers, it's important to capture a random seed value. In GDScript, you need to use the randomize() function within the ready() function first. This randomize() function captures a seed value based on the computer's clock. Since the exact time the randomize() function retrieves the time can never be predicted, this essentially creates a random seed value.

As an alternative, you can specify a seed value. However, if you use the same seed value, GDScript will calculate the same random numbers in the same order each time.

Whether you define a specific seed value or use the randomize() function to use the time as a seed value, you can create random numbers using the rand() function like the following:

```
randf()
```

This returns a random floating-point number between 0 and 1. If you want to return a random integer, use the randi() function with the modulo operator to define a range such as follows:

```
randi() % 10
```

This would return a random integer between 0 and 9. If you want a random integer between 0 and 249, you could use this:

```
randi() % 250
```

To see how to create random numbers, follow these steps:

1. Make sure you have a Godot project that consists of a Node2D and a child node Sprite2D that displays the icon.svg image in a window.

2. Click the Sprite2D node in the Scene dock.

3. Edit the script attached to the Sprite2D node as follows:

```
extends Sprite2D
func _ready():
        seed(123)
        print(randf())
        print(randi() % 10)
        print(randi() % 10)
        print(randi() % 10)
        print(randi() % 10)
```

4. Click the Run icon at the top of the window. The (DEBUG) window appears.

5.  Click the close icon of the (DEBUG) window to make it go away. Notice that the Output pane at the bottom of the Godot window displays the results of random numbers.

6.  Repeat steps 4 and 5 as often as you want. Notice that no matter how many times you run this program, the random number functions create the exact same numbers. That's because the seed value (123) is always identical each time.

7.  Delete the seed(123) line and replace it with randomize() like this:

```
extends Sprite2D
func _ready():
    randomize()
    print(randf())
    print(randi() % 10)
    print(randi() % 10)
    print(randi() % 10)
    print(randi() % 10)
```

8.  Click the Run icon at the top of the window. The (DEBUG) window appears.

9.  Click the close icon of the (DEBUG) window to make it go away. Notice that the Output pane at the bottom of the Godot window displays the results of random numbers.

10. Repeat steps 8 and 9 as many times as you wish. Notice that each time the random numbers are never the same. That's because the randomize() function uses the time you run the program as its seed value, which can never be predictable.

Unless you have a specific reason to create the same list of random numbers over and over again, it's best to use the randomize() function first before calculating a random floating-point or integer number.

# Manipulating Strings

It's easy to understand mathematical operations on numbers, but GDScript also offers different ways to manipulate strings as well. The most common way to manipulate strings is concatenation, which simply adds two strings together like this:

```
print ("Jake" + "Unger")
```

The preceding concatenation operator (+) would combine "Jake" and "Unger" together as "JakeUnger." In most cases, scrunching two strings together is not what you want, so you'll have to make sure spaces appear between concatenated strings like this:

```
print ("Jake" + " " + "Unger")
```

When working with strings, one common operation is to determine the number of characters in a string, including spaces, symbols, and punctuation marks. To do this in GDScript, simply include the string to count followed by the .length command like this:

```
print ("Hello everyone!".length())
```

This would print 15 because there are 13 letters, 1 space, and 1 exclamation mark.

Three other ways to manipulate strings involve converting a string to uppercase, converting a string to lowercase, and converting a string to snake case where text appears in all lowercase but uses an underscore to separate words like this:

```
print ("Frank Parker Katz".to_lower())      # Prints "FRANK
PARKER KATZ"
print ("Frank Parker Katz".to_upper())      # Prints "frank
parker katz"
print ("Frank Parker Katz".to_snake_case())  # Prints "frank_
parker_katz"
```

To see how to manipulate strings, follow these steps:

1. Make sure you have a Godot project that consists of a Node2D and a child node Sprite2D that displays the icon.svg image in a window.

2. Click the Sprite2D node in the Scene dock.

3. Edit the script attached to the Sprite2D node as follows:

   ```
   extends Sprite2D
   func _ready():
           var name = "Frank Parker Katz"
           print (name.length())
           print (name.to_upper())
           print (name.to_lower())
           print (name.to_snake_case())
   ```

4. Click the Run icon at the top of the window. The (DEBUG) window appears.

5.  Click the close icon of the (DEBUG) window to
    make it go away. Notice that the Output pane at the
    bottom of the Godot window displays the following:

```
17
FRANK PARKER KATZ
frank parker katz
frank_parker_katz
```

# Exercise: Randomizing an X and Y Position

In a 2D project, everything displayed on the screen can be defined by its
x and y position where the upper left corner of the Godot game window
represents (0,0). In this exercise, you'll learn how to get the game window's
size, randomly choose an x and y position, and move a Sprite2D node to
different random x and y positions.

To see how to randomly move an image within a window, follow
these steps:

1.  Create a new Godot project with a Node2D as the
    parent (root) node and a Sprite2D as a child node so
    that the Scene dock looks like Figure 5-1.

*Figure 5-1.*  *Node2D as the parent node and Sprite2D as its*
*child node*

2.  Click the Sprite2D and drag the icon.svg image into
    the Texture property displayed in the Inspector dock
    on the right side of the screen. Godot displays the
    icon.svg in the viewport.

3.  Click Node2D and click the Attach Child Node icon.
    A Create New Node dialog box appears.

4.  Click the Search text field and type **button**. The
    Create New Node dialog box displays a Button as
    shown in Figure 5-2.

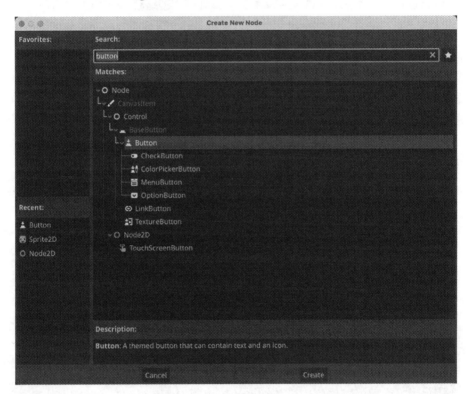

*Figure 5-2.  Searching for a Button in the Create New Node
dialog box*

5.  Click Button and then click the Create button. Godot
    adds a Button as a child node to Node2D in the
    Scene dock.

6.  Resize and move the Button to the bottom of the
    window, defined by boundaries. Notice that the
    Button will be blank.

7.  Click Button in the Scene dock and then click the
    Text property in the Inspector dock as shown in
    Figure 5-3.

***Figure 5-3.*** *The Text property of a Button in the Inspector dock*

8. Type text in the Text property such as **Choose random position**.

9. Click Node2D in the Scene dock and click the Attach Script icon. An Attach Node Script dialog box appears.

10. Click Create. Godot displays a GDScript editor window.

11. Click Button in the Scene dock and then click the Node tab in the Inspector dock.

12. Click Signals as shown in Figure 5-4.

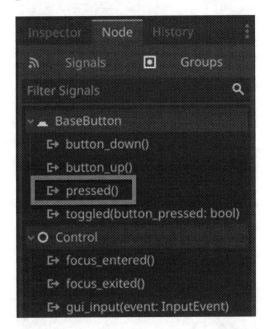

*Figure 5-4.*  *The Node tab appears next to the Inspector tab*

13. Double-click the pressed() option under the BaseButton category. A Connect a Signal to a Method dialog box appears as shown in Figure 5-5.

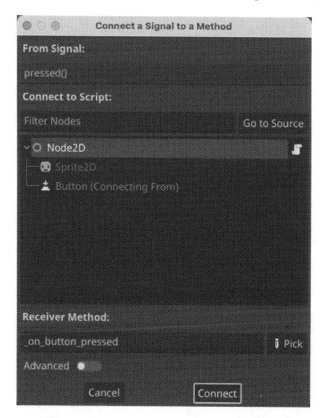

***Figure 5-5.*** *Connecting a signal (pressed) to a node*

14. Click Node2D and click the Connect button. Godot adds a func _on_button_pressed() function.

15. Edit the _on_button_pressed() function as follows:

```
func _on_button_pressed():
    var window_size = DisplayServer.window_get_size()
    randomize()
```

```
$Sprite2D.position.x = randi() % window_size.x
$Sprite2D.position.y = randi() % window_size.y
```

DisplayServer.window_get_size() retrieves the current size of the (DEBUG) window when your project runs. The randomize() function then chooses a seed value to generate unpredictable random numbers. Then the code randomly selects a value up to the window size for both the x and y positions of the Sprite2D node.

16. Click the Run icon. A dialog box asks if you want to make the current scene the main scene.

17. Click Select Current. The (DEBUG) window appears.

18. Click the Button. Notice that each time you click the Button, Godot displays the image at a random position within the window as shown in Figure 5-6.

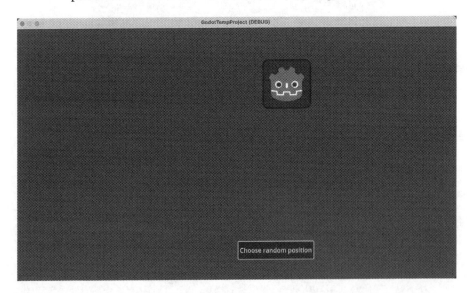

***Figure 5-6.*** *The Button lets you choose a random x and y value to move the icon*

19. Click the close icon of the window to stop running your project.

# Summary

Since computers only understand numbers, one of the most common purposes for computer programs is to calculate a numeric result. You can use common mathematical operations (addition, subtraction, multiplication, and division), but for convenience, you can also use built-in mathematical functions such as sqrt or sin to calculate common mathematical results.

When using mathematical operators, be aware of precedence, which defines which operators calculate first. For clarity, use parentheses to define which operations you want to calculate first. Parentheses help make your code easier to read while also clarifying how calculations work as well.

In video games, random numbers are especially useful. To create truly random numbers, you must understand that random numbers require a seed value. If you define a fixed seed value, you'll create the same random numbers in a fixed order every time. That's why it's better to use the randomize() function to calculate a seed value based on the time the program runs. Since this will always be unpredictable, it will create numbers that are as close to random as possible.

Mathematical calculations form the heart of most programs, so be sure you know how to calculate results, use constants to represent fixed values, and use built-in math functions. Calculating numeric results represents the foundation of nearly every program you'll need to write.

# CHAPTER 6

# Branching Statements

What makes every game fun to play are the choices players must make to get closer to winning. The challenging yet intriguing part to making a game fun is making choices that count and testing to see if the player made the right choice. Since every video game offers choices, every program controlling a video game must know how to offer choices and make decisions based on what the user does. In the programming world, you can create choices in a program through something called a branching statement.

To make a decision, a branching statement needs to check if something happened or not, such as the user pressing the space bar or if a player's character in a game has its strength reduced to 0 or less. To make decisions, branching statements rely on another data type known as Booleans. Branching statements and Boolean data types can make a game respond to different situations.

A Boolean data type holds either a true or false value. Based on this true or false value, a branching statement can make a decision on what to do next. Godot can apply Boolean statements to determine if two objects have collided, such as a player running into an obstacle. If a player did run into an obstacle, then the game needs to determine what to do next such as subtract a life from the player. To work with Boolean data types, you need to know

© Wallace Wang, Tonnetta Walcott 2024
W. Wang and T. Walcott, *Programming for Game Design*,
https://doi.org/10.1007/979-8-8688-0190-7_6

- How to declare a variable as a Boolean data type

- How to use comparison operators to define a true or false value

- How to use logical operators with Boolean values

# Working with Comparison Operators

When creating a variable to hold a Boolean data type, you can assign it a true or false value like this:

```
var alert = true
var flag = false
```

To make sure a variable can only hold a Boolean value (either true or false), you can declare a variable to hold Boolean data types like this:

```
var alert: bool = true
var flag: bool = false
```

While it's possible to store a true or false value in a variable, it's far more common to calculate a true or false value instead using a comparison operator. Essentially a comparison operator compares two values to determine if the comparison is true or false.

The comparison operator is most effective when working with integers or numbers. For example, if a variable to check a character's health in a game has been declared at "100," a comparison operator can compare how much health a player has before the health is depleted. If a player's health is less than 100, then the player loses health, and if it is below 0, then the player dies and must respawn.

This is just an example of how comparison operators could be used when working with games in Godot. Operators can also be used to determine how far a player moves or the amount of items or weapons used. The most common comparison operators are as follows:

- \> (greater than)

- \< (less than)

- == (equal to)

- >= (greater than or equal to)

- <= (less than or equal to)

- != (not equal to)

Comparison operators could compare two literal values that could calculate a Boolean value such as follows:

6 > 2 (true)

47 < 5 (false)

29 == 29 (true)

7 != 7 (false)

When comparing two fixed values, a comparison operator will evaluate to the exact same Boolean value (true or false) every time, which makes them no different than simply assigning a true or false value to a variable instead. For more flexibility, it's better to compare a fixed value to a variable or compare two different variables like this:

x > 5

y >= x + 42

z != 4

x <= y * z

Now depending on the value of each variable, a comparison operator might calculate true or false. In a video game, a comparison operator might check if a player-controlled car has hit an obstacle or not. Sometimes this will be true and sometimes it will be false, which lets a video game react to events within a game. Some events may include the player losing health or losing their life depending on how the game is programmed or other events in a story-based game.

To see how these different comparison operators work, follow these steps:

1. Make sure you have a Godot project that consists of a Node2D and a child node Sprite2D that displays the icon.svg image in a window.

2. Click the Sprite2D node in the Scene dock.

3. Edit the script attached to the Sprite2D node as follows:

```
extends Sprite2D
var x = 8
var y = 4
var z = 2
func _ready():
       print("x > y = ", x > y)
       print("x < y = ", x < y)
       print("x == y = ", x == y)
       print("x >= z = ", x >= z)
       print("x <= z = ", x <= y)
       print("x != z = ", x != z)
```

4. Click the Run icon at the top of the window. The (DEBUG) window appears.

5. Click the close icon of the (DEBUG) window to make it go away. Notice that the Output pane at the bottom of the Godot window displays the results of mathematical operations as follows:

```
x > y = true
x < y = false
x == y = false
x >= z = true
x <= z = false
x != z = true
```

Change the value of the x, y, and z variables and rerun the program again to see how your changes alter the comparison operator calculations.

# Working with Logical Operators

Imagine playing a video game where the game needs to determine if a rock you threw at a bird hit the bird or not. Now depending on the bird's health, the game next needs to know if the bird is hurt or knocked unconscious. In these situations, you need to check if multiple situations may be true or false.

To calculate a single Boolean value from multiple Boolean values, you can use one of the following logical operators:

- and
- or
- not

Both the "and" and "or" logical operators compare two Boolean values to calculate a single Boolean value. The "not" operator simply changes a single Boolean value to its opposite.

The "and" logical operator only evaluates to true if both Boolean values are true. Otherwise, the "and" logical operator evaluates to false like this:

- true and true = true
- true and false = false

- false and true = false

- false and false = false

The "or" logical operator works always evaluates to true unless both Boolean values are false like this:

- true or true = true

- true or false = true

- false or true = true

- false or false = false

The "not" logical operator simply converts a true value to false (and a false value to true) like this:

- not false = true

- not true = false

To see how logical operators work, follow these steps:

1. Make sure you have a Godot project that consists of a Node2D and a child node Sprite2D that displays the icon.svg image in a window.

2. Click the Sprite2D node in the Scene dock.

3. Edit the script attached to the Sprite2D node as follows:

```
extends Sprite2D

func _ready():
        print("true and true = ", true and true)
        print("true and false = ", true and false)
        print("false and true = ", false and true)
        print("false and false = ", false and false)
        print("true or true = ", true or true)
```

```
print("true or false = ", true or false)
print("false or true = ", false or true)
print("false or false = ", false or false)
print("not false = ", not false)
print("not true = ", not true)
```

4. Click the Run icon at the top of the window. The (DEBUG) window appears.

5. Click the close icon of the (DEBUG) window to make it go away. Notice that the Output pane at the bottom of the Godot window displays the results of mathematical operations as follows:

```
true and true = true
true and false = false
false and true = false
false and false = false
true or true = true
true or false = true
false or true = true
false or false = false
not false = true
not true = false
```

# The if Statement

Every programming language offers multiple types of branching statements, but the simplest one is called the if statement, which evaluates a Boolean value. If this Boolean value is true, then it follows one or more commands. If this Boolean value is false, then nothing happens. The if statements, and its variations, are helpful to simplify writing a program to check conditions. The if statement looks like this:

```
If Boolean value == true:
    commands
```

The key feature of the if statement is that it either runs one or more commands (if its Boolean value is true) or does nothing at all (if its Boolean value is false).

To see how the if statement works, follow these steps:

1.  Make sure you have a Godot project that consists of a Node2D and a child node Sprite2D that displays the icon.svg image in a window.

2.  Click the Sprite2D node in the Scene dock.

3.  Edit the script attached to the Sprite2D node as follows:

```
extends Sprite2D
func _ready():
        var x = 10

        if x > 5:
                print("x is greater than 5")

        if x < 5:
                print("x is less than 5")
```

4.  Click the Run icon at the top of the window. The (DEBUG) window appears.

5.  Click the close icon of the (DEBUG) window to make it go away. Notice that the Output pane at the bottom of the Godot window displays the results of mathematical operations as follows:

```
x is greater than 5
```

Change the value of the "x" variable to -10 and run the program again. Each time you change the value of the "x" variable, only one of the if statements will run, depending on whether x > 5 is true or if x < 5 is true.

# The if-else Statement

The if statement only runs if its Boolean value is true, but what if you want to do something if the Boolean value is false? You could create two separate if statements like this:

```
if x == 3:
    commands

if x != 3:
    other commands
```

While two separate if statements will work, it's clumsy because it's not obvious that the second if statement will run only if the first if statement does not run. A better solution is to use an if-else statement that offers two different commands that can run. Depending on the Boolean value, either the first set of commands will run or the second set of commands will run.

Unlike the if statement that only offers one set of commands that may or may not run, the if-else statement offers exactly two sets of commands where one set of commands will always run, depending on its Boolean value. The if-else statement looks like this:

```
if Boolean value == true:
Commands
else:
Alternate commands
```

To see how the if-else statement works, follow these steps:

1. Make sure you have a Godot project that consists of a Node2D and a child node Sprite2D that displays the icon.svg image in a window.

2. Click the Sprite2D node in the Scene dock.

3. Edit the script attached to the Sprite2D node as follows:

```
extends Sprite2D
func _ready():
        var x = 1

        if x > 5:
                print("x is greater than 5")
        else:
                print("x is less than 5")
```

4. Click the Run icon at the top of the window. The (DEBUG) window appears.

5. Click the close icon of the (DEBUG) window to make it go away. Notice that the Output pane at the bottom of the Godot window displays the results of mathematical operations as follows:

```
x is less than 5
```

Because the Boolean value of x > 5 is false (1 > 5), the else part of the if-else statement runs. Change the value of the "x" variable to 10 and run the program again. This will make the Boolean value of x > 5 (10 > 5) true, so only the first command will run and print "x is greater than 5."

# The if-elif Statement

The if-else statement offers exactly two choices. The first set of commands runs if the Boolean value is true, but the second set of commands runs if the Boolean value is false. So what if you need to check multiple Boolean values?

One option is to use multiple if statements, but this can be clumsy and doesn't make it clear that the separate if statements are related in any way. As an alternative to multiple if statements, GDScript offers an if-elif statement. The if-elif statement can check multiple Boolean values, but it's still possible that it may not run any commands at all. The if-elif statement looks like this:

```
if x > 15:
        print("x is greater than 15")
elif x <= 15:
        print("x is less than or equal to 15")
```

Notice that the if-elif statement checks two Boolean values. First, it checks if x > 15 is true. If so, then it prints "x is greater than 15." If x > 15 is false, then it checks the second Boolean value to see if x <= 15 is true or not. If so, then it prints "x is less than or equal to 15."

An if-elif statement can check multiple Boolean values such as follows:

```
if x == 5:
        print("x is equal to 5")
elif x == 10:
        print("x is equal to 10")
elif x == 15:
        print("x is equal to 15")
elif x == 20:
        print("x is equal to 20")
```

Notice that it's possible that none of the Boolean values in the if-elif statement will be true. In that case, no commands will run. To make sure that at least one set of commands will run, it's common to add a final else part to the if-elif statement like this:

```
if x == 5:
        print("x is equal to 5")
elif x == 10:
        print("x is equal to 10")
elif x == 15:
        print("x is equal to 15")
elif x == 20:
        print("x is equal to 20")
else:
        print("No Boolean value was true")
```

To see how to use an if-elif statement, follow these steps:

1. Make sure you have a Godot project that consists of a Node2D and a child node Sprite2D that displays the icon.svg image in a window.

2. Click the Sprite2D node in the Scene dock.

3. Edit the script attached to the Sprite2D node as follows:

```
extends Sprite2D
func _ready():
        var x = 15

        if x == 5:
                print("x is equal to 5")
        elif x == 10:
                print("x is equal to 10")
```

```
elif x == 15:
        print("x is equal to 15")
elif x == 20:
        print("x is equal to 20")
```

4. Click the Run icon at the top of the window. The (DEBUG) window appears.

5. Click the close icon of the (DEBUG) window to make it go away. Notice that the Output pane at the bottom of the Godot window displays "x is equal to 15."

6. Change the value of the "x" variable to 7 and run the program again. Notice that this time, nothing prints out.

7. Edit the program to change the value of the "x" variable to 7 and to include an else part at the end like this:

```
extends Sprite2D
func _ready():
        var x = 7

        if x == 5:
                print("x is equal to 5")
        elif x == 10:
                print("x is equal to 10")
        elif x -- 15:
                print("x is equal to 15")
        elif x == 20:
                print("x is equal to 20")
        else:
                print("No Boolean value was true")
```

8.  Click the Run icon at the top of the window. The (DEBUG) window appears.

9.  Click the close icon of the (DEBUG) window to make it go away. Notice that the Output pane at the bottom of the Godot window displays "No Boolean value was true."

10. Change the value of the "x" variable and repeat steps 8 and 9 as many times as you wish to see how the if-elif statement works.

# The match Statement

The if-elif statement can check multiple Boolean values until it finds one that's true. If none of them are true, then a default else part can run commands instead. While the if-elif statement can be more versatile than the if or if-else statements, they can get clumsy to write if you need to check a large number of Boolean values.

For that reason, GDScript offers a match statement. (The match statement in GDScript is similar to the switch statement in other languages like Swift, C#, and Java.) The match statement is essentially identical to the if-elif statement except it's easier to write and understand.

Consider the following if-elif statement:

```
if x == 5:
        print("x is equal to 5")
elif x == 10:
        print("x is equal to 10")
elif x == 15:
        print("x is equal to 15")
elif x == 20:
        print("x is equal to 20")
```

```
else:
        print("No Boolean value was true")
```

An equivalent match statement would look like this:

```
match x:
        5: print("x is equal to 5")
        10: print("x is equal to 10")
        15: print("x is equal to 15")
        20: print("x is equal to 20")
        _: print("No Boolean value was true")
```

The "match x" part of the match statement defines a variable to use. In the preceding example, the match statement checks the value stored in the "x" variable and tries to match it to 5, 10, 15, and 20. If x exactly matches one of those values, then the match statement runs the code linked to the matched value.

The underscore character (_) is similar to "else" in an if-elif statement. The underscore means if nothing else matches, then run the code linked to the underscore character. The underscore character ensures that at least one set of commands will run.

To see how the match statement works, follow these steps:

1. Make sure you have a Godot project that consists of a Node2D and a child node Sprite2D that displays the icon.svg image in a window.

2. Click the Sprite2D node in the Scene dock.

3. Edit the script attached to the Sprite2D node as follows:

```
extends Sprite2D
func _ready():
        var x = 15
```

```
if x == 5:
        print("x is equal to 5")
elif x == 10:
        print("x is equal to 10")
elif x == 15:
        print("x is equal to 15")
elif x == 20:
        print("x is equal to 20")
else:
        print("No Boolean value was true")

match x:
        5: print("x is equal to 5")
        10: print("x is equal to 10")
        15: print("x is equal to 15")
        20: print("x is equal to 20")
        _: print("No Boolean value was true")
```

4. Click the Run icon at the top of the window. The (DEBUG) window appears.

5. Click the close icon of the (DEBUG) window to make it go away. Notice that the Output pane at the bottom of the Godot window displays "x is equal to 15" twice. The first time it prints this message is from the if-elif statement and the second time is from the match statement. That's because the if-elif and match statements are equivalent.

6. Change the value of the "x" variable and repeat steps 4 and 5. Notice that no matter what value you store in the "x" variable, the if-elif and match statements print the same message.

Compared to the if-elif statement, the match statement is shorter and much simpler to read. When you only need to check a handful of Boolean values, the if-elif statement is fine, but when you need to check three or more Boolean values, the match statement is often a better choice.

A match statement must exactly match a specific value. However, you can list multiple values to match such as the following:

```
match x:
        1, 3, 5, 7, 9: print("Odd number")
        0, 2, 4, 6, 8: print("Even number")
        _: print("Less than 0 or greater than 10")
```

If the number is less than 0 or greater than 10, the default (underscore) part of the match statement will run, which will print "Less than 0 or greater than 10." In case you want to get the exact value that did not match any of the earlier values, you can create a new variable like this:

```
match x:
    1, 3, 5, 7, 9: print("Odd number")
    0, 2, 4, 6, 8: print("Even number")
    var new_variable: print("The value = ", new_variable)
```

To see how the match statement works, follow these steps:

1. Make sure you have a Godot project that consists of a Node2D and a child node Sprite2D that displays the icon.svg image in a window.

2. Click the Sprite2D node in the Scene dock.

3. Edit the script attached to the Sprite2D node as follows:

```
extends Sprite2D
func _ready():
        var x = 94
```

```
match x:
    1, 3, 5, 7, 9: print("Odd number")
    0, 2, 4, 6, 8: print("Even number")
    var new_variable: print("The value = ",
    new_variable)
```

4. Click the Run icon at the top of the window. The (DEBUG) window appears.

5. Click the close icon of the (DEBUG) window to make it go away. Notice that the Output pane at the bottom of the Godot window displays "The value = 94."

6. Change the value of the "x" variable and repeat steps 4 and 5. As long as you type a number that's less than 0 or greater than 10, the match statement will print out the exact value stored in the "x" variable.

# Exercise: Reacting to Different Boolean Values

Video games constantly make decisions based on the player's actions and the game's current state. If a player starts out with three lives and dies a third time, then the game ends. If a player shoots at a flying saucer, the game must react if the player hits that flying saucer or not. Boolean values, along with decision statements like the if and match statements, let any project react to changing conditions.

In this exercise, you'll see how to use comparison operators to determine a true or false value. Based on that value, your program will use an if-else statement to display two possible options within a RichTextLabel that lets you display text on the user interface.

To see how to react to different situations using Boolean values and branching statements, follow these steps:

1.  Reuse the Godot project you created in Chapter 5 that lets you click a button to randomly move an image within the Godot window.

2.  Click Node2D in the Scene dock and click the Attach Child Node icon (+). A Create New Node dialog box appears.

3.  Click the Search text field and type RichTextLabel. The RichTextLabel appears as shown in Figure 6-1.

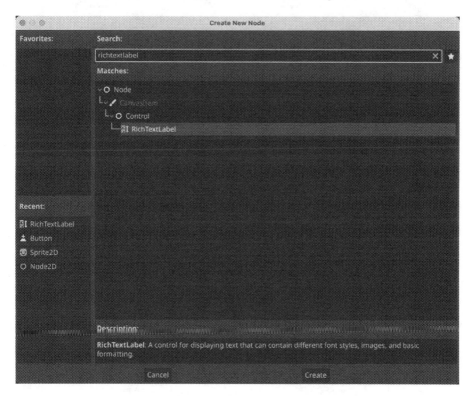

*Figure 6-1.* *Adding the RichTextLabel as a child of Node2D*

4. Click RichTextLabel and click Create. Godot adds the RichTextLabel as a child node of Node2D.

5. Click the 2D tab at the top middle of the Godot editor window. Godot displays the user interface of your project.

6. Click RichTextLabel in the Scene dock and drag and resize it so that it appears underneath the button as shown in Figure 6-2.

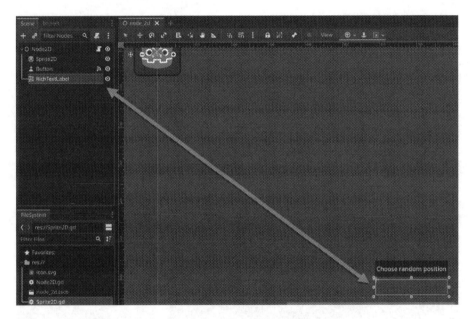

**Figure 6-2.** *Resizing and placing the RichTextLabel on the user interface*

7. Click the script icon that appears to the right of Node2D in the Scene dock. Godot displays the GDScript editor.

8. Modify the code as follows:

```
extends Node2D
func _process(delta):
        var window_size = DisplayServer.window_get_size()
        if $Sprite2D.position.y > window_size.y / 2:
            $RichTextLabel.clear()
            $RichTextLabel.append_text("In bottom half")
        else:
            $RichTextLabel.clear()
            $RichTextLabel.append_text("In top half")

func _on_button_pressed():
        var window_size = DisplayServer.window_get_size()
        randomize()
        $Sprite2D.position.x = randi() % window_size.x
        $Sprite2D.position.y = randi() % window_size.y
```

The function _process(delta) runs constantly. The if-else statement checks if the current y position is greater than the windows's height. If so, then that means the image currently appears in the bottom half of the window (since the value of y increases downward). Otherwise, the image currently appears in the top half of the window.

To display a message in the RichTextLabel involves first clearing anything currently displayed then appending new text in the RichTextLabel.

9.  Click the Run icon and then click the button to randomly move the image around the window. Notice that each time the image moves to a different location, the RichTextLabel either displays "In bottom half" or "In top half."

10. Click the close icon of the (DEBUG) window to stop running the project.

129

This exercise lets you see how different values can change a Boolean value. Based on whether a Boolean value is true or false, an if-else statement can decide to run one set of commands or an alternate set of commands. In addition, you also learned how to display text on the user interface by using a RichTextLabel node.

# Summary

To make decisions, programs need to use Boolean data types that can hold either a true or false value. One way to create a true or false value is by using comparison operators to compare two values such as a variable with a value or two variables. Depending on the value stored in the variable, the value of the comparison operator will either be true or false.

The most common comparison operators are < (less than), > (greater than), == (equal to), != (not equal to), <= (less than or equal to), and >= greater than or equal to).

Another way to calculate a Boolean value is to use logical operators that combine two Boolean values to calculate a single Boolean value. The three logical operators are

- and

- or

- not

The "and" operator evaluates to true only if both Boolean values are true such as x > 0 and x < 10 where x is 5. That means 5 > 0 is true and 5 < 10 is also true.

The "or" operator evaluates to false only if both Boolean values are false such as x > 0 or x >= 80 where x is -7. That means -7 > 0 is false and -7 >= 10 is also true.

The "not" operator simply turns a false value to true and a true value to false.

By using Boolean values, you can create branching statements so a program can make a decision. The four types of branching statements are

- if

- if-else

- if-elif

- match

The if statement checks a Boolean value, and if it's true, then it runs commands. If the Boolean value is false, it does nothing.

The if-else checks a Boolean value, and if it's true, then it runs one set of commands. If the Boolean value is false, then it runs the second set of commands.

The if-elif statement checks multiple Boolean values until it finds one that's true. If none of these Boolean values are true, the if-elif statement won't do anything unless it includes an else part at the end.

The match statement is a shorter way to write an if-elif statement. A match statement can match a single value or multiple values separated by a comma.

# CHAPTER 7

# Looping Statements

A loop repeats one or more commands multiple times. When you play a video game, the entire game represents a loop because as soon as you finish (or die in the game), the game gives you a chance to play again. That's a loop. Within a game, you have smaller loops. Enemies may pop up and move in a predictable pattern, which represents a loop. Whenever a random enemy pops up, that is called spawning, and a program can run a loop to spawn more enemies. Fighting a single enemy represents a loop. Repeating the same game animation to fight an enemy is a loop. Any time you have repetitive action, that's a loop.

Looping statements let you repeat code. That way you can write smaller programs that are easier to write and understand. In GDScript, there are two types of loops:

- For loops
- While loops

The main difference between these two loops is that the for loop is used most often when you know exactly how many times you want a loop to repeat. On the other hand, a while loop is used most often when the number of times the loop may repeat can vary, so it's never a fixed number

© Wallace Wang, Tonnetta Walcott 2024
W. Wang and T. Walcott, *Programming for Game Design*,
https://doi.org/10.1007/979-8-8688-0190-7_7

# Using a For Loop

A for loop counts how many times to repeat. The simplest for loop defines a fixed number like this:

```
for x in 5:
    print(x)
```

As simple as this for loop might look, there are actually several parts to understand:

- The "x" variable counts, starting from 0.

- The for loop increases the value of the "x" variable by 1 each time it repeats.

- The fixed number, 5, defines when to stop the loop, which is when x is exactly equal to 4 (counting five times from 0, 1, 2, 3, and 4).

To see how a for loop works, follow these steps:

1. Make sure you have a Godot project that consists of a Node2D and a child node Sprite2D that displays the icon.svg image in a window.

2. Click the Sprite2D node in the Scene dock.

3. Edit the script attached to the Sprite2D node as follows:

```
extends Sprite2D
func _ready():
    for x in 5:
        print(x)
```

4. Click the Run icon at the top of the window. The (DEBUG) window appears.

5.  Click the close icon of the (DEBUG) window to
    make it go away. Notice that the Output pane at the
    bottom of the Godot window displays the results of
    the for loop as follows:

    0

    1

    2

    3

    4

6.  Change the value from 5 to another positive integer
    value and rerun the program again. No matter what
    integer value you choose, the for loop will always
    start counting at 0 and stop at the defined number
    minus one (such as 5 – 1 = 4).

    To make it clearer that the for loop is repeating over
    a range of values, starting with 0, you can also define
    the upper value of a for loop like this:

    ```
    for x in range(5):
            print(x)
    ```

    This is equivalent to

    ```
    for x in 5:
            print(x)
    ```

# Using a For Loop to Count with Different Values

An ordinary for loop always starts counting at 0 and stops at the upper limit value – 1. However, what if you want to start counting from a nonzero value? In that case, you can define a range of values that define the starting number and an upper limit value like this:

```
for x in range(5, 11):
        print(x)
```

The preceding code starts counting at 5 and stops at the upper limit – 1 (11 – 1 = 10). To see how this for loop works, follow these steps:

1.  Make sure you have a Godot project that consists of a Node2D and a child node Sprite2D that displays the icon.svg image in a window.

2.  Click the Sprite2D node in the Scene dock.

3.  Edit the script attached to the Sprite2D node as follows:

```
extends Sprite2D
func _ready():
        for x in range(5, 11):
                print(x)
```

4.  Click the Run icon at the top of the window. The (DEBUG) window appears.

5.  Click the close icon of the (DEBUG) window to make it go away. Notice that the Output pane at the bottom of the Godot window displays the results of the for loop as follows:

5

6

7

8

9

10

6.  Change the starting value from 5 to another positive
    integer value and change the ending value from 11
    to another positive integer value larger than 6. Then
    rerun the program again. No matter what integer
    value you choose, the for loop will always start
    counting at the starting value and stop at the ending
    value minus one (such as 11 – 1 = 10).

So far, we've created for loops that count from a lower value to a higher
value, incrementing by one. Rather than increment by 1, you can define a
number to increment by such as 2 or 3 like this:

```
for x in range(5, 13, 2):
    print(x)
```

The preceding code starts counting at 5 but increments by 2. So the
second number is 7, the third number is 9, the fourth number is 11, and
then it stops because the upper limit minus the increment value (13 – 2 =
11) has been reached or exceeded.

To see how a for loop can increment by values other than 1, follow
these steps:

1.  Make sure you have a Godot project that consists of
    a Node2D and a child node Sprite2D that displays
    the icon.svg image in a window.

2.  Click the Sprite2D node in the Scene dock.

3.  Edit the script attached to the Sprite2D node as follows:

```
extends Sprite2D
func _ready():
        for x in range(5, 13, 2):
            print(x)
```

4.  Click the Run icon at the top of the window. The (DEBUG) window appears.

5.  Click the close icon of the (DEBUG) window to make it go away. Notice that the Output pane at the bottom of the Godot window displays the results as follows:

```
5
7
9
11
```

6.  Change the starting value from 5 to another positive integer value and change the ending value from 13 to another positive integer value larger than 6. Change the increment value from 2 to another positive number such as 3 or 4. Then rerun the program again. No matter what integer value you choose, the for loop will always start counting at the starting value and stop at the ending value minus the increment value (such as 13 – 2 = 11).

So far, we've been counting from a lower value to a higher value by increments of 1 or another value we choose. A for loop can also count down from a higher value to a lower value by a negative increment such as -1 or -3. To do that, just switch the numbers defined in the range like this:

```
for x in range(13, 5, -1):
    print(x)
```

This for loop starts counting at 13 then decrements by 1 (or increases by -1) until it reaches the second limit of 5 – -1 = 6. To see how this for loop works, follow these steps:

1. Make sure you have a Godot project that consists of a Node2D and a child node Sprite2D that displays the icon.svg image in a window.

2. Click the Sprite2D node in the Scene dock.

3. Edit the script attached to the Sprite2D node as follows:

```
extends Sprite2D
func _ready():
        for x in range(13, 5, -1):
            print(x)
```

4. Click the Run icon at the top of the window. The (DEBUG) window appears.

5. Click the close icon of the (DEBUG) window to make it go away. Notice that the Output pane at the bottom of the Godot window displays the results as follows:

```
13
12
11
10
9
8
7
6
```

6.  Change the starting value from 13 to another positive integer value and change the ending value from 5 to another positive integer value. Change the increment value from -1 to another negative number such as -2 or -3. Then rerun the program again. No matter what integer value you choose, the for loop will always start counting at the starting value and stop at the ending value minus the increment value (such as 5 – -1 = 6).

# Using the For Loop with Strings and Arrays

The for loop normally repeats based on numeric values that define the starting and ending values. However, a for loop can repeat based on the number of items in a string or an array. (Arrays are a data structure that you'll learn about in Chapter 8.)

A string can be a single word (such as "Hello") or multiple words separated by spaces or punctuation marks (such as "Hello, world!"). Every character in a string, including spaces and punctuation marks, counts as 1 character, so the string "Hello" consists of 5 characters, while the string "Hello, world!" consists of 13 characters.

Because every string contains one or more characters, a for loop can use the total number of characters to define how many times it repeats like this:

```
for x in "Hello":
    print(x)
```

Since the string "Hello" contains five characters, the preceding for loop repeats five times. Besides defining how many times a for loop repeats, a string can also define what value the for loop can retrieve. In the preceding example, the for loop retrieves and prints each character of the string.

To see how a for loop can work with a string, follow these steps:

1.  Make sure you have a Godot project that consists of a Node2D and a child node Sprite2D that displays the icon.svg image in a window.

2.  Click the Sprite2D node in the Scene dock.

3.  Edit the script attached to the Sprite2D node as follows:

```
extends Sprite2D
func _ready():
        for x in "Hello":
                print(x)
```

4.  Click the Run icon at the top of the window. The (DEBUG) window appears.

5.  Click the close icon of the (DEBUG) window to make it go away. Notice that the Output pane at the bottom of the Godot window displays the results as follows:

```
H
e
l
l
o
```

6.  Change the string "Hello" to another string, even one containing spaces and punctuation marks. Then run the program again. Each time you change the length and contents of the string, the for loop will repeat based on the number of characters in the string and print each character in that string.

Besides looping through a string, a for loop can also loop through an array where the number of items in an array determines how many times the for loop repeats and the contents of the array determine what a for loop variable can retrieve like this:

```
for x in ["Hello", "Bye", "Cat", "Dog", "Bird"]:
    print(x)
```

The array contains five strings (["Hello", "Bye", "Cat", "Dog", "Bird"]), so it repeats five times. Then it prints each item in the array.

To see how a for loop can use an array to define how many times to repeat, follow these steps:

1. Make sure you have a Godot project that consists of a Node2D and a child node Sprite2D that displays the icon.svg image in a window.

2. Click the Sprite2D node in the Scene dock.

3. Edit the script attached to the Sprite2D node as follows:

```
extends Sprite2D
func _ready():
        for x in ["Hello", "Bye", "Cat", "Dog", "Bird"]:
            print(x)
```

4. Click the Run icon at the top of the window. The (DEBUG) window appears.

5. Click the close icon of the (DEBUG) window to make it go away. Notice that the Output pane at the bottom of the Godot window displays the results as follows:

```
Hello
Bye
Cat
Dog
Bird
```

6. Change the strings stored in the array by adding new strings. Then run the program again. Each time you change the length and contents of the string, the for loop will repeat based on the number of items in the array and print each item in that array.

A for loop can repeat a fixed number of times or over a range where that range can be two numeric values, a string, or an array. When you know exactly how many times a loop should repeat, use a for loop. When you don't know how many times a loop should repeat, use a while loop instead.

# The While Loop

The for loop repeats until it reaches a numeric limit. On the other hand, the while loop repeats as long as a Boolean value remains true. The moment this Boolean value becomes false, the while loop stops repeating. To use a while loop, you must include the following:

- A variable that will change within the while loop

- A Boolean value that uses this variable with a comparison operator to check if it's true or false

- A way to change this variable within the loop so that the Boolean value will eventually become false

A while loop looks like this:

```
    var x = 0      # A variable that will change within
the loop
    while x < 5:  # A Boolean value that will eventually
be false
        print(x)
        x += 1 # A way to change the variable within
the loop
```

If you don't create and store an initial value in a variable before the while loop, the while loop's Boolean value won't be able to evaluate to either true or false.

If you create a Boolean value that never evaluates to true, the while loop will never run. If this Boolean value never evaluates to false, the while loop will never stop running, creating an endless loop.

If you never change the variable within the while loop, the Boolean value can never evaluate to false, creating an endless loop.

To see how the while loop works, follow these steps:

1.  Make sure you have a Godot project that consists of a Node2D and a child node Sprite2D that displays the icon.svg image in a window.

2.  Click the Sprite2D node in the Scene dock.

3.  Edit the script attached to the Sprite2D node as follows:

```
extends Sprite2D
func _ready():
        var x = 0      # A variable that will change
within the loop
        while x < 5:  # A Boolean value that will
eventually be false
```

```
        print(x)
        x += 1 # A way to change the variable
within the loop
```

4.  Click the Run icon at the top of the window. The (DEBUG) window appears.

5.  Click the close icon of the (DEBUG) window to make it go away. Notice that the Output pane at the bottom of the Godot window displays the results of mathematical operations as follows:

0

1

2

3

4

6.  Change the value of "x" from 0 to 9 and repeat steps 4 and 5. Notice that nothing happens because the Boolean value (9 < 5) is false, so the while loop never runs.

7.  Change the value of "x" back to 0 and delete the "x += 1" line, so the variable never changes. Then repeat steps 4 and 5. Notice that the program keeps printing 0 and never stops running because the while loop's Boolean value (x < 5) is always true and never changes. This creates an endless loop. To stop Godot from running, you'll need to Force Quit Godot.

# Comparing For and While Loops

A for loop is best for counting, but a while loop can do that too. A while loop is best for running until a Boolean value becomes false, but a for loop can do that too. In programming, there are often multiple ways to do the same task, but some ways are shorter and easier than others.

Consider the following for loop that runs exactly five times:

```
for x in 5:
    print(x)
```

This for loop starts counting at 0, counts 1, 2, 3, and 4, then stops. An equivalent while loop might look like this:

```
var x = 0
while x < 5:
    print(x)
    x += 1
```

Both loops count from 0 to 4, but the for loop is shorter and easier to understand. On the other hand, the while loop is longer and harder to understand with more ways the loop can work incorrectly. If you fail to initialize a variable before the while loop, the while loop's Boolean value (x < 5) may never be true, so the loop never runs at all. If you fail to change the "x" variable within the loop (x += 1), then the loop risks never stopping.

To see how to create equivalent for and while loops, follow these steps:

1. Make sure you have a Godot project that consists of a Node2D and a child node Sprite2D that displays the icon.svg image in a window.

2. Click the Sprite2D node in the Scene dock.

3. Edit the script attached to the Sprite2D node as follows:

```
extends Sprite2D
func _ready():
        for x in 5:
                print("for loop = ", x)
        var y = 0
        while y < 5:
                print("while loop = ", y)
                y += 1
```

4.  Click the Run icon at the top of the window. The
    (DEBUG) window appears.

5.  Click the close icon of the (DEBUG) window to
    make it go away. Notice that the Output pane at the
    bottom of the Godot window displays the results of
    mathematical operations as follows:

```
for loop = 0
for loop = 1
for loop = 2
for loop = 3
for loop = 4
while loop = 0
while loop = 1
while loop = 2
while loop = 3
while loop = 4
```

The while loop is best for repeating until a Boolean value becomes
false. Video games often use a loop to continue playing the game until the
user quits. So a while loop might look like this:

```
var play_game: bool = true
var games_played = 0
```

```
while play_game == true:
        games_played += 1
        print("Play game ", games_played)
        if games_played == 5:
                play_game = false
```

This while loop runs until the number of games played equals 5. Then it changes its Boolean value to false, so the while loop eventually ends.

To duplicate this in a for loop, we need to use a "break" command like this:

```
for games in range(1, 100):
        print("For loop game ", games)
        if games == 5:
                break
```

This for loop would normally continue looping 100 times, but the if statement combined with the break command prematurely exits this for loop after 5 times. Although the for loop may look shorter, there's one huge problem.

The while loop can continue looping indefinitely until its Boolean value changes to false. With the for loop, we must choose an arbitrarily large value (100) to make the for loop keep repeating. If this arbitrary value is too low, the for loop could end too soon.

If the for loop controlled a video game, there's no way of knowing how many times someone might want to play a video game before stopping. No matter what arbitrarily large value we define for the for loop, it may not be high enough. In this case, the while loop does not need an arbitrary value to define how many times to loop because a while loop repeats endlessly until someone chooses to quit the game.

To see how the while and for loops compare when stopping when a Boolean value changes, follow these steps:

1.  Make sure you have a Godot project that consists of a Node2D and a child node Sprite2D that displays the icon.svg image in a window.

2.  Click the Sprite2D node in the Scene dock.

3.  Edit the script attached to the Sprite2D node as follows:

```
extends Sprite2D
func _ready():
        var play_game: bool = true
        var games_played = 0
        while play_game == true:
                games_played += 1
                print("While loop game ", games_played)
                if games_played == 5:
                        play_game = false

        for games in range(1, 100):
                print("For loop game ", games)
                if games == 5:
                        break
```

4.  Click the Run icon at the top of the window. The (DEBUG) window appears.

5.  Click the close icon of the (DEBUG) window to make it go away. Notice that the Output pane at the bottom of the Godot window shows the while loop and the for loop both ending after five times as follows:

```
While loop game 1
While loop game 2
```

```
While loop game 3
While loop game 4
While loop game 5
For loop game 1
For loop game 2
For loop game 3
For loop game 4
For loop game 5
```

When creating loops, choose between the for loop and the while loop. Both have their advantages and disadvantages, so use the loop that's best for your particular needs.

# Exercise: Repeating Code with Loops

Writing multiple, often repetitive commands can clarify what a program does at the expense of taking up a lot of space. On the other hand, loops take up much less space but can be harder to understand. Ultimately, programming is a trade-off between clarity (takes time to write) and efficiency (harder to understand).

In this exercise, you'll create a simple loop to see how to rotate an image and eventually stop at a specific angle to keep the loop from running endlessly.

To see how to use a loop, follow these steps:

1.  Create a new Godot project and create a Node2D in the Scene dock.

2.  Click Node2D in the Scene dock and click the Attach Child Node icon (+). A Create New Node dialog box appears.

3.  Click the Search text field and type **sprite2d**.

4.  Click Sprite2D in the Create New Node dialog box and click Create. Godot creates a Sprite2D as a child node under Node2D.

5.  Click Sprite2D. Notice that the Inspector dock displays an empty Texture property.

6.  Drag and drop the icon.svg image from the FileSystem dock to the Texture property of the Sprite2D node. The icon.svg appears on the user interface.

7.  Drag the Sprite2D node so that it appears within the borders of the user interface window.

8.  Click Node2D in the Scene dock and then click the Attach Script icon. An Attach Node Script dialog box appears.

9.  Click Create. Godot displays a GDScript.

10. Edit the GDScript code as follows:

```
extends Node2D
var degrees = 0
@export var final_angle = 0
func _process(delta):
        while degrees <= final_angle:
                $Sprite2D.rotation_degrees = degrees
                degrees += 10
```

The final_angle variable appears in the Inspector dock for Node2D. This lets you type in a value, and then the while loop will rotate the icon.svg image to the angle you chose.

11.  Click Node2D in the Scene dock. Notice that the
     final_angle variable is visible in the Inspector dock
     as shown in Figure 7-1.

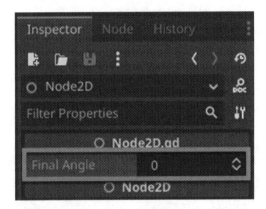

**Figure 7-1.** *The final_angle variable appears in the Inspector dock*

12.  Click the Final Angle property in the Inspector dock
     and type an angle such as 45 and press Enter. The
     while loop will use this value to rotate the image to
     your defined Final Angle value.

13.  Click the Run icon. A dialog box asks for you to
     choose a main scene.

14.  Click Select Current. A dialog box appears, asking
     you to save your files.

15.  Click Save. Godot runs your project. Notice that the
     image appears rotated at the angle you defined in
     the Final Angle property in the Inspector dock.

16.  Click the close icon of the (DEBUG) window to stop
     your project.

The while loop keeps rotating the image until it has rotated the image beyond the value stored in the final_angle variable. Although we can't see the while loop running, we can see the results when the while loop finishes running when it displays a rotated image in the (DEBUG) window.

# Summary

A loop repeats one or more commands multiple times. This can make programs more compact but also harder to understand. The two types of available loops are for loops and while loops.

A for loop can run a fixed number of times. A while loop may never run, but once it starts running, it keeps running until a Boolean value changes to false.

When creating a for loop, you can define a fixed number to define how many times to repeat the for loop, a range of values, and an increment value. A for loop can also use a string or an array to define how many times it repeats.

When creating a while loop, make sure you define a variable before the loop and then change that variable somewhere inside the loop to make a Boolean value change from true to false eventually. Failure to do this could create an endless loop that freezes or hangs the program and keeps it from working.

Both a for loop and a while loop can work identically although in most cases, one loop will be simpler and easier to use than the other. Loops simply give you a way to repeat code.

# CHAPTER 8

# Understanding Arrays

Every program needs to store data, and that data usually gets stored in one or more variables. However, the more data a program needs to store, the more variables you need to create. Rather than create multiple variables, it's much easier to use an array.

An array essentially acts like a single variable but with the ability to store any number of items. A number of items are grouped together, making arrays handy for storing data in one place that share a common characteristic. A video game might use one array to store a list of supplies such as a medical kit, ammunition for a rifle, and food and a second array to store a list of weapons the player can use.

Another array can even be used to store the characteristics of a player in an RPG-type game such as hair, torso, legs, etc. You can use an array for just about anything when it comes to making a game. It just depends on the type of game that you are making. Arrays are especially useful when dealing with multiple variables.

Arrays represent the most commonly used way to store data besides single variables. So it's important to understand how to create arrays, fill them with data, and retrieve data from them.

© Wallace Wang, Tonnetta Walcott 2024
W. Wang and T. Walcott, *Programming for Game Design*,
https://doi.org/10.1007/979-8-8688-0190-7_8

# Using Arrays

A variable acts like a single box that can hold exactly one chunk of data. To access the value in a variable, you just have to use the variable name. The main limitation of a variable is that it can only hold one chunk of data at a time.

To create a variable, just define three parts as shown in Figure 8-1:

- Variable name

- (Optional) Data type

- (Optional) Initial value

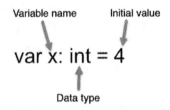

**Figure 8-1.**  *The three parts of creating a variable*

To create an array, you just need two parts:

- Array name

- (Optional) One or more initial values

Unlike variables that can be defined to hold a specific data type, arrays can hold any data type such as integers, strings, and floating-point numbers. The variables stored in an array are ordered by index. The first index of an array begins at 0 then continues onward. Arrays consist of a list of data enclosed by square brackets as shown in Figure 8-2.

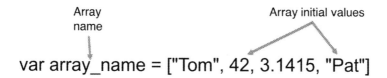

Array name          Array initial values

var array_name = ["Tom", 42, 3.1415, "Pat"]

*Figure 8-2.* *The two parts of creating an array*

Where a variable can only hold one chunk of data at a time, arrays can hold multiple chunks of data in a single variable name. A variable acts like a single box, but an array acts like a collection of boxes where each box can hold a different chunk of data as shown in Figure 8-3.

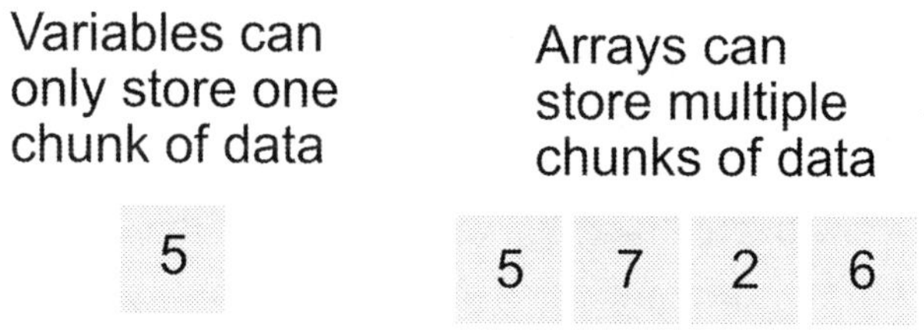

Variables can only store one chunk of data

5

Arrays can store multiple chunks of data

5   7   2   6

*Figure 8-3.* *The difference between a variable and an array*

To retrieve data stored in a variable, just use the variable name like this:

```
var x = 4
print("The value in x = ", x)
```

However, to retrieve data stored in an array, you need both the variable name and its position (also called an index value) within the array. The leftmost position in an array is index value 0, the second position is index value 1, and so on as shown in Figure 8-4.

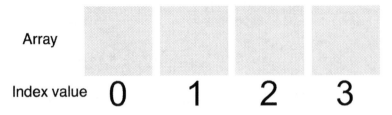

**Figure 8-4.** *An array stores data in specific positions identified by an index number*

Suppose you needed to track the health of two different characters. You could create two separate variables like this:

```
var healthPerson = 40
var healthDog = 15
```

The problem with creating separate variables is that there is no visible relationship between similar variables. Using an array, you can group related data together such as follows:

```
var healthArray = [healthPerson, healthDog]
```

An array can hold multiple elements in a single location. To access a specific item in an array, we need to define the array name plus the index position. The first item in an array is at index 0, the second at index 1, and so on. Suppose we ran the following code:

```
print(healthArray[0])
```

The first item in the healthArray is healthPerson, which has a value of 40. So the preceding command would print 40.

If we want to print out all the elements within an array, we could omit the index value and only specify the array name like this:

```
print(healthArray)
```

Arrays can be versatile. For example, we could create a character creation menu in a game that stores the different elements of the character, such as the legs, torso, and head, in an array. There are multiple ways to get creative with strings, arrays, and integers when programming in Godot, so take the time to discover different functions to make your game.

To see how to create an array and retrieve data from that array, follow these steps:

1. Make sure you have a Godot project that consists of a Node2D and a child node Sprite2D that displays the icon.svg image in a window.

2. Click the Sprite2D node in the Scene dock.

3. Edit the script attached to the Sprite2D node as follows:

```
extends Sprite2D
func _ready():
        var name_array = ["Tom", 42, 3.1415, "Pat"]
        print("Index 2 = ", name_array[2])
        print("Index 0 = ", name_array[0])
        print("Index 3 = ", name_array[3])
        print("Index 1 = ", name_array[1])
```

4. Click the Run icon at the top of the window. The (DEBUG) window appears.

5. Click the close icon of the (DEBUG) window to make it go away. Notice that the Output pane at the bottom of the Godot window displays the following:

```
Index 2 = 3.1415
Index 0 = Tom
Index 3 = Pat
Index 1 = 42
```

To retrieve data from an array, you must specify the array name followed by an index value enclosed in square brackets. So if you want to retrieve the first item in an array, you would specify the array name with an index value of 0 like this:

```
array_name[0]
```

When retrieving data, be careful to specify an index value that actually contains data. For example, suppose you had an array like this:

```
var name_array = ["Tom", 42, 3.1415, "Pat"]
```

The index numbers correspond to each chunk of data like this:

| Index value | Data |
| --- | --- |
| 0 | "Tom" |
| 1 | 42 |
| 2 | 3.1415 |
| 3 | "Pat" |

If you use the index value of 3, you'll retrieve the data stored in the index 3 position, which is "Pat." However, if you use an index value of 4 or greater, there is no data stored in those index positions in the array, so trying to retrieve nonexistent data will cause an error.

To see what happens if you try to retrieve nonexistent data in an array, follow these steps:

1. Make sure you have a Godot project that consists of a Node2D and a child node Sprite2D that displays the icon.svg image in a window.

2. Click the Sprite2D node in the Scene dock.

3.  Edit the script attached to the Sprite2D node as
    follows:

```
extends Sprite2D
func _ready():
        var name_array = ["Tom", 42, 3.1415, "Pat"]
        print("Index 32 = ", name_array[32])
```

4.  Click the Run icon at the top of the window. The
    (DEBUG) window appears.

5.  Click the close icon of the (DEBUG) window to make
    it go away. Notice that the program crashes. Any
    time you try to retrieve data using an index value
    that doesn't exist, your program will always crash.

# Creating and Adding Items to an Array

The simplest way to create an array is to define an array name and assign it
an initial array by using square brackets such as follows:

```
var pet_array = ["Dog", "Cat", "Bird", "Fish", Turtle"]
```

If you want to create an array but don't want to define initial values,
you have two options:

- var pet_array = Array()

- var pet_array = []

Both methods create an empty array. Whether you start with an empty
array or with an array containing one or more items, you can always add
new data to an array at any time. Two ways to add items to an array include

- append

- insert

161

The append command always adds a new item at the end of an array. The insert command lets you define the position (index value) where you want a newly added item to appear. This index value must be an existing value, which means it already contains data. When you use the insert command, it moves all existing data to the right as shown in Figure 8-5.

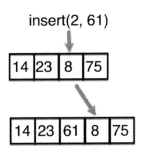

**Figure 8-5.** *The insert command pushes existing data to the right, increasing their index value by 1*

To see how both the append and insert commands can add items to an array, follow these steps:

1. Make sure you have a Godot project that consists of a Node2D and a child node Sprite2D that displays the icon.svg image in a window.

2. Click the Sprite2D node in the Scene dock.

3. Edit the script attached to the Sprite2D node as follows:

```
extends Sprite2D
func _ready():
        var number_array = [14, 23, 8]
        number_array.append(75)
        print("Append ", number_array)
        number_array.insert(2, 61)
        print("Insert ", number_array)
```

4. Click the Run icon at the top of the window. The (DEBUG) window appears.

5. Click the close icon of the (DEBUG) window to make it go away. Notice that the Output pane at the bottom of the Godot window displays the results of the append and insert commands as follows:

```
Append [14, 23, 8, 75]
Insert [14, 23, 61, 8, 75]
```

Notice that the append command puts 75 at the end (rightmost) side of the array while the insert(2, 61) commands puts 61 at the third position (index value 2) and pushes everything else to the right.

When using the insert command, be careful to only specify index values that exist. If you try to insert an item into an array using an invalid index number, the program will crash.

# Getting Information About Arrays

Once you've created an array and stored items in them, you may need to get information about the array such as whether it's empty, how many items it may hold, what's the largest item stored, and what's the smallest item stored in the array.

To get information about an array, GDScript offers the following commands:

- is_empty

- size

- max/min

The is_empty command lets you know if an array is empty. The size command returns the total number of items in an array. The max and min commands retrieve the maximum or minimum items stored in an array.

For numeric values, the max command retrieves the largest value, and the min command retrieves the smallest value.

To see how these commands work with arrays, follow these steps:

1.  Make sure you have a Godot project that consists of a Node2D and a child node Sprite2D that displays the icon.svg image in a window.

2.  Click the Sprite2D node in the Scene dock.

3.  Edit the script attached to the Sprite2D node as follows:

```
extends Sprite2D
func _ready():
        var number_array = []
        print("Is_empty = ", number_array.is_empty())
        number_array.append(40)
        print("Is_empty = ", number_array.is_empty())
        number_array.append(25)
        number_array.append(37)
        number_array.append(94)
        print(number_array)
        print("Maximum value = ", number_array.max())
        print("Minimum value = ", number_array.min())
        print(number_array)
        print("Size = ", number_array.size())
```

4.  Click the Run icon at the top of the window. The (DEBUG) window appears.

5.  Click the close icon of the (DEBUG) window to make it go away. Notice that the Output pane at the bottom of the Godot window displays the results of the is_empty, commands as follows:

```
Is_empty = true
Is_empty = false
[40, 25, 37, 94]
Maximum value = 94
Minimum value = 25
[40, 25, 37, 94]
Size = 4
```

Notice that initially, the array is empty, so the is_empty command returns true. Then the append command stores 40 in the array, so the second time the is_empty command returns false.

Multiple append commands add 25, 37, and 94 to the array. That means the maximum value in the array is 94 and the minimum value is 25. Finally, the size command returns the size or total number of items stored in the array, which is 4 (40, 25, 37, 94).

When working with strings, the max and min commands use alphabetical order to determine a minimum and maximum value. Strings that begin with "a" are considered lower, while strings that begin with "z" are considered higher.

To see how to use the min and max commands with strings, follow these steps:

1.  Make sure you have a Godot project that consists of a Node2D and a child node Sprite2D that displays the icon.svg image in a window.

2.  Click the Sprite2D node in the Scene dock.

3.  Edit the script attached to the Sprite2D node as follows:

```
extends Sprite2D
func _ready():
```

```
var name_array = ["Fred", "Barney", "Wilma",
"Betty"]
print("Max = ", name_array.max())
print("Min = ", name_array.min())
```

4.  Click the Run icon at the top of the window. The (DEBUG) window appears.

5.  Click the close icon of the (DEBUG) window to make it go away. Notice that the Output pane at the bottom of the Godot window displays the results of the max and min commands as follows:

```
Max = Wilma
Min = Barney
```

6.  Experiment with different names in the array and repeat steps 4 and 5.

# Retrieving Data from Arrays

After you've stored data in an array, you can retrieve that data by specifying the index value of the data you want to retrieve such as follows:

```
var name_array = ["Fred", "Barney", "Wilma", "Betty"]
print(name_array[1])
```

The preceding code creates an array with four strings and then prints the string stored at index 1, which is "Barney." One trouble with arrays is that if you add or delete items from an array, the index values of the data will constantly change. To make retrieving data from an array easier, GDScript offers three commands:

- front

- back

- pick_random

The front command retrieves the first item in an array, which is always at index 0. The back command retrieves the last item in an array. Since an array can be of any size, trying to specify the index value of the last item in an array can be dangerous since it will change when you add or delete items from an array.

The pick_random command simply chooses an item from the array at random. This can be handy for video games that use an array to store playing card values or need to create other forms of random activity.

To see how to use these commands, follow these steps:

1.  Make sure you have a Godot project that consists of a Node2D and a child node Sprite2D that displays the icon.svg image in a window.

2.  Click the Sprite2D node in the Scene dock.

3.  Edit the script attached to the Sprite2D node as follows:

```
extends Sprite2D
func _ready():
        var name_array = ["Fred", "Barney", "Wilma",
        "Betty"]
        print("Front = ", name_array.front())
        print("Back = ", name_array.back())
        print("Pick random = ", name_array.pick_random())
```

4.  Click the Run icon at the top of the window. The (DEBUG) window appears.

5.  Click the close icon of the (DEBUG) window to
    make it go away. Notice that the Output pane at the
    bottom of the Godot window displays the results of
    the is_empty, commands as follows:

```
Front = Fred
Back = Betty
Pick random = Barney
```

Note that if you run the program again, the front ("Fred") and back
("Betty") results will always be the same, but the pick_random command
will likely retrieve a different name.

The front and back commands retrieve an item from an array but do
not remove it from the array. Three other commands not only retrieve an
item from an array but remove it as well:

- pop_at

- pop_back

- pop_front

The pop_at command retrieves and removes an item from a specific
index value. The pop_back and pop_front commands retrieve and remove
an item from the back and front of an array, respectively.

To see how these three pop commands work, follow these steps:

1.  Make sure you have a Godot project that consists of
    a Node2D and a child node Sprite2D that displays
    the icon.svg image in a window.

2.  Click the Sprite2D node in the Scene dock.

3.  Edit the script attached to the Sprite2D node as
    follows:

```
extends Sprite2D
func _ready():
     var name_string = ""
     var name_array = ["Fred", "Barney", "Wilma",
     "Betty"]
     print(name_array)
     name_string = name_array.pop_front()
     print("Pop front = ", name_string)
     print(name_array)

     name_string = name_array.pop_back()
     print("Pop back = ", name_string)
     print(name_array)

     name_string = name_array.pop_at(1)
     print("Pop at = ", name_string)
     print(name_array)
```

4.  Click the Run icon at the top of the window. The
    (DEBUG) window appears.

5.  Click the close icon of the (DEBUG) window to
    make it go away. Notice that the Output pane at the
    bottom of the Godot window displays the results of
    the is_empty, commands as follows:

```
["Fred", "Barney", "Wilma", "Betty"]
Pop front = Fred
["Barney", "Wilma", "Betty"]
Pop back = Betty
["Barney", "Wilma"]
Pop at = Wilma
["Barney"]
```

Notice that each time a pop command runs, it retrieves and removes an item from the array. Thus the array gradually shrinks each time another pop command runs.

If a pop command tries to retrieve an item from an array that does not exist, it will only return a <null> value. Change the array in the preceding code to an empty array [] like this:

```
var name_array =[]
```

Then run the program again. The Output pane will display the following:

```
[]
Pop front = <null>
[]
Pop back = <null>
[]
Pop at = <null>
[]
```

Remember that all pop commands retrieve and remove items from an array. If you only want to retrieve an item without removing that item from the array, use the front or back command, or access the name of the array and an index value such as name_array[2].

# Manipulating Arrays

You can store data in any order in an array, so two arrays can contain the exact same data but arranged in different order. This chaotic way of storing data can make arrays difficult to use since you never know where data might be stored at any given time.

To change the order of data in an array, you can use the following commands:

- Sort

- Reverse

- Shuffle

Sort rearranges the order of an array in alphabetical or numeric order from lowest to highest. Reverse rearranges the order of an array in reverse alphabetical or numeric order from highest to lowest. Shuffle randomly rearranges the order of an array.

To see how these commands work to change the order of data stored in an array, follow these steps:

1.  Make sure you have a Godot project that consists of a Node2D and a child node Sprite2D that displays the icon.svg image in a window.

2.  Click the Sprite2D node in the Scene dock.

3.  Edit the script attached to the Sprite2D node as follows:

```
extends Sprite2D
func _ready():
        var name_array = ["Fred", "Barney", "Wilma",
"Betty"]
        name_array.sort()
        print(name_array)
        name_array.reverse()
        print(name_array)
        name_array.shuffle()
        print(name_array)

        var number_array = [5, -21, 47, 68, 13]
        number_array.sort()
        print(number_array)
```

```
number_array.reverse()
print(number_array)
number_array.shuffle()
print(number_array)
```

4. Click the Run icon at the top of the window. The (DEBUG) window appears.

5. Click the close icon of the (DEBUG) window to make it go away. Notice that the Output pane at the bottom of the Godot window displays the results as follows:

```
["Barney", "Betty", "Fred", "Wilma"]
["Wilma", "Fred", "Betty", "Barney"]
["Betty", "Barney", "Fred", "Wilma"]
[-21, 5, 13, 47, 68]
[68, 47, 13, 5, -21]
[68, 47, -21, 5, 13]
```

Notice how the reverse command does the complete opposite of the sort command. Also note that the shuffle command will return a different result each time you run the program, so the results of the shuffle command on your computer won't likely exactly match the results listed earlier.

By sorting data, you can make the position of data more predictable on where it's stored in the array. The shuffle command is good for scrambling data in random order, which can be handy for listing items a player might encounter in a video game such as different types of treasures or enemies.

# Searching for Data in an Array

When an array contains multiple items, you may want to know if an array contains certain data and if so, where that data might exist. To do this, GDScript offers two commands:

- has

- bsearch

The has command checks if a certain item is in an array and returns a true or false value. The bsearch command must always work with a sorted array (created using the sort command). Then it can search a sorted array to return the index value of a specific item. (If you try to use the bsearch command on an unsorted array, the results can be unpredictable and unreliable.)

To see how to search for specific items in an array, follow these steps:

1. Make sure you have a Godot project that consists of a Node2D and a child node Sprite2D that displays the icon.svg image in a window.

2. Click the Sprite2D node in the Scene dock.

3. Edit the script attached to the Sprite2D node as follows:

```
extends Sprite2D
func _ready():
        var index_value = 0
        var name_array = ["Fred", "Barney", "Wilma",
"Betty", "Daphne", "Shaggy"]

        name_array.sort()
        print(name_array)
        if name_array.has("Shaggy"):
```

```
                    index_value = name_array.bsearch("Shaggy")
                    print("Shaggy is in the array at index = ",
                    index_value)
            else:
                    print("Shaggy is not in the array")
            if name_array.has("Melvin"):
                    index_value = name_array.bsearch("Melvin")
                    print("Melvin is in the array at index = ",
                    index_value)
            else:
                    print("Melvin is not in the array")
```

4. Click the Run icon at the top of the window. The (DEBUG) window appears.

5. Click the close icon of the (DEBUG) window to make it go away. Notice that the Output pane at the bottom of the Godot window displays the results as follows:

```
["Barney", "Betty", "Daphne", "Fred", "Shaggy",
"Wilma"]
Shaggy is in the array at index = 4
Melvin is not in the array
```

The sort command first sorts the array. Then the first if statement uses the "has" command to see if "Shaggy" is in the array. If so, then it uses the bsearch command to find the index value of "Shaggy," which is 4. The second if statement also uses the "has" command to see if "Melvin" is in the array. Since "Melvin" isn't stored in the array, the else part of the if-else statement runs and prints "Melvin is not in the array."

# Deleting Data from an Array

After storing data in an array, another common task is to delete items. One way to delete and retrieve values from an array is through the various pop (pop_at, pop_front, and pop_back) commands. If you just want to delete items in an array, you can use these commands:

- clear

- erase

- remove_at

The clear command completely empties an array no matter how many items might be stored. The erase command lets you specify the data you want to remove without knowing its index value. The remove_at lets you specify which item to delete, based on its index value.

The erase command searches for data to delete, but if that data does not exist in the array, the erase command does nothing.

To see how these commands work to delete items from an array, follow these steps:

1. Make sure you have a Godot project that consists of a Node2D and a child node Sprite2D that displays the icon.svg image in a window.

2. Click the Sprite2D node in the Scene dock.

3. Edit the script attached to the Sprite2D node as follows:

```
extends Sprite2D
func _ready():
        var name_array = ["Fred", "Barney", "Wilma",
"Betty", "Daphne", "Shaggy"]
        name_array.erase("Betty")
```

```
print(name_array)
name_array.remove_at(1)
print(name_array)
name_array.clear()
print(name_array)
```

4.  Click the Run icon at the top of the window. The
    (DEBUG) window appears.

5.  Click the close icon of the (DEBUG) window to
    make it go away. Notice that the Output pane at the
    bottom of the Godot window displays the results as
    follows:

```
["Fred", "Barney", "Wilma", "Daphne", "Shaggy"]
["Fred", "Wilma", "Daphne", "Shaggy"]
[]
```

# Exercise: Using Arrays

Arrays can be useful for storing multiple chunks of data in a single location.
Once that information has been stored in an array, you can retrieve that
information later. In this exercise, you'll use an array to store the x and y
position of an image that appears in random positions on the screen. Each
time the image moves to a different location, the array will keep track of all
previous locations and list them at the top of the screen.

To see how to store the location data of an image in an array, follow
these steps:

1.  Create a Godot project that consists of a Node2D
    as the parent node and the following nodes as its
    children nodes: Sprite2D, Button, and Label.

2.   Rename the Label node as ArrayLabel.

3.   Click the Sprite2D node in the Scene dock and
     create a Label as its child node. The structure of the
     scene should look like Figure 8-6.

***Figure 8-6.*** *The scene should consist of a Node2D, Sprite2D, Button,*
*and two Labels*

4.   Click Node2D and click the Attach Script icon. An
     Attach Node Script dialog box appears.

5.   Click Create. Godot displays a GDScript file.

6.   Click the Sprite2D node and drag the icon.svg image
     from the FileSystem dock to the Texture property in
     the Inspector dock.

7.   Click Button in the Scene dock. Resize and move the
     button so that it appears near the bottom middle
     of the user interface window (defined by a faint
     rectangle border).

8.   Click the Text property in the Inspector dock and
     type **Random Position**.

9.  Click the Node tab in the Inspector dock on the right side of the window.

10. Double-click **pressed()**. A Connect a Signal to a Method dialog box appears.

11. Click Node2D and click Connect. Godot creates a _on_button_pressed() function.

12. Click 2D and then click Sprite2D in the Scene dock and move it near the middle of the user interface.

13. Click the Label child node underneath Sprite2D and move it underneath the icon.svg image displayed by the Sprite2D node as shown in Figure 8-7.

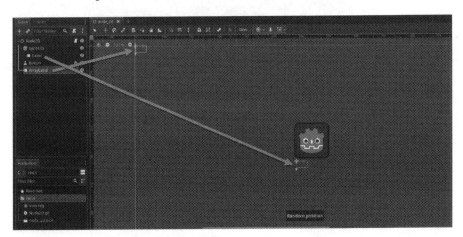

***Figure 8-7.*** *The position of Label and ArrayLabel on the user interface*

14. Move the ArrayLabel to the upper left corner of the user interface window.

15. Click the script icon that appears to the right of Node2D in the Scene dock. Godot displays the GDScript editor.

16. Modify the code as follows:

```
extends Node2D
var array_position = []
func _on_button_pressed():
        var window_size = DisplayServer.window_get_size()
        var format_string = "(%d, %d)"

        randomize()
        $Sprite2D.position.x = randi() %  window_size.x
        $Sprite2D.position.y = randi() %  window_size.y
        var actual_string = format_string % [$Sprite2D.
        position.x, $Sprite2D.position.y]
        $Sprite2D/Label.text = actual_string

        array_position.append(actual_string)
        $ArrayLabel.text = (array_join(array_position))

func array_join(my_array: Array, glue: String = ", ")
-> String:
        var string: String = ""
        for index in range(0, my_array.size()):
                string += str(my_array[index])
                if index < my_array.size() - 1:
                        string += glue
        return string
```

Each time the user clicks the button, the code randomly moves the Sprite2D (with the icon.svg image) to a new random position on the screen. This x and y position gets stored in an array. Since the ArrayLabel can only hold a text string, the array_join function takes each item from the array, separates each item with a comma, and creates one long string so it can appear in the ArrayLabel at the top left of the user interface window.

17.  Click the Run icon. A dialog box appears, asking you to select a main scene.

18.  Click Select Current. A dialog box appears, asking to save the current scene.

19.  Click Save. The user interface of your project appears.

20.  Click the Random Position button several times. The image moves to a random position and displays its current x and y position underneath. Notice that the top of the screen also displays a list of all the positions the image has been as shown in Figure 8-8.

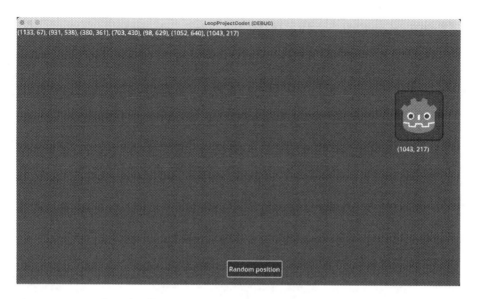

***Figure 8-8.*** *The child node Label underneath Sprite2D displays the current location of the image*

21.   Click the close icon of the (DEBUG) window.

# Summary

Arrays let you store multiple items in a single variable name. The number of items an array can hold can constantly expand or shrink. When storing items in an array, you can identify that data by the array's name and the index value of that item where the first item in an array is stored at index 0, the second at index 1, and so on.

Each time you add, delete, or rearrange items in an array, the index values of data may change. Normally you can retrieve data by specifying the array name and an index value, but you can also use the various pop commands (pop_at, pop_front, and pop_back) to retrieve and remove data from an array at the same time.

181

Data can be stored in an array in any order. To organize data in an array, you can sort the array in alphabetical or numeric order. Once you've sorted an array, you can search for specific items in an array without knowing its index value.

Arrays represent one of the most commonly used data structures in any program. By understanding how to add, sort, retrieve, and delete data from an array, you can store related data together in an array instead of creating multiple, separate variables. Using arrays can save up some time when working with multiple variables and help with writing a simpler program for the game that you would want to create. After all, programming anything, especially a video game, is all about creativity.

# CHAPTER 9

# Understanding Dictionaries

Every program needs to store data and that data usually gets stored in one or more variables. However, the more data a program needs to store, the more variables you need to create. Even worse, multiple variables make it hard to know which variables might be related to one another. This is why it is important to declare variables early on and to make your program as simple as possible.

Two ways to avoid using multiple variables are to use an array or a dictionary. The main drawback of an array is that data can be stored in any order, making it difficult to find and retrieve specific data.

A dictionary overcomes this drawback of arrays by using keys. Like an array, dictionaries also store data in any order, but dictionaries always store data with a key, known as a key-value pair. The value is the data you want to store, and the key represents a way to identify the data so you can retrieve it later.

Because you can always retrieve data using a key, the unordered state of the dictionary doesn't matter. Thus dictionaries are handy for retrieving data quickly that's not as simple to do with arrays. Two arrays can contain the same data, but the index used to retrieve identical data can greatly differ. On the other hand, the order that you store data in a dictionary doesn't matter. As long as you know the key associated with the data you want to retrieve, you'll always be able to retrieve that data from a dictionary at any time.

© Wallace Wang, Tonnetta Walcott 2024
W. Wang and T. Walcott, *Programming for Game Design*,
https://doi.org/10.1007/979-8-8688-0190-7_9

# Creating Dictionaries

One advantage of a dictionary is that it can store data that can be related to each other. Suppose a program needs to store someone's name and phone number. A phone number by itself means nothing without a name, but if you store this data in two separate variables, it's not clear they're related to each other like this:

```
var first_name: String = "Frank"
var phone_number: String = "555-1234"
```

Separate variables don't make it clear which data is related to other data. Even though we may know that "Frank" has the "555-1234" phone number, the computer does not because each data chunk is stored in a separate variable.

Dictionaries can store related data together in a pair known as a key-value pair. The value is the data you want to save and the key is any related data that you want to use to help find and retrieve the value as shown in Figure 9-1.

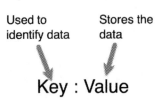

*Figure 9-1.* *Dictionaries store data as a key-value pair*

To create a dictionary, you need to define just three parts:

- Dictionary name
- Curly brackets to enclose one or more key-value pairs of data
- One or more key-value pairs of data separated by a colon (:)

A dictionary stores data in key-value pairs where the key is used to retrieve data and the value is the actual data itself like this:

"Frank" : "555-1234"

In the preceding example, the key is "Frank" and the value is "555-1234." The key and value can be any data type such as follows:

3.1415 : "Pi"

In this example, the key is 3.1415 and the value is "Pi." When creating a dictionary, you need to define a name for the dictionary and set it equal to one or more key-value pairs enclosed within curly brackets, where each key-value pair is separated by a comma like this:

```
var contacts = {
        "Frank" : "555-1234",
        3.1415 : "Pi",
        "Amount" : 12.25
    }
```

In the preceding code, the name of the dictionary is "contacts," and it contains three key-value pairs enclosed within curly brackets. Each key-value pair consists of two values separated by a colon. Then each key-value pair must be separated with a comma except the last key-value pair.

Make sure every key in a dictionary is unique because dictionaries use these keys to find data. If you had duplicate keys, then the dictionary wouldn't know which data you wanted to retrieve.

To see how to create a dictionary, follow these steps:

1.  Make sure you have a Godot project that consists of a Node2D and a child node Sprite2D that displays the icon.svg image in a window.

2.  Click the Sprite2D node in the Scene dock.

3. Edit the script attached to the Sprite2D node as follows:

```
extends Sprite2D
func _ready():
        var contacts = {
                "Frank" : "555-1234",
                3.1415 : "Pi",
                "Amount" : 12.25
        }
        print(contacts)
```

4. Click the Run icon at the top of the window. The (DEBUG) window appears.

5. Click the close icon of the (DEBUG) window to make it go away. Notice that the Output pane at the bottom of the Godot window displays the following:

```
{ "Frank": "555-1234", 3.1415: "Pi", "Amount": 12.25 }
```

This code creates a dictionary, stores three key-value pairs, and then prints out the whole dictionary.

## Retrieving Data from a Dictionary

Once you've stored data in a dictionary, the next step is retrieving that data. The simplest way to retrieve data is to use the dictionary name followed by the key linked to the data that you want. Suppose you had a dictionary like this:

```
var contacts = {
        "Frank" : "555-1234",
        3.1415 : "Pi",
```

```
    "Amount" : 12.25
}
```

In each key-value pair, the key comes first, followed by a colon and its associated value. So to retrieve "555-1234," you could reference the dictionary name and the key linked to the data you want like this:

```
contacts["Frank"]
```

Rather than retrieve individual data from a dictionary, you can also use a for loop to retrieve everything stored in a dictionary. Such a for loop defines a variable that will retrieve each key-value pair from a dictionary. Then the number of key-value pairs automatically defines how many times the for loop repeats.

Inside the for loop, you can access each individual key-value pair by specifying the dictionary name followed by the key inside square brackets such as follows:

```
for x in contacts:
    print(contacts[x])
```

To see how to retrieve data from a dictionary, follow these steps:

1. Make sure you have a Godot project that consists of a Node2D and a child node Sprite2D that displays the icon.svg image in a window.

2. Click the Sprite2D node in the Scene dock.

3. Edit the script attached to the Sprite2D node as follows:

```
extends Sprite2D
func _ready():
        var contacts = {
                "Frank" : "555-1234",
```

```
                    3.1415 : "Pi",
                    "Amount" : 12.25
          }
          print(contacts["Frank"])
          print(contacts[3.1415])
          print(contacts["Amount"])

          print("Now using a for loop")
          for x in contacts:
                    print(contacts[x])
```

4. Click the Run icon at the top of the window. The (DEBUG) window appears.

5. Click the close icon of the (DEBUG) window to make it go away. Notice that the Output pane at the bottom of the Godot window displays the results of the append and insert commands as follows:

```
555-1234
Pi
12.25
Now using a for loop
555-1234
Pi
12.25
```

The first three values appear by retrieving the data from the dictionary using the key of each value. The second three values appear using a for loop.

# Getting Information About Dictionaries

Once you've created a dictionary and stored key-value pairs in them, you may need to get information about the dictionary such as whether it's empty, how many items it may hold, what are all the keys, and what are all the values.

To get this type of information about a dictionary, GDScript offers the following commands:

- is_empty

- size

- keys

- values

The is_empty command lets you know if a dictionary is empty. The size command returns the total number of key-value pairs stored in the dictionary. The keys command returns an array of all the keys in the dictionary, while the values command returns an array of all the values in the dictionary.

To see how these commands work with dictionaries, follow these steps:

1. Make sure you have a Godot project that consists of a Node2D and a child node Sprite2D that displays the icon.svg image in a window.

2. Click the Sprite2D node in the Scene dock.

3. Edit the script attached to the Sprite2D node as follows;

```
extends Sprite2D
func _ready():
        var key_array = Array()
        var value_array = []
```

```
var contacts = {
        "Frank" : "555-1234",
        3.1415 : "Pi",
        "Amount" : 12.25
}
print(contacts)
if contacts.is_empty() == true:
        print("Empty dictionary")
else:
        print("Number of key-value pairs = ",
        contacts.size())

key_array = contacts.keys()
value_array = contacts.values()
print(key_array)
print(value_array)
```

4.  Click the Run icon at the top of the window. The
    (DEBUG) window appears.

5.  Click the close icon of the (DEBUG) window to
    make it go away. Notice that the Output pane at the
    bottom of the Godot window displays the results of
    the is_empty, commands as follows:

```
{ "Frank": "555-1234", 3.1415: "Pi", "Amount": 12.25 }
Number of key-value pairs = 3
["Frank", 3.1415, "Amount"]
["555-1234", "Pi", 12.25]
```

This code creates two empty arrays using two different methods:
Array() and []. Both methods are equivalent. After creating two empty
arrays, the code then creates a dictionary and stores three key-value pairs,
which prints out to display all three key-value pairs in the dictionary.

The size command returns the number of key-value pairs in the dictionary (3), and then the keys() command retrieves all the keys in the dictionary and stores them in an array. Finally, the values() command retrieves all the values in the dictionary and stores them in another array. Notice that the number of keys and values must be exactly equal since every key in a dictionary must be linked to a single value.

# Changing and Deleting Data in Dictionaries

After you've stored data in a dictionary, you can change data by using that data's key. To do this, you must specify the dictionary name and the key where you want to store new data. Then you store new data that erases the current data like this:

```
var contacts = {
        "Frank" : "555-1234",
        3.1415 : "Pi",
        "Amount" : 12.25
}
```

If we wanted to change the value 12.25, we notice it's linked to the key "Amount." Therefore, we just need to assign the dictionary name (contacts) and the "Amount" key with new data like this:

```
contacts["Amount"] = 987
```

Since the "Amount" key originally contains the value 12.25, this value gets replaced by 987. Now the "Amount" key is linked to the value 987. By assigning new data to an existing key, you can replace data with new data much like storing new data in a single variable.

When you want to delete data stored in a dictionary, you need to use the key. If you don't know the key but only know the data you want to delete, you can use the data to find the key by using the find_key()

191

command. Once you know the key linked to the data you want to delete, you can then use the erase command to delete the key and its linked data from a dictionary.

To see how to change and delete data in a dictionary, follow these steps:

1.  Make sure you have a Godot project that consists of a Node2D and a child node Sprite2D that displays the icon.svg image in a window.

2.  Click the Sprite2D node in the Scene dock.

3.  Edit the script attached to the Sprite2D node as follows:

```
extends Sprite2D
func _ready():
        var contacts = {
                "Frank" : "555-1234",
                3.1415 : "Pi",
                "Amount" : 12.25
        }
        print(contacts)

        contacts["Amount"] = 987
        print(contacts)

        print("The key is ", contacts.find_key(987))

        contacts.erase("Amount")
        print(contacts)
```

4.  Click the Run icon at the top of the window. The (DEBUG) window appears.

5.  Click the close icon of the (DEBUG) window to
    make it go away. Notice that the Output pane at the
    bottom of the Godot window displays the results as
    follows:

```
{ "Frank": "555-1234", 3.1415: "Pi", "Amount": 12.25 }
{ "Frank": "555-1234", 3.1415: "Pi", "Amount": 987 }
The key is Amount
{ "Frank": "555-1234", 3.1415: "Pi" }
```

This code works by creating a dictionary called contacts and storing
three key-value pairs, which it prints out so you can see the entire contents
of the dictionary. Then it stores 987 to replace the current data (12.25)
linked to the "Amount" key and prints the contents of the dictionary again
so you can see that 987 is now linked to the "Amount" key.

The find_key(987) command searches the contacts dictionary for
the value 987. When it finds it, it returns the key linked to 987, which is
"Amount." Finally, the code uses the erase command to erase the key
"Amount" and the data it's linked to (987). The last print command prints
out the dictionary's contents to show that the "Amount" : 987 key-value
pair has been deleted from the dictionary.

If you want to completely empty a dictionary, use the clear command.
To see how the clear command works, follow these steps:

1.  Make sure you have a Godot project that consists of
    a Node2D and a child node Sprite2D that displays
    the icon.svg image in a window.

2.  Click the Sprite2D node in the Scene dock.

3.  Edit the script attached to the Sprite2D node as
    follows:

```
extends Sprite2D
func _ready():
```

```
var contacts = {
    "Frank" : "555-1234",
    3.1415 : "Pi",
    "Amount" : 12.25
}
print(contacts)

contacts.clear()
print(contacts)
```

4.  Click the Run icon at the top of the window. The (DEBUG) window appears.

5.  Click the close icon of the (DEBUG) window to make it go away. Notice that the Output pane at the bottom of the Godot window displays the results as follows:

```
{ "Frank": "555-1234", 3.1415: "Pi", "Amount": 12.25 }
{ }
```

The first print command shows the entire contents of the dictionary. Then the clear command runs before the second print command. Since the clear command deleted everything out of the dictionary, the second print command reveals the dictionary is completely empty.

## Exercise: Using Dictionaries

In this exercise, you'll use a dictionary to store a location name (such as "Top" or "Middle") and link each location name to a specific value. Then the project will randomly select a location, retrieve an actual value from a dictionary, and move an image to that location on the screen.

To see how to store location data in a dictionary, follow these steps:

1. Create a Godot project that consists of a Node2D as the parent node and the following nodes as its children nodes: Sprite2D, Button, and Label.

2. Click Sprite2D in the Scene dock and drag the icon.svg from the FileSystem dock into the Texture property of the Sprite2D node in the Inspector dock.

3. Move the Sprite2D node in the middle of the user interface.

4. Click Button and type **Random Position** in the Text property in the Inspector dock.

5. Move the Button near the bottom, middle of the user interface.

6. Click Label and move it above the Button as shown in Figure 9-2.

*Figure 9-2.* *The design of the user interface*

7.  Click Node2D in the Scene dock and click the
    Attach Script icon. An Attach Node Script dialog box
    appears.

8.  Click Create. Godot displays a GDScript file.

9.  Click Button in the Scene dock and then click the
    Node tab in the Inspector dock.

10. Double-click **pressed()**. A Connect a Signal to a
    Method dialog box appears.

11. Click Node2D and click Connect. Godot creates an
    _on_button_pressed() function in the GDScript file.

12. Edit the GDScript file as follows:

```
extends Node2D
var window_size = DisplayServer.window_get_size()
var x_dictionary = {
            "Left" : 0,
            "Middle" : window_size.x / 2,
            "Right" : window_size.x
}
var y_dictionary = {
            "Top" : 0,
            "Middle" : window_size.y / 2,
            "Bottom" : window_size.y
}

func _on_button_pressed():
        var random_x = 0
        var random_y = 0
        var direction_x = ""
        var direction_y = ""
        randomize()
```

```
random_x = randi() %  3
random_y = randi() %  3
match random_x:
        0: direction_x = "Left"
        1: direction_x = "Middle"
        _: direction_x = "Right"
match random_y:
        0: direction_y = "Top"
        1: direction_y = "Middle"
        _: direction_y = "Bottom"
$Sprite2D.position.x = x_dictionary[direction_x]
$Sprite2D.position.y = y_dictionary[direction_y]
$Label.text = direction_x + ", " + direction_y
```

Notice that this code creates two dictionaries that define three different x and y positions (left, middle, and right for the x axis and top, middle, and bottom for the y axis). When the user clicks the Button, the code randomly selects a value between 0 and 2. Using that value, the code then retrieves a specific location from the two dictionaries.

13. Click the Run icon. A dialog box appears, asking you to select a main scene.

14. Click Select Current. A dialog box appears to save your scene.

15. Click Save

16.    Click the Random Position button to move the icon. svg image to different parts of the user interface window. Notice that each time the image moves, the label above the Button describes where the image appears such as left, bottom, middle, or top.

17.    Click the close icon in the (DEBUG) window.

# Summary

Dictionaries let you link data with a unique key in a key-value pair. By using this key, you can retrieve the data you want. Unlike an array that uses an index value to identify data, dictionaries use a key to identify data. Therefore, key-value pairs can be more useful than arrays at times. Arrays are sometimes nice for grouping variables together, but they have no relation to each other. The main drawback is that the index value of data in an array can constantly change as you add or delete items from that array. On the other hand, data is always linked to a unique key in a dictionary.

To create a dictionary, define a dictionary name and store one or more key-value pairs within curly brackets. Make sure each key-value pair is separated by a colon and each key-value pair is separated from the other key-value pairs by a comma (except for the last key-value pair).

The keys and the data can be of any data type such as integers, floating-point numbers, or strings. The only restriction is that every key must be unique.

Dictionaries give you another way to store data beyond arrays or individual variables. While not as commonly used as arrays, the unique key-value link makes dictionaries useful for storing related data together.

# CHAPTER 10

# Functions

You can attach a script to any item in Godot to make it interactive. To avoid creating one massive script of code, it's better to divide a large program into smaller ones that work together. Such small programs that make up a larger program are called functions.

Ideally, a function should perform one task and take up no more than one page or screen. By keeping a function small, it's easy to understand how it works. Large amounts of code can be difficult to search to find errors. Therefore it's best to make code as small and simple as possible. By making a function perform a single task, it makes it easy to know what a function is supposed to do, so you know whether it's working correctly or not.

In the old days, computer programs were often simple and small enough to understand. As programs got larger and more complicated, understanding how an entire program worked became difficult. That's why programmers started dividing large programs into collections of smaller ones called functions.

Functions act like building blocks. Each function should be as independent as possible from the rest of a program. That way you can modify a function without accidentally affecting any other part of a program. Once a function proves it works, you can reuse it in another project. Ultimately, this lets you create a library of proven functions that you can reuse and create other programs faster.

© Wallace Wang, Tonnetta Walcott 2024
W. Wang and T. Walcott, *Programming for Game Design*,
https://doi.org/10.1007/979-8-8688-0190-7_10

# Understanding Functions

You can create as many functions as you need, but Godot provides several functions for every script you create. You can also access a function to a node within a Godot project by selecting the node and then searching for the function under the "Nodes" category under the Inspector. Some of these built-in functions are

- _init()
- _ready()
- _process(delta)

All of these functions already exist, so you just need to add your own custom code to make them work. The _init() and _ready() functions automatically run every time a script starts running. The _init() function runs first and is often used to load data.

The _ready() function runs second and starts only when the node that its script is attached to has completely loaded.

The _process(delta) function runs continuously to respond to user input such as pressing a key or clicking the mouse.

To see how these three built-in functions work, follow these steps:

1. Make sure you have a Godot project that consists of a Node2D and a child node Sprite2D that displays the icon.svg image in a window.

2. Click the Sprite2D node in the Scene dock.

3. Edit the script attached to the Sprite2D node as follows:

```
extends Sprite2D
func _ready():
        print("Ready function here")
```

```
func _init():
     print("Init function here")
```

4.  Click the Run icon at the top of the window. The
    (DEBUG) window appears.

5.  Click the close icon of the (DEBUG) window to
    make it go away. Notice that the Output pane at the
    bottom of the Godot window displays the following:

```
Init function here
Ready function here
```

This shows that the _init() function runs before the
_ready() function.

6.  Edit the script attached to the Sprite2D node as
    follows:

```
extends Sprite2D
func _ready():
     print("Ready function here")

func _init():
     print("Init function here")

func _process(delta):
     print("Process(delta) function here")
```

7.  Click the Run icon at the top of the window. The
    (DEBUG) window appears.

8. Click the close icon of the (DEBUG) window to make it go away. Notice that the Output pane at the bottom of the Godot window displays the following:

```
Init function here
Ready function here
Process(delta) function here
Process(delta) function here
Process(delta) function here
Process(delta) function here
```

The Output pane should show multiple "Process(delta) function here" messages because this _process(delta) function runs continuously until you stop running the project.

If you examine the names of these three functions, you'll notice how functions are defined in three parts:

- func keyword

- A function name

- A parameter list enclosed in parentheses

The func keyword (short for "function") creates a function. In the Godot editor, all GDScript keywords appear in magenta to make them easy to recognize. If a keyword does not appear in magenta, that's a visual clue that you may have typed something wrong.

Function names can be anything, but it's best to choose a descriptive name that helps explain what the function does. Godot's built-in function names all start with an underscore (_) character to identify them easily. When making a game, make functions related to that game.

For example, if you want to attack an enemy or shoot, you could name your function "func shoot()" or " func attack()." If you want to have an inventory and drop items, you could also have a function such as " func dropItem()" or "func drop_item()." There are many ways to name a function when creating a game for Godot. Just make sure that your functions are relative to the game so that it is easy to track what each function does for the game to work. When you name your own functions, it's more common to omit an underscore character at the beginning of the function name.

The parameter list is enclosed in parentheses and identifies any data the function expects to receive. In both the _init() and _ready() functions, this parameter list is empty, which means these functions can work without receiving any outside data.

The _process(delta) function runs continuously, but it runs based on frames displayed on the screen, which appear at slightly irregular intervals, which is measured in seconds by the "delta" parameter.

To see how this delta value constantly changes each time the _process function runs, follow these steps:

1. Make sure you have a Godot project that consists of a Node2D and a child node Sprite2D that displays the icon.svg image in a window.

2. Click the Sprite2D node in the Scene dock.

3. Edit the script attached to the Sprite2D node as follows:

```
extends Sprite2D
func _process(delta):
        print("Delta = ", delta)
```

4. Click the Run icon at the top of the window. The (DEBUG) window appears.

5.   Click the close icon of the (DEBUG) window to make it go away. Notice that the Output pane at the bottom of the Godot window displays the results as follows:

```
Delta = 0.01666666666667
Delta = 0.01111111111111
Delta = 0.00277555555556
Delta = 0.00833333333333
Delta = 0.00833333333333
Delta = 0.00833333333333
```

The actual values for delta will likely be different on your computer, but you should see slight variations that show how the _process() function runs continuously but at slightly irregular intervals.

## Creating Functions

To create your own function, you must define a unique function name, an optional parameter list, and code within the function to make it do something. The simplest function has an empty parameter list and one line of code such as follows:

```
func my_function():
        print("My function running now")
```

Godot's built-in functions run when certain events occur, but functions that you create won't run until they're specifically called by name. To call or run a function, you must specify the function name followed by its parameter list like this:

```
my_function()
```

Any code stored in that function now runs. Without functions, you would have to type code throughout your program in multiple locations. If you later needed to change that code to fix a problem or add new features, you would have to modify it everywhere you used it in your program.

Any time you duplicate code that performs identical tasks, you risk omitting one copy of the code that needs to be fixed. Over time, you could wind up with several different versions of the same code.

By storing frequently used code in a function, you create a single copy of the code. Now if you need to fix or modify that code, you change it in one place, and those changes automatically appear throughout your program wherever that function might be used. This saves time to correct a code in one place rather than in multiple locations.

To see how to create and call a function, follow these steps:

1. Make sure you have a Godot project that consists of a Node2D and a child node Sprite2D that displays the icon.svg image in a window.

2. Click the Sprite2D node in the Scene dock.

3. Edit the script attached to the Sprite2D node as follows:

```
extends Sprite2D
func my_function():
        print("My function running now")

func _init():
        print("Init function")
        my function()

func _ready():
        print("Ready function")
        my_function()
```

4.  Click the Run icon at the top of the window. The
    (DEBUG) window appears.

5.  Click the close icon of the (DEBUG) window to
    make it go away. Notice that the Output pane at the
    bottom of the Godot window displays the results as
    follows:

```
Init function
My function running now
Ready function
My function running now
```

In the preceding code, the init() function runs first and runs two lines
of code. The first line of code prints "Init function." Then the second line of
code calls my_function(). Now in the code within my_function(), the code
prints "My function running now."

Then the ready() function runs its two lines of code. The first line of
code prints "Ready function." Then the second line of code also calls my_
function(), which prints "My function running now."

Notice that my_function() does the exact same thing each time it runs,
which is to print "My function running now." In most cases, you want a
function to run slightly differently each time, and to do that, you need to
accept parameters.

# Using Parameters with Functions

When a function has an empty parameter list, its code can only do the
same thing over and over again. In most cases, you want a function to
behave slightly differently based on new data. To accept new data, a
parameter list can contain one or more variable names like this:

```
func my_function(new_data):
```

Each variable name within the parameter list can contain one chunk of data. The preceding parameter list displays a variable (new_data). To call this function and pass data, you have to use the function name and include data to send to the function, listed within parentheses, like this:

```
my_function("Passed data")
```

This example passes a string ("Passed data") to the function, but you could also pass an integer or a floating-point number as well. If you want to limit the parameter variable to a specific data type, you could do the following:

```
func my_function(new_data: String):
```

The preceding code specifies that any data passed to the function must be a String data type. If you wanted, you could also define an int or float data type instead. Rather than pass one chunk of data, you can pass two or more chunks of data by defining two or more variables in a function's parameter list like this:

```
func another_function(x: int, y: int):
```

To call this function, you would use the function name (another_function) and pass in two integers like this:

```
another_function(-24, 95)
```

To see how to use parameters in a function, follow these steps:

1. Make sure you have a Godot project that consists of a Node2D and a child node Sprite2D that displays the Icon.svg image in a window.

2. Click the Sprite2D node in the Scene dock.

3.  Edit the script attached to the Sprite2D node as follows:

```
extends Sprite2D
func my_function(new_data: String):
        print("Called from this function = ", new_data)

func another_function(x: int, y: int):
        print ("The x value you sent = ", x)
        print ("The y value you sent = ", y)

func _init():
        my_function("Init")
        another_function(-24, 95)

func _ready():
        my_function("Ready")
        another_function(74, -827)
```

4.  Click the Run icon at the top of the window. The (DEBUG) window appears.

5.  Click the close icon of the (DEBUG) window to make it go away. Notice that the Output pane at the bottom of the Godot window displays the results as follows:

```
Called from this function = Init
The x value you sent = -24
The y value you sent = 95
Called from this function = Ready
The x value you sent = 74
The y value you sent = -827
```

This code creates two functions called my_function and another_ function. The my_function can accept one string, which gets stored in its new_data variable. The another_function can accept two integers. The first integer gets stored in the x variable, and the second gets stored in the y variable.

In the preceding example, the init() function runs first and sends the string "Init" to my_function, which prints out "Called from this function = Init." Then it calls another_function and sends -24 and 95, which prints out "The x value you sent = -24" and "The y value you sent = 95."

The ready() function runs next and calls my_function, passing the string "Ready." This prints out "Called from this function = Ready." Then it calls another_function and sends 74 and -827, which prints out "The x value you sent = 74" and "The y value you sent = -827."

Because my_function and another_function accept parameters, they can receive data when they're called, which allows them to change their behavior slightly.

In the preceding example, another_function accepts two parameters (x and y), which are both integer data types. You can have multiple parameters where each one can be a different data type.

To see how multiple parameters can be of different data types, follow these steps:

1. Make sure you have a Godot project that consists of a Node2D and a child node Sprite2D that displays the icon.svg image in a window.

2. Click the Sprite2D node in the Scene dock.

3. Edit the script attached to the Sprite2D node as follows:

```
extends Sprite2D
func big_function(my_name: String, age: int,
weight: float):
```

```
        print("Hello, ", my_name, ". You are ", age, "
        years old and weigh ", weight, " pounds.")

func _init():
    big_function("Randy", 38, 134.5)

func _ready():
    big_function("Sally", 25, 124.8)
```

4. Click the Run icon at the top of the window. The
   (DEBUG) window appears.

5. Click the close icon of the (DEBUG) window to
   make it go away. Notice that the Output pane at the
   bottom of the Godot window displays the results as
   follows:

```
Hello, Randy. You are 38 years old and weigh
134.5 pounds.
Hello, Sally. You are 25 years old and weigh
124.8 pounds.
```

The big_function accepts three parameters: my_name, age, and
weight. When using multiple parameters, you must always call that
function using the exact number of parameters it expects and make sure
each parameter is the correct data type.

If you pass too many (or too few) parameters, the function call won't
work. If you try to pass a string into a parameter that's expecting a number
(or vice versa), you'll get an error as shown in Figure 10-1.

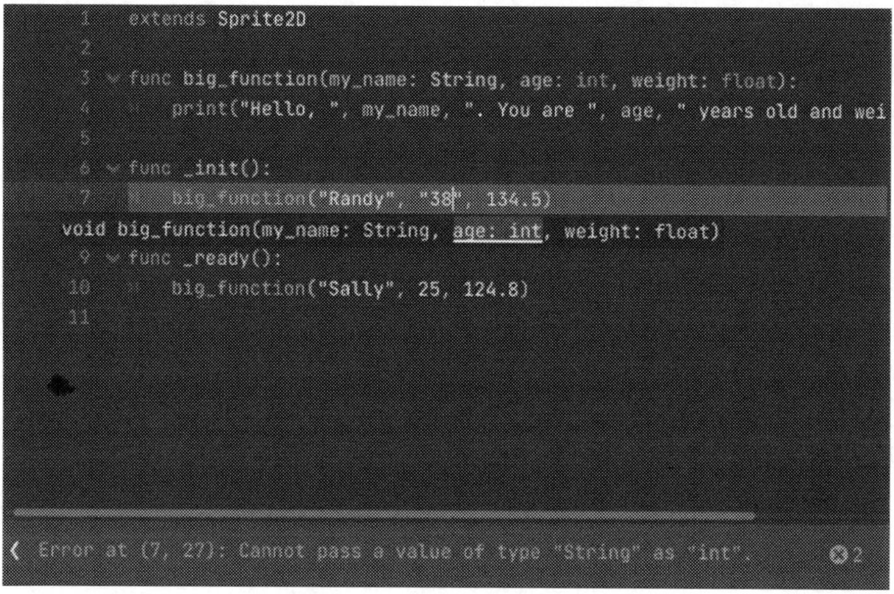

```
1    extends Sprite2D
2
3 ∨ func big_function(my_name: String, age: int, weight: float):
4        print("Hello, ", my_name, ". You are ", age, " years old and wei
5
6 ∨ func _init():
7        big_function("Randy", "38", 134.5)
void big_function(my_name: String, age: int, weight: float)
9 ∨ func _ready():
10       big_function("Sally", 25, 124.8)
11
```

Error at (7, 27): Cannot pass a value of type "String" as "int".    ⊗2

*Figure 10-1.* *Passing the wrong data type to a function will cause an error*

# Optional Parameters

When functions define one or more parameters, calling that function must provide the exact number of values in the right order. If a function expects two different parameters, every function call must pass exactly two values. Suppose you had a function like this:

```
func my_function(x: int, y: String):
```

To call this function, you must include an integer and a string inside a parameter list like this:

```
my_function(34, "Hello")
```

Since this function expects two parameters (an integer and a string), it would not work if you only called the function with one value (either an integer or a string), three or more values, or even two values but in the wrong order (the integer must be first and the string must be second).

If you want the option of calling a function without specifying the exact number of parameters, you can use something called optional parameters. An optional parameter defines a default value for a parameter. That way you can either call the function using all parameters or only the non-optional parameters.

To define an optional parameter, set a default value to that parameter like this:

```
func my_function(x: int, y: String = "Bye"):
```

Since this function defines its second parameter as an optional parameter, you can call the function in one of two ways:

- my_function(25, "Hello")

- my_function(25)

The first method calls the function and passes it two parameters (25 and "Hello"). The second method calls the function but passes it only one parameter (25). Since the second parameter is missing, the function will use its default value ("Bye").

When defining optional parameters, the optional parameters must be last, so the following is invalid because a non-optional parameter appears last:

```
func my_function(x: int = 0, y: String):
```

You can also have two or more optional parameters as well such as follows:

```
func my_function(x: int = 0, y: String = "Hello"):
```

The general rule is that when you use an optional parameter, all parameters afterward must also be optional parameters.

To see how to use optional parameters, follow these steps:

1. Make sure you have a Godot project that consists of a Node2D and a child node Sprite2D that displays the icon.svg image in a window.

2. Click the Sprite2D node in the Scene dock.

3. Edit the script attached to the Sprite2D node as follows:

```
extends Sprite2D
func _init():
        my_function(15, "Hello")

func my_function(x: int = 0, y: String = "Default"):
        print("Integer = ", x)
        print("String = ", y)
```

4. Click the Run icon at the top of the window. The (DEBUG) window appears.

5. Click the close icon of the (DEBUG) window to make it go away. Notice that the Output pane at the bottom of the Godot window displays the results as follows:

```
Integer = 15
String = Hello
```

Because the function call includes two parameters (15 and "Hello"), the function uses both parameters. Edit the function call as follows and rerun the program:

```
my_function(-99)
```

Notice that this function call omits the second parameter. As a result, the function uses its default value for that second parameter, which is "Default." The result in the Output pane is now:

```
Integer = -99
String = Default
```

It's possible to have a function consisting of nothing but optional parameters such as the following:

func my_function(x: int = 0, y: String = "Default"):

To call this function with two optional parameters, you have three options:

| Function call | Result |
| --- | --- |
| my_function(3, "Frank") | Completely overrides all optional parameter values. |
| my_function(3) | Passes a value for the first parameter only but uses the default value for the second optional parameter. |
| my_function() | Passes no values so the function uses both default values. |

The preceding three function calls are the only valid options for calling a function with two optional parameters. If you do not pass a value to the first parameter, you cannot pass values to any other parameters as well. That's because the function won't know which default value to use for its optional parameters. That's why the following function call is invalid:

```
my_function("Frank")
```

With the preceding function call, GDScript misinterprets the function call as sending "Frank" to the first parameter, which expects an integer. Since "Frank" is a string, this causes an error.

The general rule is to put all non-optional parameters first in a function's parameter list. Then when calling the function, send specific values. The moment you omit a specific value to use a default value, all remaining parameters to the right must also use default values. Optional parameters are just one way to make functions more flexible.

# Returning Values with Functions

At the simplest level, a function performs a single task using one or more parameters. However, you can also create a function that returns a single value. This allows functions to calculate a useful result and send this result back to another part of the program. Essentially, this lets functions represent a single, calculated value.

One example of a function that returns a value is Godot's square root function that looks like this:

```
sqrt(x)
```

When you want to calculate the square root of a number, you can just pass that number into the sqrt function. After the sqrt function calculates the result, it stores that result in the function name, which represents that single value. So if we wanted to calculate the square root of 9, we could call the sqrt function and pass it a parameter of 9 like this:

```
sqrt(9)
```

To use this value, we'd have to assign it to a variable or treat it like a value like this:

```
print(sqrt(9))
```

This code sends 9 to the sqrt function, which calculates an answer of 3. Then it prints 3. The main idea behind a function that returns a value is that it calculates a useful result that another part of a program can use.

If you want a function to return a value, you must place the "return" keyword on the last line in the function, followed by the data you want to return. So if you wanted a function to return a string, the entire function might look like this:

```
func greeting(my_name: String):
   var salutation: String
   salutation = "Hello, " + my_name
   return salutation
```

To call a function that returns a value, treat that function name as if it were a single value such as a string or a number. To see how to create and call a function that returns a value, follow these steps:

1. Make sure you have a Godot project that consists of a Node2D and a child node Sprite2D that displays the icon.svg image in a window.

2. Click the Sprite2D node in the Scene dock.

3. Edit the script attached to the Sprite2D node as follows:

```
extends Sprite2D
func greeting(my_name: String, income: float):
      const tax_bracket = 0.25
      var tax_owed : float
      tax_owed = income * tax_bracket
      return "Hello, " + my_name + ". You owe " +
      str(tax_owed) + " in taxes."

func _init():
      print(greeting("Oliver", 125000))

func _ready():
      print(greeting("Elsa", 79000))
```

4. Click the Run icon at the top of the window. The (DEBUG) window appears.

5. Click the close icon of the (DEBUG) window to make it go away. Notice that the Output pane at the bottom of the Godot window displays the results as follows:

```
Hello, Oliver. You owe 31250 in taxes.
Hello, Elsa. You owe 19750 in taxes.
```

This code creates a function called "greeting," which accepts two parameters called "my_name" (that can hold a String data type) and "income" (that can hold a float data type). Within the "greeting" function is code that multiplies a constant by the income parameter and then creates a string that it sends back.

The init() function calls the greeting function by sending it "Oliver" and 125000. Then the greeting function calculates the taxes owed and uses this value in a string that it returns. Thus the init() function prints "Hello, Oliver. You owe 31250 in taxes."

The ready() function runs next and calls the greeting function by sending it "Elsa" and 79000. Then the greeting function returns the string "Hello, Elsa. You owe 19750 in taxes."

If you want to define the data type that a function returns, you can add this symbol -> followed by the data type the function returns such as follows:

```
func greeting(my_name: String, income: float) -> String:
```

When a function returns a value, you can call that function by treating it as if it were a single value. When a function does not return a value, you can call that function as if it were a command.

217

# Exercise: Using Functions

Godot provides functions to respond to a variety of different events such as when the mouse appears over an object or when an object changes size. Godot's built-in functions let you respond to different types of events. However, you can write your own functions to perform specialized tasks unique to your particular project.

In this exercise, you'll get a chance to use both types of functions: the built-in functions to respond to the user and the specialized functions that you create yourself.

To see how to use functions, follow these steps:

1. Create a Godot project that consists of a Node2D as the parent node and the following nodes as its children nodes: Sprite2D, Button, Label, and ColorRect.

2. Click Sprite2D in the Scene dock and drag the icon.svg from the FileSystem dock into the Texture property of the Sprite2D node in the Inspector dock.

3. Click Button in the Scene dock, click the Text property in the Inspector dock, and type **Reset**.

4. Move all the nodes so they look like Figure 10-2.

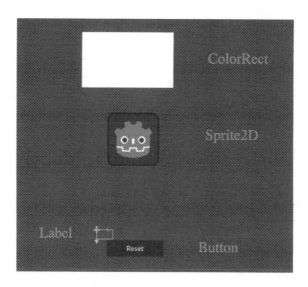

***Figure 10-2.*** *Designing the user interface*

5.  Click Node2D in the Scene dock and click the
    Attach Script icon. An Attach Node Script dialog box
    appears.

6.  Click Create. The GDScript editor appears.

7.  Click Button in the Scene dock and then click Node
    and Signals in the Inspector dock. A list of signals
    appears.

8.  Double-click **pressed()**. A Connect a Signal to a
    Method dialog box appears.

9.  Click Node2D and click Connect. Godot creates
    an _on_button_pressed() function in the
    GDScript editor.

10. Click ColorRect in the Scene dock and then click
    Node and Signals in the Inspector dock. A list of
    signals appears.

11.    Double-click **mouse_entered()**. A Connect a Signal to a Method dialog box appears.

12.    Click Node2D and click Connect. Godot creates an _on_color_rect_mouse_entered() function in the GDScript editor.

13.    Double-click **mouse_exited()**. A Connect a Signal to a Method dialog box appears.

14.    Click Node2D and click Connect. Godot creates an _on_color_rect_mouse_exited() function in the GDScript editor.

15.    Edit the GDScript as follows:

```
extends Node2D
func _on_button_pressed():
      $Sprite2D.rotation = 0
      $Label.text = ""

func _on_color_rect_mouse_entered():
      $Label.text = "Mouse entered the color rectangle"
      rotate_me(20)

func _on_color_rect_mouse_exited():
      $Label.text = "Mouse exited the color rectangle"
      rotate_me(-40)

func rotate_me(radians: float):
      $Sprite2D.rotate(radians)
```

The Button function resets the image and clears the Label. The _on_color_rect_mouse_entered() and _on_color_rect_mouse_exited() functions respond when the mouse pointer appears over or outside of the ColorRect boundaries by displaying a message in the Label and calling a rotate_me function. This rotate_me function is a function that accepts a float value and uses that value to rotate the Sprite2D node that displays the icon.svg image.

16. Click the Run icon. A dialog box appears, asking you to select a main scene.

17. Click Select Current. A dialog box appears to save your scene.

18. Click Save.

19. Move the mouse pointer over the ColorRect. The "Mouse entered the color rectangle" text appears in the Label and the Sprite2D node rotates to the right.

20. Move the mouse pointer away from the ColorRect. The "Mouse exited the color rectangle" text appears in the Label and the Sprite2D node rotates to the left.

21. Click the Reset Button. The Label clears all text and the Sprite2D straightens itself.

22. Click the close icon in the (DEBUG) window.

This example used several built-in functions (on_button_pressed(), on_color_rect_mouse_entered(), and on_color_rect_mouse_exited()) along with a separate user-defined function called rotate_me that accepts a float data type. In general, functions should perform a single task and fit within one screen, so it's easy to see all the code at a glance.

# Summary

A function lets you divide a large program into multiple smaller programs like building blocks. Ideally, a function should be as completely independent from the rest of the program as possible. That way it will be easy to modify in the future without worrying if any changes might affect the way another part of a program works.

A function consists of a name, a parameter list, and one or more lines of code that do something. The simplest function has an empty parameter list, so the function does the same thing over and over again. A more flexible function accepts one or more parameters that can be defined to hold only certain data types such as strings, integers, or floating-point numbers.

Godot comes with built-in functions that run automatically, but when you define your own functions, you'll need to call them by name and pass any values to their parameter list to make these functions run. A function can run and complete a task, or a function can run and return a value by using the "return" keyword on the last line of the function.

Ultimately, functions let you reuse and isolate code to help you write more reliable programs.

# CHAPTER 11

# Object-Oriented Programming

The main idea behind object-oriented programming is to help write more reliable software. Smaller programs are easier to write and understand than larger programs, which is why programmers divide large programs into multiple, smaller functions. Every program consists of data to manipulate and algorithms that provide step-by-step instructions for manipulating that data.

One problem with functions is that they isolate algorithms, but each function can potentially access data used by other functions. This can make programs less reliable because you never know when data might change. To fix this problem, computer scientists have created object-oriented programming.

The idea behind object-oriented programming is to isolate both data and the algorithms that manipulate them into self-contained, isolated objects. Where functions isolated algorithms, objects isolate algorithms and the data those algorithms directly affect.

Because data and the algorithms that manipulate them are stored together, it's easy to see which code might change data. Grouping together data and the algorithms that change them is called encapsulation, which represents one key advantage of object-oriented programming.

© Wallace Wang, Tonnetta Walcott 2024
W. Wang and T. Walcott, *Programming for Game Design*,
https://doi.org/10.1007/979-8-8688-0190-7_11

# Creating a Class

The basis of object-oriented programming is classes. A class defines variables (called properties) and functions (called methods) that are related. Properties are simply variables defined in a class, and methods are functions defined in a class.

To create a class, simply use the "class" keyword followed by a descriptive name that usually begins with an uppercase letter such as follows:

```
class GameObjects:
```

A class is meant to contain properties and methods that are common to multiple items in your program. In a video game, a class often defines objects in a game such as cars, planes, and birds since they all share common characteristics of a location and the ability to move. When a class is accessed, you have the ability to access all the characteristics, properties, and methods of that class.

When designing user interfaces, programmers often use classes to define the size, appearance, and position of an object on the screen such as a button, slider, or text field. A class defines the shared characteristics of multiple items. Then each multiple item can add additional features that are unique such as a button that can detect clicks or touches or a text field that can hold text.

When creating a class, start with the basic characteristics shared among multiple items. For this example, we'll pretend to design a class for a video game object that has an x and y position along with code to make it move.

To add properties (variables), just declare one or more variables and an optional data type like this:

```
class GameObjects:
    var x: int
    var y: int
```

To add a method (function), declare a function name and a parameter list along with the code to run when that method is called like this:

```
class GameObjects:
    var x: int
    var y: int
    func move(x_position: int, y_position: int):
        x += x_position + 2
        y += y_position
```

A class by itself acts like a data type, so you need to create a variable to create an object by specifying a new class like this:

```
var car = GameObjects.new()
```

In this example, the "car" variable creates an object from the GameObjects class using the new() method. Now the "car" object has all the properties and methods defined by the GameObjects class such as an x and y property and a move method. To access these x and y properties, you need to specify the object name followed by the property you want to use such as car.x or car.y.

To run the move method, you have to specify the object name followed by the method name such as car.move with two integers in the parameter list.

To see how to define a class and create an object from this class, follow these steps:

1.  Make sure you have a Godot project that consists of a Node2D and a child node Sprite2D that displays the icon svg image in a window.

2.  Click the Sprite2D node in the Scene dock.

3. Edit the script attached to the Sprite2D node as
   follows:

```
extends Sprite2D
class GameObjects:
        var x: int
        var y: int
        func move(x_position: int, y_position: int):
                x += x_position + 2
                y += y_position

func _init():
        var car = GameObjects.new()
        car.x = 0
        car.y = 0
        print("Car x position = ", car.x, " Car y
        position = ", car.y)
        car.move(3, 1)
        print("Car x position = ", car.x, " Car y
        position = ", car.y)
```

4. Click the Run icon at the top of the window. The
   (DEBUG) window appears.

5. Click the close icon of the (DEBUG) window to
   make it go away. Notice that the Output pane at the
   bottom of the Godot window displays the following:

```
Car x position = 0 Car y position = 0
Car x position = 5 Car y position = 1
```

The init() function first creates an object using the GameObjects class
and the new() command. The next two lines define the x and y properties
as 0. Then it prints 0 for both the x and y positions of the car.

Then the car.move(3,1) command calls the move method (function) inside the car object, passing 3 and 1. The 3 value gets stored in the x_position parameter, and the 1 value gets stored in the y_position parameter. The x property then gets set to the x_position parameter added to 2 for a total of 5. This gets added to the current value of x, which is 0.

The y property adds the y_position value to the current value of y, which is 0. So now y equals 1. Then the last line in the init() function prints out the car's x and y position again to show that it changed based on the move method defined in the GameObjects class.

Suppose we create another object from the GameObjects class like this:

```
var bird = GameObjects.new()
```

This bird object would have x and y properties that you could access by referencing the object name followed by the property you want such as follows:

```
bird.x = 12
bird.y = 35
```

Then you could call the move method for that bird object like this:

```
bird.move(2, 5)
```

When creating multiple objects from the same class, objects will share the same properties and methods defined by the class. The object name (car or bird) helps define the specific property and method you want to access. So the combination of the object name (which should always be unique) and the property or method name lets you access properties and methods.

Since the name of the object is always separated from the property or method name by a period or dot, the appearance of code like car.x or bird.move(2, 5) is known as "dot-syntax." Any time you see this dot-syntax in code, chances are good that you're looking at objects defined by a class.

# Initializing Properties

When you create a class, you need to define one or more properties that can hold specific data types. The simplest way to define properties is to declare a name and the data type it can hold such as follows:

```
var strength: int
```

However, such properties are initially undefined, which means if you try to use them, your program will crash. As a safer alternative, it's better to initialize all properties using a special constructor method, which works in one of two ways:

- Assign a default initial value to each property.

- Assign a value to each property when creating an object.

To assign initial values to properties, you need to create an init() function, called a constructor, in a class like this:

```
class GameObjects:
      var x: int
      var y: int
      func _init():
            x = -999
            y = -111
```

Each time you create an object from this class, the x and y properties will always start with these defined initial values (-999 for x and -111 for y).

To see how to assign initial values to properties, follow these steps:

1. Make sure you have a Godot project that consists of a Node2D and a child node Sprite2D that displays the icon.svg image in a window.

2. Click the Sprite2D node in the Scene dock.

3.  Edit the script attached to the Sprite2D node as
    follows:

```
extends Sprite2D
class GameObjects:
        var x: int
        var y: int
        func _init():
                x = -999
                y = -111

func _init():
        var car = GameObjects.new()
        print("Car x position = ", car.x, " Car y
        position = ", car.y)
```

4.  Click the Run icon at the top of the window. The
    (DEBUG) window appears.

5.  Click the close icon of the (DEBUG) window to
    make it go away. Notice that the Output pane at the
    bottom of the Godot window displays the results as
    follows:

```
Car x position = -999 Car y position = -111
```

Defining initial values for each property prevents your code from trying
to access a property that has no value at all, which will crash the program.
However, initial values likely won't be useful, so you'll need to take a
second step to assign valid values to each property. Each time you create
another object from the same class, this new object will always start with
the same initial values, which may not be what you want.

A better solution is to use the init() constructor method to assign values to each property when you create the object. If you notice in the previous code, creating an object from a class used the new() method where the new parameter list is empty.

When creating a new object from a class, it's better to assign initial values to that object when it's created. To do this, you need to create an init() constructor method like this:

```
class GameObjects:
    var x: int
    var y: int
    func _init(x_value, y_value):
        x = x_value
        y = y_value
```

This init() constructor method accepts two integer values and assigns them to the x and y properties when creating an object. To create an object, you must declare an object using the new command but also pass in values for the x_value and y_value parameters like this:

```
var car = GameObjects.new(123, 456)
```

This creates an object called "car," based on the GameObjects class. The new method creates an object and defines initial values (123 and 456) at the same time. In this way, every time you create an object, you can define different initial values for that object.

To see how to assign initial values to properties, follow these steps:

1.  Make sure you have a Godot project that consists of a Node2D and a child node Sprite2D that displays the icon.svg image in a window.

2.  Click the Sprite2D node in the Scene dock.

3. Edit the script attached to the Sprite2D node as follows:

```
extends Sprite2D
class GameObjects:
        var x: int
        var y: int
        func _init(x_value, y_value):
                x = x_value
                y = y_value
        func move(x_position: int, y_position: int):
                x += x_position + 2
                y += y_position

func _init():
        var car = GameObjects.new(123, 456)
        print("Car x position = ", car.x, " Car y
        position = ", car.y)
```

4. Click the Run icon at the top of the window. The (DEBUG) window appears.

5. Click the close icon of the (DEBUG) window to make it go away. Notice that the Output pane at the bottom of the Godot window displays the results as follows:

```
Car x position = 123 Car y position = 456
```

When defining a class, you have three options as shown in Figure 11-1:

- Define properties but do not assign any initial values.

- Define properties that always have an initial value.

- Define initial values for properties when creating an object.

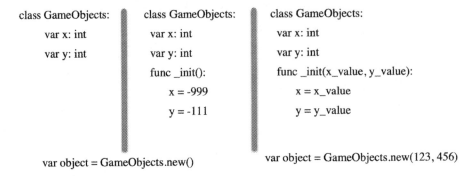

*Figure 11-1.* *Three ways to define properties in a class*

If you do not initialize properties or if you do give properties an initial value, you can create a class from that object by using the new method with an empty parameter list such as GameObjects.new(). If you create an init() constructor method that accepts parameters to assign to each property, then you must create that object by passing in initial values such as GameObjects.new(123, 456).

# Inheriting Classes

A class lets you define common features shared among different items. A video game might need to define the x and y positions of every item in the game. However, a tree would be stationary, but a car would be mobile. So even though both a tree and a car would need to define an x and y position, a car would need additional code to make it move around.

You could create two separate classes, one for a plant and one for a car, that define their x and y properties like this:

```
class Plant:              class Car:
    x: int                    x: int
    y: int                    y: int
```

However, creating two separate classes creates duplicate x and y properties. If you need to change the x or y properties in the future, you'll have to change them in each class. If you duplicated this code through a dozen separate classes, you'll need to revise this code in every location.

Duplicate code causes two problems. First, duplicate code takes up space. Second, duplicate code increases the risk of introducing bugs. If you need to fix problems in your code, you must update every copy of that code. Failure to do so means you risk having two or more different versions of the code.

Inheritance avoids duplication. Instead of physically copying code, inheritance lets you define code in one class that you can virtually copy into another class. Now this second class gets all the code defined in the first class without physically creating duplicate code. If you need to change this code, you change it in one class, and those changes automatically change everywhere that code is used.

To copy or inherit code from an existing class, you just need to use the "extends" keyword followed by the class you want to copy code from such as follows:

```
class Car extends Plant:
```

The preceding code tells the computer to copy all code defined in the Plant class and reuse them in the Car class. Now whatever code is defined in the Plant class can also be used in the Car class.

To see how to use parameters in a function, follow these steps:

1. Make sure you have a Godot project that consists of a Node2D and a child node Sprite2D that displays the icon.svg image in a window.

2. Click the Sprite2D node in the Scene dock.

3.  Edit the script attached to the Sprite2D node as follows:

```
extends Sprite2D
class Plant:
        var x: int
        var y: int
        func _init():
                x = 55
                y = 66

class Car extends Plant:
        pass

func _init():
        var ford = Car.new()
        print("Ford x position = ", ford.x)
        print("Ford y position - ", ford.y)
```

4.  Click the Run icon at the top of the window. The (DEBUG) window appears.

5.  Click the close icon of the (DEBUG) window to make it go away. Notice that the Output pane at the bottom of the Godot window displays the results as follows:

```
Ford x position = 55
Ford y position = 66
```

Notice that the Plant class defines an x and y property along with an init() method that sets an initial value of 55 for x and 66 for y. Then the Car class inherits from the Plant class. Even though the Car class is completely empty (the "pass" command does nothing), the Car class inherits everything defined in the Plant class. That means the Car class inherits a value of 55 for its x property and a value of 66 for its y property.

The init() function creates a new object (ford) from the Car class. Then it prints the x and y properties of the ford object to show that it inherited the value of 55 for x and the value of 66 for y even though the Car class itself does nothing. The Car class simply copied everything in the Plant class.

Simply inheriting everything defined in one class isn't useful since you might as well just use the class that defines everything. The more common use for inheritance is to extend (hence the keyword "extends") a class by inheriting code from one class but adding new code as well.

Suppose you wanted to define a Car class with an x and y property to define a location but also a speed property to define how fast it's going. A clumsy way would be to create a class that defines an x and y property like this:

```
class Plant:
      var x: int
      var y: int
      func _init():
           x = 55
           y = 66
```

Then you could copy that class and add a speed property like this:

```
class Car:
      var x: int
      var y: int
      var speed: int
      func _init():
           x = 55
           y - 66
```

As you can see, this duplicates code. A far better solution is to use inheritance to define the Car class only with the properties and methods that are unique to that class such as follows:

```
class Car extends Plant:
    var speed: int
```

Notice that the Car class just adds a new speed property, but it inherits all the properties and methods defined in the Plant class. By inheriting code from one class while adding new code, a class can define custom properties and methods quickly and easily.

To see how inheritance lets you create custom classes, follow these steps:

1. Make sure you have a Godot project that consists of a Node2D and a child node Sprite2D that displays the icon.svg image in a window.

2. Click the Sprite2D node in the Scene dock.

3. Edit the script attached to the Sprite2D node as follows:

```
extends Sprite2D
class Plant:
        var x: int
        var y: int
        func _init():
                x = 55
                y = 66

class Car extends Plant:
        var speed: int
```

```
func _init():
    var ford = Car.new()
    ford.speed = 123
    print("Ford x position = ", ford.x)
    print("Ford y position = ", ford.y)
    print("Ford speed = ", ford.speed)
```

4.  Click the Run icon at the top of the window. The (DEBUG) window appears.

5.  Click the close icon of the (DEBUG) window to make it go away. Notice that the Output pane at the bottom of the Godot window displays the results as follows:

```
Ford x position = 55
Ford y position = 66
Ford speed = 123
```

Notice that the Car class defined a custom property (speed) that is not available in the Plant class. If you create an object from the Plant class and try to use the speed property, you'll get an error because the speed property is not defined in the Plant class.

# Polymorphism

Inheritance lets one class virtually copy code from another class while also adding its own unique code. One problem with inheritance is that it copies all methods defined in one class. Polymorphism lets you rewrite code in a method so that way you can use the same method name but replace it with entirely different code.

For example, a video game might create an Animal class that defines an x and y property along with a move method like this:

```
class Animal:
      var x: int
      var y: int
      func move(x_position: int, y_position: int,
      z_position: int):
            x += x_position
            y += y_position
```

This Animal class defines an x and y property along with a move method. Now we can create a new class that inherits from this Animal class like this:

```
class Bird extends Animal:
      var z: int
      func move(x_position: int, y_position: int,
      z_position: int):
            x += x_position + 3
            y += y_position + 4
            z += z_position + 2
```

Notice that this Bird class inherits the x and y properties from the Animal class while adding its own z property as well. Also notice that the move method contains a different code. Polymorphism lets you change the code within a method, but you must keep the function name and parameter list exactly the same. That's why the Animal class defines a move method with three parameters since that third parameter (z_position) will be needed for the Bird class.

To see how to use polymorphism, follow these steps:

1. Make sure you have a Godot project that consists of a Node2D and a child node Sprite2D that displays the icon.svg image in a window.

2. Click the Sprite2D node in the Scene dock.

3. Edit the script attached to the Sprite2D node as follows:

```
extends Sprite2D
class Animal:
        var x: int
        var y: int
        func move(x_position: int, y_position: int,
        z_position: int):
                x += x_position
                y += y_position

class Bird extends Animal:
        var z: int
        func move(x_position: int, y_position: int,
        z_position: int):
                x += x_position + 3
                y += y_position + 4
                z += z_position + 2

func _init():
        var dog = Animal.new()
        dog.move(2, 3, 4)
        print("Dog x position = ", dog.x, " Dog y
        position = ", dog.y)
```

```
var bird = Bird.new()
bird.move(2, 3, 4)
print("Bird x position = ", bird.x, "
Bird y position = ", bird.y, " Bird z
position = ", bird.z)
```

4.  Click the Run icon at the top of the window. The
    (DEBUG) window appears.

5.  Click the close icon of the (DEBUG) window to
    make it go away. Notice that the Output pane at the
    bottom of the Godot window displays the results as
    follows:

```
Dog x position = 2 Dog y position = 3
Bird x position = 5 Bird y position = 7 Bird z
position = 6
```

Notice that the dog.move(2,3,4) command is identical to the bird.
move(2,3,4) command yet creates different results. That's because the
dog.move(2,3,4) method is defined by the code in the Animal class while
the bird.move(2,3,4) method has rewritten the code to calculate different
results.

Polymorphism lets you rewrite code in methods and reuse method
names. While you can completely modify the code within a method using
polymorphism, you cannot change the parameter list of that method.
That's why the move method in both the Animal class and the Bird class is
identical like this:

```
func move(x_position: int, y_position: int, z_position: int):
```

Polymorphism lets you reuse method names and parameter lists while
replacing them with completely different code. That way you don't get
stuck inheriting methods you don't need.

# Exercise: Understanding How Object-Oriented Programming Works in Godot

Each time you create a scene by adding nodes, you're using object-oriented programming without even knowing it. That's because the base class is a Node, and from that class, Godot derives variations of a Node such as Node2D and Node3D. Within both Node2D and Node3D are further variants based on the Node2D and Node3D classes.

The main idea behind Godot is that most nodes inherit properties from an existing node. Once you understand the properties you can modify in one node, you'll know how to modify those same properties in another node.

Object-oriented principles can be especially useful when you want to create duplicate nodes such as multiple trees, rocks, or enemies within a video game. While you could create a single node, customize it, and then duplicate it, this creates completely separate and isolated nodes. If you later change one node, you'll need to change all duplicate copies of that same node. So if a video game contains 100 trees and you want to change their color or size, you'll need to change all 100 of them individually.

Obviously, this can be tedious to do, so the solution is to rely on object-oriented programming, specifically the idea of inheritance. That way you can define a single node file (.tscn), customize it, and place it in your video game. Then you create duplicate copies of that node within your video game.

Now if you want to customize the appearance of all nodes, you change it once in its separate .tscn file, and those changes automatically change all copies placed elsewhere in your video game. Instead of making 100 changes to 100 individual nodes, you make a single change to one node, and those changes get inherited (copied) to all copies of that node.

To see how Godot uses objects to create the various nodes used to define a scene, follow these steps:

1. Create a new Godot project.

2. Click Other Node. A Create New Node dialog box appears as shown in Figure 11-2.

*Figure 11-2.*   *The list of nodes in the Create New Node dialog box*

3. Click Node in the Create New Node dialog box. A description of that node's purpose appears at the bottom of the Create New Node dialog box.

4. Click the disclosure triangle that appears to the left of Node2D. A list of nodes that inherit from Node2D appears as shown in Figure 11-3.

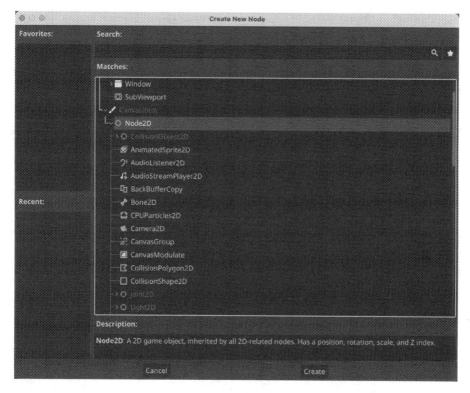

***Figure 11-3.*** *The list of nodes derived from Node2D*

5.  Click Node2D and then click Create. Godot makes Node2D the parent node.

6.  Choose Scene ➤ Save Scene. A Save Scene As dialog box appears.

7.  Click the File text field and type **Main.tscn**. Then click Save.

8.  Click the + (Attach Child Node) icon. A Create New Node dialog box appears.

9.  Click the Search text field and type **Sprite2D**. Then
    click Create. Godot makes the Sprite2D a child node
    of Node2D in the Scene dock.

10. Click Sprite2D in the Scene dock. Then drag and
    drop the icon.svg image file from the FileSystem
    dock into the Texture property in the Inspector
    dock. The icon.svg image now appears in the
    Sprite2D node.

11. Right-click Sprite2D in the Scene dock. A pop-up
    menu appears.

12. Click Save Branch as Scene as shown in Figure 11-4.
    A Save New Scene As dialog box appears.

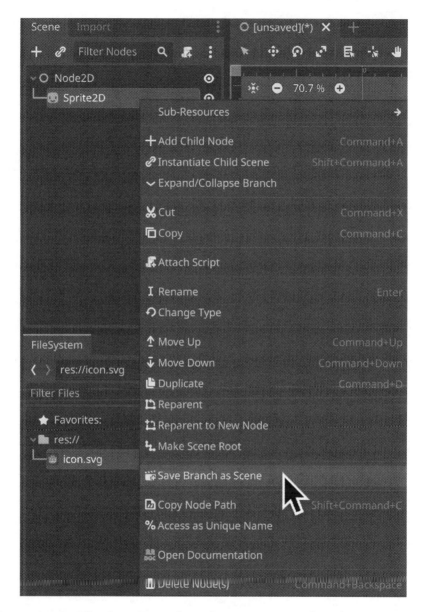

**Figure 11-4.** *The Save Branch as Scene command in the pop-up menu*

13. Click the File text field and type **Player.tscn**.
    Then click Save. Notice that your Player.tscn file
    now appears in the FileSystem dock as shown in
    Figure 11-5.

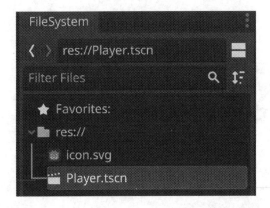

***Figure 11-5.*** *Godot creates a new scene file in the FileSystem dock*

14. Double-click the Main.tscn file in the FileSystem
    dock. This displays the Main.tscn file, which is the
    main scene for the project.

15. Drag and drop the Player.tscn file in the FileSystem
    dock into the viewport three times as shown in
    Figure 11-6.

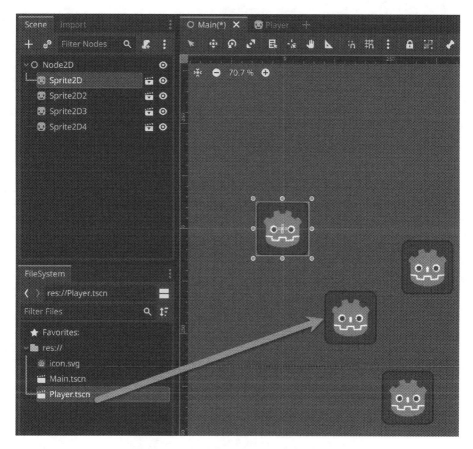

***Figure 11-6.*** *Dragging and dropping the Player.tscn file into the Main.tscn file three times*

16. Double-click the Player.tscn file in the FileSystem dock. Godot displays the contents of the Player.tscn file, which displays the icon.svg image. Notice that Sprite2D is the parent node in the Scene dock.

17. Click Sprite2D in the Scene dock. The Inspector dock displays all the properties available to customize.

247

18.    Click the disclosure triangle to the left of the
       Visibility property under the CanvasItem category as
       shown in Figure 11-7.

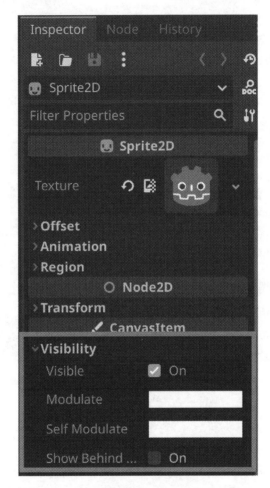

*Figure 11-7.* *The Visibility property under the CanvasItem category*
*in the Inspector dock*

19.    Click the Modulate property (that appears as a white
       rectangle). A color dialog box appears.

20. Click the various color options to choose a color as shown in Figure 11-8. This color will change the appearance of the icon.svg image file displayed in the Sprite2D node.

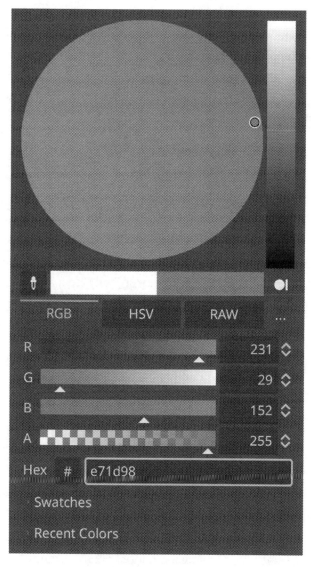

***Figure 11-8.*** *The Color dialog box*

21.  Choose Scene ➤ Save Scene (or press Ctrl/
     Command+S) to save your changes.

22.  Double-click the Main.tscn file in the FileSystem
     dock. Notice that all the icon.svg images now
     display the color changes you selected earlier. By
     changing one node, you changed multiple nodes
     automatically using inheritance.

# Summary

Object-oriented programming is a way to group data, and the algorithms
that manipulate that data, in one place. The first step to using object-
oriented programming is to create a class that defines one or more
properties (variables) and one or more methods (functions). After creating
a class, the second step is to create an object based on that class.

Three advantages of object-oriented programming include
encapsulation, inheritance, and polymorphism. Encapsulation means that
a class represents a self-contained entity that's as independent as possible.
This lets you modify a class without affecting the rest of a program.

Inheritance lets one class virtually copy code from another class.
In this way, you can avoid physically duplicating code so only one copy
of code exists. That way you can modify this code, and the changes
automatically affect any other classes.

Polymorphism means that a class can inherit code from another class
but rewrite an inherited method to contain a completely different code.
This prevents a class from inheriting methods that aren't needed.

Object-oriented programming is just one way to help write software
that's easy to modify without affecting the rest of a program. In addition,
object-oriented program can make it easy to reuse code without physically
duplicating that code. Reusing tested code makes a program more reliable
and faster to write.

# CHAPTER 12

# Getting Input from the User

All programs, such as word processors, spreadsheets, and databases, must accept input from the user. In video games, players commonly control a game object through the keyboard, mouse, joystick, or touch screen. By defining how specific keys on the keyboard function, how different buttons on a mouse or joystick work, and how to detect different types of touch gestures, you can detect user input for your game's particular needs.

Godot offers two ways to get input from input devices:

- Detect specific hardware interactions such as pressing the space bar.

- Assign your own hardware interactions for common events.

In the first approach, your code must detect specific hardware interactions. So your game might let you shoot a missile by pressing the space bar or clicking the left mouse. That means whenever your code needs to detect if the user wants to shoot a missile, your program must detect when the user presses the space bar or clicks the left mouse button. Unfortunately, just detecting if the user presses the space bar or clicks the left mouse button doesn't make it clear exactly what event your code is responding to.

© Wallace Wang, Tonnetta Walcott 2024
W. Wang and T. Walcott, *Programming for Game Design*,
https://doi.org/10.1007/979-8-8688-0190-7_12

In the second approach, you define an arbitrarily named input category such as "fire missile" and then assign one or more hardware interactions to trigger that action. Now your code just needs to identify when the user triggers the "fire missile" action and not exhaustively check for all hardware actions such as pressing the space bar or clicking the left mouse button.

In most cases, this second approach is preferable because it makes your code easier to understand and write. The drawback is that you must define an Input Map that defines all possible actions to respond to and the hardware actions that trigger that action.

# Detecting Keyboard and Mouse Input

The GDScript command for detecting when specific keys are pressed is as follows:

```
Input.is_key_pressed()
```

In parentheses, you must specify the exact key to detect such as KEY_F1, KEY_TAB, or KEY_A. (For a complete list of keys Godot can detect, visit https://docs.godotengine.org/en/stable/classes/class_%40globalscope.html#enum-globalscope-key.)

To see how to detect keyboard input by detecting specific keys, follow these steps:

1. Create a new Godot project and make Node2D the parent node and Sprite2D a child node.

2. Drag and drop the icon.svg image into the Texture property of Sprite2D.

3. Click Sprite2D in the Scene dock and click the Attach Script icon. Godot displays the GDScript editor.

4.  Edit the GDScript file as follows:

```
extends Sprite2D

var speed = 300

func _process(delta):
        var velocity = Vector2.ZERO

        if Input.is_key_pressed(KEY_RIGHT) or Input.
        is_key_pressed(KEY_D):
        velocity = Vector2.RIGHT * speed

        if Input.is_key_pressed(KEY_LEFT) or Input.is_
        key_pressed(KEY_A):
        velocity = Vector2.LEFT * speed

        if Input.is_key_pressed(KEY_UP) or Input.is_key_
        pressed(KEY_W):
        velocity = Vector2.UP * speed

        if Input.is_key_pressed(KEY_DOWN) or Input.is_
        key_pressed(KEY_S):
        velocity = Vector2.DOWN * speed

        position += velocity * delta
```

This code checks if certain keys are pressed such
as the right arrow (KEY_RIGHT) or the S key
(KEY_S). Since many games use the WASD keys as
alternatives to the up/down, right/left arrow keys,
the preceding code checks if the user pressed either
one of the WASD keys or one of the equivalent arrow
keys. Most games use WASD or arrow keys to detect
player movement.

Then it multiples a direction (such as Vector2. DOWN) with a speed to calculate a velocity, which gets multiplied by the delta variable to define the Sprite2D's position. Notice that the beginning of the _process(delta) function sets the velocity variable to Vector2.ZERO. Without this Vector2.ZERO value, the Sprite2D will keep moving in the direction the user last selected such as up, down, left, or right.

5. Click the Run icon. A dialog box appears, asking you to select a main scene.

6. Click Select Current. A dialog box appears to save your scene.

7. Click Save.

8. Press the WASD or up/down, right/left arrow keys to move the image around the window. Notice that as soon as you release a key, the image stops moving.

9. Click the close icon in the (DEBUG) window when you're done.

Detecting the left or right mouse button is just as easy. The GDScript command for detecting when a mouse button is pressed is as follows:

```
Input.is_mouse_button_pressed()
```

Inside the parentheses, you can define MOUSE_BUTTON_LEFT, MOUSE_BUTTON_RIGHT, or MOUSE_BUTTON_MIDDLE. To see how to detect mouse buttons, follow these steps:

1. Click the script icon that appears to the right of Sprite2D in the project you created previously.

2.  Modify the GDScript as follows:

```
extends Sprite2D

var speed = 300

func _process(delta):
    var velocity = Vector2.ZERO

    if Input.is_key_pressed(KEY_RIGHT) or
    Input.is_key_pressed(KEY_D):
    velocity = Vector2.RIGHT * speed

    if Input.is_key_pressed(KEY_LEFT) or
    Input.is_key_pressed(KEY_A):
    velocity = Vector2.LEFT * speed

    if Input.is_key_pressed(KEY_UP) or
    Input.is_key_pressed(KEY_W):
    velocity = Vector2.UP * speed

    if Input.is_key_pressed(KEY_DOWN) or
    Input.is_key_pressed(KEY_S):
    velocity = Vector2.DOWN * speed

    if Input.is_mouse_button_pressed
    (MOUSE_BUTTON_RIGHT):
    velocity = Vector2.RIGHT * speed

    if Input.is_mouse_button_pressed
    (MOUSE_BUTTON_LEFT):
    velocity = Vector2.LEFT * speed

    if Input.is_mouse_button_pressed
    (MOUSE_BUTTON_MIDDLE):
    velocity = Vector2.DOWN * speed

    position += velocity * delta
```

This additional code detects when the user presses the left, right, or middle mouse button.

3.  Click the Run icon.

4.  Hold down the right mouse button. The image moves to the right.

5.  Hold down the left mouse button. The image now moves to the left.

6.  Hold down the middle mouse button. The image now moves down.

# Defining an Input Map

Checking for specific keys or mouse buttons pressed can be fine, but many times a game may offer multiple ways to perform the same task such as letting the user move an object by pressing the WASD keys, the arrow keys, a joystick, or a mouse. Checking multiple types of input can be tedious, so Godot offers an input map instead.

With an input map, you define event categories to detect such as "move_right" or "move_down." Within each category, you can then define all the different ways to accomplish that task such as through a keyboard, mouse, or joystick. In Figure 12-1, there's a move_left event that can be triggered in four ways:

• Press the A key

• Press the left arrow key

• Press the joystick button

• Pull the joystick to the left

***Figure 12-1.*** *An Input Map can assign multiple input devices to the same action*

Once you've defined one or more ways to detect input (such as through a keyboard, mouse, or joystick), you can assign equivalent inputs to the same category. Now instead of checking for multiple pressed keys, mouse buttons, or joystick buttons, your code can just check if the user selected a specific input event such as move_left. This makes your code easier to read and understand while also being shorter to write.

To see how to create and use an input map, follow these steps:

1. Create a new Godot project and make Node2D the parent node and Sprite2D a child node.

2. Drag and drop the icon.svg image into the Texture property of Sprite2D.

257

3. Choose Project ➤ Project Settings. A Project Settings dialog box appears.

4. Click the Input Map tab.

5. Click the Show Built-in Actions switch in the upper right corner of the Project Settings dialog box. A list of predefined actions appears as shown in Figure 12-2.

*Figure 12-2.* *The Built-in Actions available in the Input Map*

6. Click the Show Built-in Actions switch again to hide all built-in actions since we want to create our own event categories.

7.  Click the Add New Action text field and type **move_
    left**. Then click Add. Godot creates a new action
    category.

8.  Click the Add New Action text field and type **move_
    right**. Then click Add.

9.  Click the Add New Action text field and type **move_
    up**. Then click Add.

10. Click the Add New Action text field and type ***move_
    down***. Then click Add. The Input Map displays four
    categories as shown in Figure 12-3.

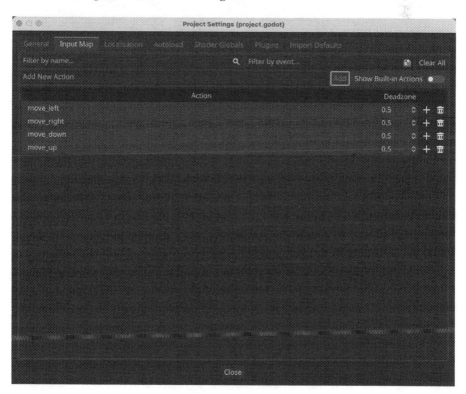

***Figure 12-3.*** *The Input Map with four empty categories displayed*

11.  Click the + icon that appears to the right of move_
     left. An Event Configuration dialog box appears as
     shown in Figure 12-4.

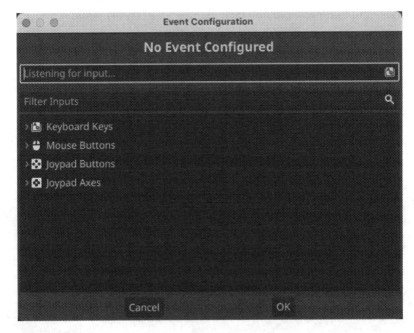

*Figure 12-4. The Event Configuration dialog box*

12.  Click the disclosure triangle to the left of Keyboard
     Keys and then click Left to define the left arrow key.
     Then click OK. Godot adds the Left key to the move_
     left event. As an alternative to choosing a key from a
     list of options, you can also press the key you want to
     represent an event category.

13.  Click the + icon to the right of move_left. The Event
     Configuration dialog box appears (see Figure 12-4).

14.  Press the A key and click OK. Godot now assigns
     the A key to the move_left event as shown in
     Figure 12-5.

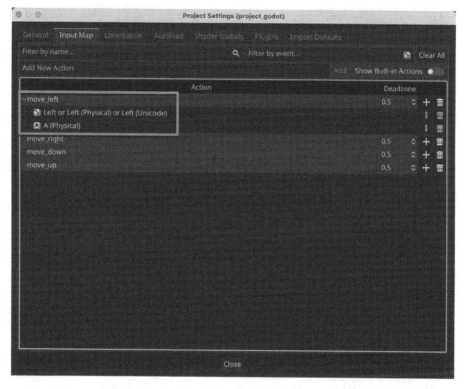

***Figure 12-5.*** *The Event Configuration dialog box listing two ways to represent the move_left event*

15. Click the + icon that appears to the right of move_ right. The Event Configuration dialog box appears (see Figure 12-4).

16. Press the D key and click OK.

17. Click the + icon that appears to the right of move_right again to open the Event Configuration dialog box.

18. Click the disclosure triangle that appears to the left of Keyboard Keys, click Right, and click OK.

261

19. Click the + icon that appears to the right of move_ down to open the Event Configuration dialog box.

20. Press the W key and click OK.

21. Click the + icon that appears to the right of move_down again to open the Event Configuration dialog box.

22. Click the disclosure triangle that appears to the left of Keyboard Keys, click Down, and click OK.

23. Click the + icon that appears to the right of move_up to open the Event Configuration dialog box.

24. Press the S key and click OK.

25. Click the + icon that appears to the right of move_up again to open the Event Configuration dialog box.

26. Click the disclosure triangle that appears to the left of Keyboard Keys, click Up, and click OK. The Input Map tab in the Project Settings dialog box should now display an arrow key (Up, Left, Down, or Right) and a letter key (W, A, S, or D) for each event as shown in Figure 12-6.

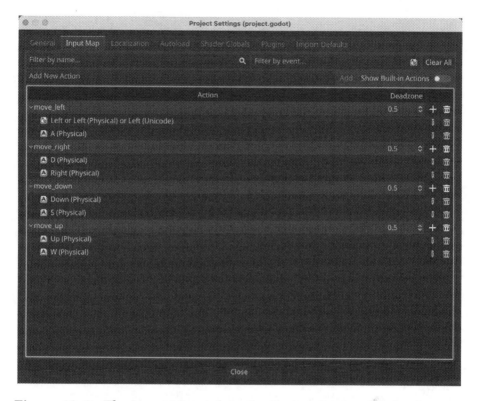

***Figure 12-6.*** *The Input Map tab in the Project Settings dialog box listing two ways to represent each event*

27.  Click Close to make the Project Settings dialog box go away.

28.  Click Sprite2D in the Scene dock and click the Attach Script icon. Godot displays the GDScript editor.

29.  Edit the GDScript file as follows:

```
extends Sprite2D
var speed = 400
func _process(delta):
        var velocity = Vector2.ZERO
```

263

```
if Input.is_action_pressed("move_left"):
    velocity = Vector2.LEFT * speed

if Input.is_action_pressed("move_right"):
    velocity = Vector2.RIGHT * speed

if Input.is_action_pressed("move_up"):
    velocity = Vector2.UP * speed

if Input.is_action_pressed("move_down"):
    velocity = Vector2.DOWN * speed

position += velocity * delta
```

30. Click the Run icon at the top of the window. The (DEBUG) window appears.

31. Press the left/right, up/down arrow keys to move the icon.svg image around the screen.

32. Press the WASD keys to move the icon.svg image around the screen. Notice that the code no longer looks for specific keys but looks for specific events (move_down).

33. Click the close icon of the (DEBUG) window to make it go away.

When assigning keys to an event, Godot gives you two choices. First, you can select a key from the list of available options displayed in the Event Configuration dialog box. Second, you can press a key. Either method lets you choose all available keys to detect.

Besides letting you detect keys, the Input Map can also detect mouse buttons and joystick actions. Any time you want to modify an action, click the Edit icon (it looks like a pencil). Any time you want to remove an action, click the Delete icon (it looks like a trash can) as shown in Figure 12-7.

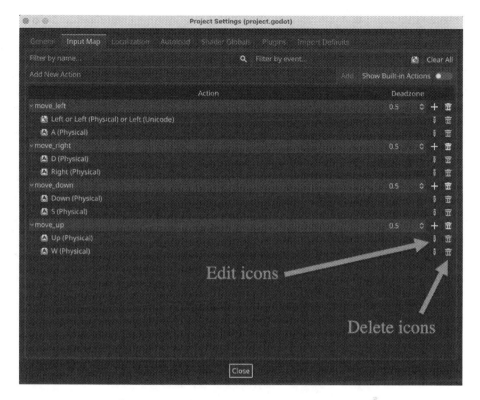

**Figure 12-7.** *Editing or deleting an Input Map*

# Detecting Modifier Keys in an Input Map

So far we've detected physical keys that the user can press such as the left arrow key or the W key. However, Godot's Input Map can also detect modifier keys such as Control, Alt (Windows/Linux), Option (Macintosh), and Shift. Being able to detect modifier keys with other keys lets Godot detect keystroke combinations such as Ctrl+P or Shift+F2.

Detecting modifier keys involves selecting a check box while choosing a specific key. So if you selected the A key, you could choose a Shift, Control, or Alt/Option key modifier. If you choose a single modifier, the keystroke combination might look like Control+A. If you choose two modifiers, the keystroke combination might look like Control+Shift+A.

265

To see how to use modifiers, follow these steps:

1.  Open the Godot project you created and edited in the previous section.

2.  Choose Project ➤ Project Settings to open the Project Settings dialog box.

3.  Click the Input Map tab.

4.  Click the Add New Action text field and type **rotate_left**. Then click Add.

5.  Click the Add New Action text field and type **rotate_right**. Then click Add.

6.  Click the + icon that appears to the right of rotate_ left. An Event Configuration dialog box appears.

7.  Press the left arrow key. A list of modifier keys appears at the bottom of the Event Configuration dialog box as shown in Figure 12-8.

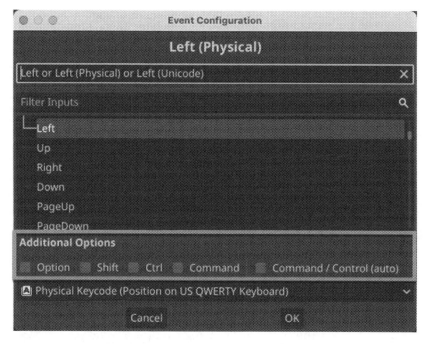

***Figure 12-8.*** *The modifier keys appear at the bottom of the Event Configuration dialog box*

8.  Select the Shift check box and click OK.

9.  Click the + icon that appears to the right of rotate_ right. An Event Configuration dialog box appears.

10. Press the right arrow key. A list of modifier keys appears at the bottom of the Event Configuration dialog box (see Figure 12-8).

11. Select the Shift check box and click OK.

12. Click Close to make the Event Configuration dialog box go away.

13.  Click the script icon that appears to the right of
     Sprite2D in the Scene dock. Godot opens the
     GDScript editor.

14.  Edit the GDScript as follows:

```
extends Sprite2D
var speed = 400
var spin_speed = 5
func _process(delta):
        var velocity = Vector2.ZERO
        spin_speed = 0
        if Input.is_action_pressed("move_left"):
                velocity = Vector2.LEFT * speed
        if Input.is_action_pressed("move_right"):
                velocity = Vector2.RIGHT * speed
        if Input.is_action_pressed("move_up"):
                velocity = Vector2.UP * speed
        if Input.is_action_pressed("move_down"):
                velocity = Vector2.DOWN * speed
        position += velocity * delta
        if Input.is_action_pressed("rotate_left"):
                spin_speed = -5
        if Input.is_action_pressed("rotate_right"):
                spin_speed = 5
        rotation += spin_speed * delta
```

The rotation code works similar to the movement
code where the beginning of the _process(delta)
function sets the spin_speed variable to 0.
Otherwise, the image would keep rotating even
after we let go of the Shift+left arrow or Shift+right
arrow key.

Then the code checks to see if the rotate_left or rotate_right event occurs, which can only happen if the user presses the Shift+left arrow or Shift+right arrow. If that occurs, then the if statement sets spin_speed to either 5 or -5, depending on which arrow key the user pressed.

15. Click the Run icon. The (DEBUG) window appears.

16. Press the left/right and up/down arrow keys to move the icon.svg image around the screen.

17. Hold down Shift and press the left arrow key. Notice that the icon.svg image rotates to the left. The image appears to roll to the left because the Shift+Left arrow key rotates it but the Left arrow also moves it to the left at the same time.

18. Hold down Shift and press the right arrow key. Notice that the icon.svg image rotates to the right.

19. Click the close icon in the (DEBUG) window.

You can also use the modifier keys for non-keyboard input devices such as with the mouse. To see how to use modifier keys with the mouse, follow these steps:

1. Open the Godot project that contains the code that can move and rotate the icon.svg image.

2. Choose Project ➤ Project Settings. The Project Settings dialog box appears.

3. Click the Input Map tab. The rotate_left and rotate_right events should already be defined.

4. Click the + icon to the right of rotate_left. An Event Configuration dialog box appears.

5. Click the disclosure triangle to the left of mouse buttons.

6. Click Left Mouse Button. A list of modifiers appears at the bottom of the Event Configuration dialog box (see Figure 12-8).

7. Select the Shift check box and click OK.

8. Click Right Mouse Button. A list of modifiers appears at the bottom of the Event Configuration dialog box (see Figure 12-8).

9. Select the Shift check box and click OK.

10. Click Close to make the Event Configuration dialog box go away. The rotate_left and rotate_right categories should now display a Shift+Left Mouse Button and a Shift+Right Mouse Button action as shown in Figure 12-9.

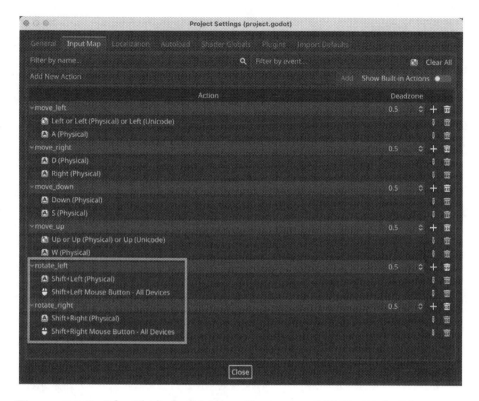

***Figure 12-9.*** *The Shift+Left Mouse Button and Shift+Right Mouse Button actions added to the Input Map*

11.  Click Close to make the Project Settings window go away.

12.  Click the Run icon.

13.  Hold down the Shift key and hold the left mouse button. The icon.svg image rotates to the left

14.  Hold down the Shift key and hold down the right mouse button. The icon.svg image rotates to the right.

15.  Click the close icon of the (DEBUG) window.

271

# Summary

Every video game needs to let the user control objects within the game through the keyboard, mouse, joystick, or touch screen. You could write code to detect specific input actions such as when the user presses the K key or clicks the left mouse button. However, it's more convenient to create an Input Map instead.

An Input Map lets you define one or more event categories that represent a particular type of movement such as up, down, left, or right. Then within each category, you can detect multiple inputs through different keys, the mouse, or a joystick.

Besides detecting individual keys, the Input Map can also detect keystroke combinations through one or more modifiers such as the Shift, Control, or Alt/Option modifier keys. By combining two or more modifiers together, you can create keystroke combinations such as Control+Shift+F1 or Shift+Option+Left mouse button.

Once you know how to detect input from the user through a variety of input devices (keyboard, mouse, joystick), you'll be able to create a game that can respond to the user in the way players like best.

# CHAPTER 13

# Shooting Projectiles

Moving is one of the most common tasks in any video game. The second most common task is shooting a projectile to attack enemies. Even though a player can move around in the game, it makes the game boring over time. Therefore making more interactions such as shooting projectiles, unlocking items, or other options can make a game more interesting.

Firing a projectile involves creating another object, aiming it, and moving it in the direction it was aimed. Later, shooting a projectile also means detecting if it collides with anything. It is important to check for collision, or else shooting a projectile is void. If it hits something, then the game must make the projectile disappear and respond to the projectile hitting an object.

First you must create a projectile as a separate scene. This scene defines the projectile's appearance and must also include GDScript code to make it move.

After you've created a projectile as a separate scene, the second step is to link the projectile scene with the scene that defines your player in a video game such as an airplane, tank, or gun. Once you've connected the projectile scene with your player scene, you'll need to write GDScript to create the projectile at a specific location and a direction using a Marker2D node. Wherever you place this Marker2D node is where your projectile will appear, such as shooting out of the mouth of a cartoon dragon or out of the tip of a laser cannon.

© Wallace Wang, Tonnetta Walcott 2024
W. Wang and T. Walcott, *Programming for Game Design*,
https://doi.org/10.1007/979-8-8688-0190-7_13

# Creating a Projectile Scene

A projectile scene consists of three nodes as shown in Figure 13-1:

- Area2D (parent)

- Sprite2D (child) – Defines the image of the projectile in the Texture property

- CollisonShape2D (child) – Defines the shape and size of the collision boundaries of the projectile

***Figure 13-1.***  *The scene structure of a projectile*

The Area2D node can detect collisions, which can be useful if the projectile hits another object such as an enemy. However, by itself, the Area2D node cannot detect collisions without the help of a CollisionShape2D child node. When you add the CollisionShape2D node, you can then define the Shape property.

The Shape property lets you define the physical shape of the collision boundaries such as a rectangle or ellipse. You can move and resize the Shape boundary to closely match the visible image of the projectile. You want to match the Shape boundary as close to the image as possible in order to detect collisions better.

The Sprite2D node lets you choose an image for the projectile. Ideally, you should create custom images for your projectile, but any image file will work.

To see how to create a projectile, follow these steps:

1. Create a new Godot project and click Other Node when the new project loads. A Create New Node dialog box appears.

2. Click the Search text field, type **Area2D,** and click Create. Godot makes the Area2D node the parent node in the Scene dock.

3. Click the + (Add Child Node) icon. The Create New Node dialog box appears.

4. Click the Search text field, type **Sprite2D**, and click Create. Godot makes the Sprite2D a child node underneath Area2D.

5. Click Area2D in the Scene dock and click the + (Add Child Node) icon. The Create New Node dialog box appears.

6. Click the Search text field, type **CollisionShape2D**, and click Create. Godot makes the CollisionShape2D a child node of Area2D (see Figure 13-1).

# Changing the Name of a Node

Each time you create a scene out of multiple nodes, Godot uses the default, generic name for that node such as Area2D or Sprite2D. However, it's often better to give specific, descriptive names for your nodes. That way you can better understand what they actually represent. If you want to give a specific name to a node such as "Player" for Sprite2D, you simply double-click the name of the node and type in your preferred name. Giving nodes specific names will better help you track each object used in the game and help you indicate how you will let the objects function.

In our project, the scene consists of an Area2D node with a Sprite2D and CollisionShape2D node as two child nodes. However, it's not clear exactly what Area2D represents. In this particular case, the Area2D represents a projectile, so it might be better to rename Area2D with a more descriptive name such as "Bullet" or "Missile."

To see how to rename a node, follow these steps:

1.  Make sure you have created a Godot project where a scene consists of an Area2D node with two child nodes: Sprite2D and CollisionShape2D (see Figure 13-1).

2.  Double-click Area2D in the Scene dock. Godot highlights the entire node name.

3.  Edit the Area2D name to **Bullet** as shown in Figure 13-2.

*Figure 13-2.* *Changing the name of Area2D to Bullet*

4.  Press Enter.

You can rename any node to give it a more descriptive name. For our projectile, it's enough just to change the Area2D name to Bullet, so it's easier to see what this scene represents in the game.

1.  Press Ctrl/Command+S to save your scene. A Save Scene As dialog box appears. Since you changed the root node to Bullet, Godot assumes you want to save your scene using that root node name such as Bullet.tscn as shown in Figure 13-3.

***Figure 13-3.** Saving a scene for the first time*

2. Click Save. Godot saves your scene using the .tscn
   file extension in the FileSystem dock as shown in
   Figure 13-4.

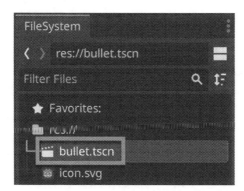

***Figure 13-4.** A saved scene's file name appears in the FileSystem dock*

# Adding a Projectile Image

A projectile needs an image to make it visible within a game. Ideally, you (or an artist) should create a custom projectile image, but for our purposes, we can use the icon.svg image that appears in every Godot project.

Since we're going to use the icon.svg image to represent our player that we control as well, we need to change the appearance of the icon.svg image to represent our projectile. One simple way to do that is to change the scale of the image.

By changing the scale, we can shrink (or expand) an image beyond its original size. For a project, we want to shrink the icon.svg image. We could change its scale manually by dragging the mouse, but it's more precise to use the Scale properties in the Inspector dock instead.

To see how to create and scale an image for a projectile, follow these steps:

1. Click Sprite2D in the Scene dock to select it.

2. Drag and drop the icon.svg image into the Texture property of Sprite2D.

3. Click the disclosure triangle that appears to the left of the Transform category that appears under Node2D.

4. Click the x field under the Scale property and type 0.25. Then press Enter. Notice that Godot automatically scales the y property to 0.25 as shown in Figure 13-5.

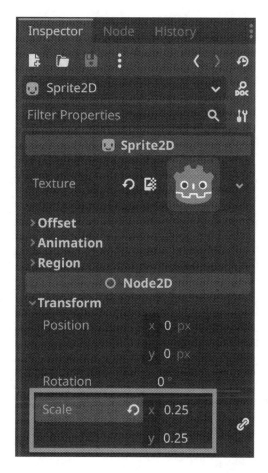

*Figure 13-5.* *Changing the Scale properties of the Sprite2D node*

# Adding a Collision Shape

At this point, you might notice a yellow warning icon that appears to the right of the CollisionShape2D node in the Scene dock as shown in Figure 13-6.

**Figure 13-6.** *A warning about the CollisionShape2D node*

Godot displays warnings whenever it detects incomplete tasks. In this case, we've added a CollisionShape2D node to define the collision boundaries around our projectile. However, we haven't defined this collision boundary yet. To do this, we'll need to modify the Shape property in the CollisionShape2D node.

To see how to define a collision shape, follow these steps:

1. Open the Godot project you created and edited in the previous section.

2. Click CollisionShape2D in the Scene dock to select it.

3. Click the <empty> field that appears in the Shape property. A list of options appears in a pull-down menu as shown in Figure 13-7.

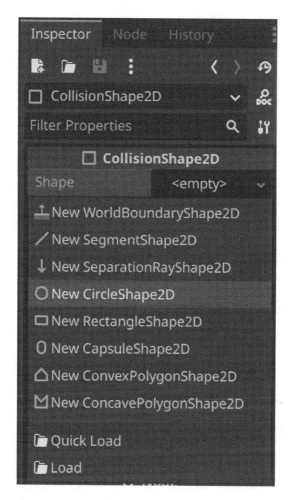

***Figure 13-7.*** *Choosing the shape of a collision boundary around a node*

4.  Click New RectangleShape2D. Godot displays a rectangular box with orange handles around the sides and corners as shown in Figure 13-8.

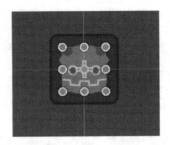

*Figure 13-8.* *Resizing the shape of a collision boundary*

5.  Drag the orange handles until the collision
    boundary rectangle covers the icon.svg image.
    Notice that the yellow warning icon no longer
    appears in the Scene dock.

At this point, we've created a projectile out of three nodes (Area2D,
Sprite2D, and CollisonShape2D). The Sprite2D node defines the
appearance of the projectile, and the CollisionShape2D node defines a
collision boundary around the image.

# Making the Projectile Move

The Sprite2D node defines the appearance of the projectile, but it won't
move. To make it move, we need to write GDScript code. Because we want
the entire projectile to move, we need to attach a script to the root node
(Bullet) in the Scene dock.

The GDScript code needs to change the position of the entire scene
along either the x or y axis. The exact axis you choose doesn't matter
because it simply defines the projectile to move in a straight line. The
direction that the projectile will actually move within a game depends
entirely on where you define the projectile to appear and in which
direction the x or y axis appears. This will be defined in the next chapter
when we create a player and define how to shoot the projectile.

To see how to write GDScript code to make the projectile move, follow these steps:

1.  Make sure the Godot project you created earlier is open.

2.  Click the Bullet node in the Scene dock and click the Attach Script icon. An Attach Node Script dialog box appears. Notice that the default script name is the name of the root node (Bullet) followed by the .gd file extension such as bullet.gd.

3.  Click Create. Godot displays the contents of the newly created GDScript.

4.  Edit the bullet.gd file as follows:

```
extends Area2D
@export var speed = 700
func _process(delta):
        position += transform.x * speed * delta
```

5.  Press Ctrl/Command+S to save your GDScript code.

The first line in the preceding code (extends Area2D) simply inherits all code associated with the Area2D node. One particular property we want to use from the Area2D node is the position property, which defines the node's position on the screen.

The second line (@export var speed = 700) defines a variable called "speed" and sets its value to 700. The @export keyword in front of "var speed" means this variable (speed) appears in the Inspector dock. That means we can change the value of the speed variable either by modifying the GDScript code or by changing the speed variable within the Inspector dock as shown in Figure 13-9.

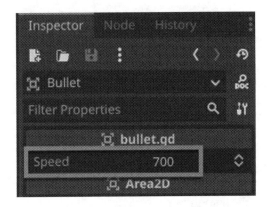

*Figure 13-9.* *The @export keyword makes a variable accessible through the Inspector dock*

The third line (func _process(delta)) defines a function that runs every time the game displays another frame. Since every computer runs at different speeds, the delta variable represents how much time has passed since the previous frame appeared. By using this delta variable, we can create smoother movement regardless of the speed of the computer that the project runs on.

The fourth line changes the position of the Bullet node. In this case, we want to move along the x axis (transform.x) based on the speed variable (speed = 700) and the delta variable.

To see how this code works, follow these steps:

1.  Click the Run icon. A dialog box appears, asking if you want to use the current scene as the main scene.

2.  Click Select Current. After a while, you should see the icon.svg move along the top of the Godot (DEBUG) window.

3.  Click the close icon of the (DEBUG) window.

Each time you click the Run icon, you'll see the icon.svg image move to the right across the top of the (DEBUG) window. This lets you see that the projectile looks and behaves the way we want. In the next chapter, we'll create a player and write GDScript code to make the projectile shoot out of the player image as it moves and rotates around the screen.

# Summary

Many video games create flying projectiles from the player (to hit enemies) or from enemies (to hit the player). Shooting objects that fly across the screen is a common mechanic used in nearly every video game, so it's important to know how to create a flying projectile.

A projectile consists of a single scene with an Area2D node as its root node. Attached to this Area2D node are two child nodes: a Sprite2D node and a CollisionShape2D node. The Sprite2D node lets you choose an image to represent the projectile. The CollisionShape2D node lets you define a collision boundary around your projectile.

To make a projectile move, you need to write GDScript code that changes the position of the projectile along the x or y axis. Once you've defined a projectile and made it move, you'll be ready to add it to a player scene. Creating separate scenes, made out of different nodes, and putting them together to build larger scenes is what makes the Godot game engine easy to use for creating all types of video games. Once you understand the key concepts of shooting projectiles at enemies, you can also add health or a scoreboard. Be as creative as you want when making a game.

# CHAPTER 14

# Adding Projectiles to a Player

Creating a projectile and making it move is the first step. The second step is making that projectile appear when and where you want it during a game. In most cases, you want a projectile to appear where you aim, so this chapter is about adding a projectile to a player that you can move and rotate. No matter how you move or rotate the player, you can fire a projectile from the top of the player image. This chapter focuses on adding projectiles in case you want to make a simple 2D shooter game.

In Godot, a game consists of multiple scenes made up of nodes. You can have as many scenes and modes as you want, but it's best to keep the project simple. Nodes act like building blocks to create scenes, and scenes act as much larger building blocks to create more complex scenes. Once you create a projectile as a scene, you need to create a new scene that defines a player that you can control.

The most important part about shooting a projectile is defining where it appears and what direction it will go. To do this, you need to link a projectile to a special Marker2D node that defines the position and direction where you want a projectile to appear around a player. In simpler terms, the Marker2D will help with aiming and shooting at enemies in the game that you are making.

© Wallace Wang, Tonnetta Walcott 2024
W. Wang and T. Walcott, *Programming for Game Design*,
https://doi.org/10.1007/979-8-8688-0190-7_14

# Creating a Player Scene

Before you can shoot a projectile, you need to create a player that people can move, rotate, and aim. A player scene can consist of the following nodes as shown in Figure 14-1:

- CharacterBody2D (parent)

- Sprite2D (child) – Defines the image of the player in the Texture property

- CollisonShape2D (child) – Defines the shape and size of the collision boundaries of the player

- Marker2D (child of Sprite2D) – Defines the location and direction where the projectile will appear and move

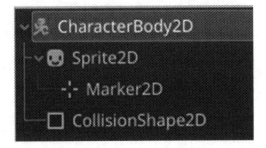

***Figure 14-1.***  *The scene structure of a player*

The CharacterBody2D node is a node designed for creating objects in a game that GDScript code can control and move within a game. Most importantly, GDScript code must create a link to the projectile scene so that it can fire and move in the direction defined by a Marker2D node.

The Sprite2D node lets you choose an image for the player. Ideally, you should create custom images for your projectile, but any image file will work. More importantly, the Marker2D node must be a child of Sprite2D. This Marker2D node defines the position and direction where a projectile will appear and move.

The CollisionShape2D node defines a collision boundary around the player. This is useful for detecting when the player runs into objects or gets hit by flying projectiles fired by enemy objects.

To see how to create a player, follow these steps:

1. Make sure you have opened the previous Godot project where you created a projectile scene called bullet.tscn.

2. Choose Scene ➤ New Scene. Godot creates a new scene.

3. Click 2D at the top of the Godot window to view your newly created scene.

4. Click Other Node in the Scene dock. A Create New Node dialog box appears.

5. Click the Search text field, type **CharacterBody2D**, and click Create. Godot makes the CharacterBody2D node the parent node of the newly created scene.

6. Click the + (Attach Child Node) icon in the Scene dock. A Create New Node dialog box appears.

7. Click the Search text field, type **Sprite2D**, and click Create. Godot makes the Sprite2D node the child node of the CharacterBody2D parent node.

8. Click Sprite2D in the Scene dock and click the + (Attach Child Node) icon. A Create New Node dialog box appears.

9. Click the Search text field, type **Marker2D**, and click Create. Godot makes the Sprite2D node the child node of the Sprite2D node.

10. Click CharacterBody2D in the Scene dock and click the + (Attach Child Node) icon. A Create New Node dialog box appears.

11. Click the Search text field, type **CollisionShape2D**, and click Create. Godot makes the CollisionShape2D node the child node of the CharacterBody2D node (see Figure 14-1).

# Changing the Name of a Node

When we created the projectile scene, the parent node was Area2D. We changed this name to "Bullet" to make it more descriptive of what that scene actually represents. Likewise, our current player scene displays a CharacterBody2D node as its parent node, so we'll need to rename this node to something more descriptive such as "Player."

To see how to rename a node, follow these steps:

1. Make sure you have created a Godot project where a scene consists of a CharacterBody2D node with two child nodes: Sprite2D and CollisionShape2D (see Figure 14-1).

2. Double-click CharacterBody2D in the Scene dock. Godot highlights the entire node name.

3. Edit the CharacterBody2D name to **Player** as shown in Figure 14-2.

***Figure 14-2.*** *Changing the name of CharacterBody2D to Player*

4. Press Enter.

5. Press Ctrl/Command+S to save your scene. A Save Scene
   As dialog box appears. Since you changed the root node
   to Player, Godot assumes you want to save your scene
   using that root node name such as Player.tscn.

6. Click Save. Godot saves your scene using the .tscn
   file extension in the FileSystem dock as shown in
   Figure 14-3.

***Figure 14-3.*** *A saved scene's file name appears in the FileSystem dock*

# Adding a Player Image and Collision Shape

The Sprite2D node contains a Texture property where you can add an image that represents the player in a game. Ideally, you should create multiple images to represent a player as it moves where each image appears in rapid succession to create a simple animation. In another chapter, we will discuss more about sprites and animations to add some flare to your game. For our purposes, we'll use a simple static image to represent the player using the icon.svg image.

To see how to create and scale an image for a player, follow these steps:

1. Click Sprite2D in the Scene dock to select it.

2. Drag and drop the icon.svg image into the Texture property of Sprite2D.

3. Click CollisionShape2D in the Scene dock to select it.

4. Click the <empty> field that appears in the Shape property. A list of options appears in a pull-down menu.

5. Click New RectangleShape2D. Godot displays a rectangular box with orange handles around the sides and corners.

6. Drag the orange handles until the collision boundary rectangle covers the icon.svg image.

# Using the Marker2D Node to Define the Projectile Location

To fire a projectile, we need to define where it starts and which direction it should move. The way to do that is through the Marker2D node that's attached as a child node to the Sprite2D node. The Marker2D node lets you define

- Where the projectile should appear

- Which direction the projectile should move

The position of the Marker2D defines where the projectile appears. The orientation of the Marker2D defines which direction the projectile will move.

To see how to customize the Marker2D node to define the projectile location and direction, follow these steps:

1. Make sure the Godot project you created earlier is open.

2. Click the Marker2D node in the Scene dock to select it. Godot highlights the Marker2D node, which should look like an orange cross.

3. Click the Move Mode icon. Godot displays an x and y axis arrow on the Marker2D node.

4. Drag the Marker2D to the top middle of the icon.svg image (the Sprite2D node) as shown in Figure 14-4. The red arrow represents the x axis and the green arrow represents the y axis.

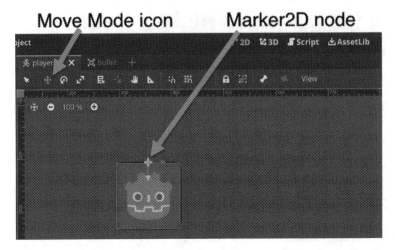

*Figure 14-4.* *Using the Move Mode icon to position a Marker2D node*

5. Click the disclosure triangle to the left of Transform in the Inspector dock and then double-click the Rotation text field.

6. Type -90 and press Enter. This rotates the x axis (red arrow) to point vertically as shown in Figure 14-5. This will define the direction that the projectile will move.

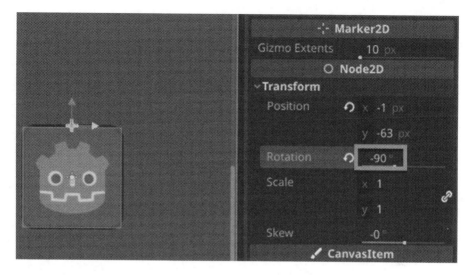

***Figure 14-5.*** *Rotating the Marker2D orients its x axis*

7.   Press Ctrl/Command+S to save your scene.

# Defining Ways to Control the Player

Now that we've created a player out of multiple nodes, the next step is to define ways to control the player by moving it, rotating it, and firing a projectile by pressing various keys on the keyboard. To define the actions of certain keys, we need to identify the actions we want (such as rotate_left or shoot) and then assign specific keys to each action. The seven actions we need to detect are as follows:

- Up

- Down

- Left

- Right

- Rotate left

- Rotate right

- Shoot

To see how to define keys to control specific actions on the player, follow these steps:

1. Make sure the Godot project you created earlier is open.

2. Choose Project ➤ Project Settings. A Project Settings window appears.

3. Click the Input Map tab as shown in Figure 14-6.

***Figure 14-6.*** *The Input Map tab in the Project Settings window*

4. Click the Add New Action text field, type **up**, and press Enter.

5. Click the Add New Action text field, type **down**, and press Enter.

6. Click the Add New Action text field, type **left**, and press Enter.

7. Click the Add New Action text field, type **right**, and press Enter.

8. Click the Add New Action text field, type **rotate_left**, and press Enter.

9.  Click the Add New Action text field, type **rotate_right**, and press Enter.

10. Click the Add New Action text field, type *shoot*, and press Enter. You should now have defined seven different actions as shown in Figure 14-7.

*Figure 14-7. Defining seven actions to detect*

At this point, we've defined seven different actions. Now we need to define specific keys to trigger each action. To move up/down, left/right, games typically use both the arrow keys and the WASD keys as well. To rotate left and rotate right, we can use the comma and period keys. To shoot a projectile, we can use the space bar.

When you want to assign specific keys to an action, you have two choices. First, you can simply press the key you want to assign to each action. Second, you can click the list of all available keys to choose the key to assign to each action. The first method is faster and more intuitive, so that's the method we'll use.

To assign specific keys to each action, follow these steps.

1.  Click the + (Add Event) icon that appears to the right of the **up** action. An Event Configuration window appears as shown in Figure 14-8.

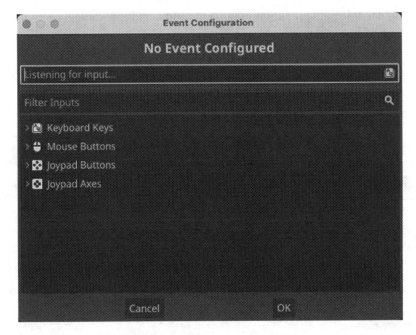

***Figure 14-8.*** *The Event Configuration window*

2.  Press the up arrow key and click OK. The Event
    Configuration window displays the Up (Physical)
    key under the **up** action.

3.  Click the + (Add Event) icon that appears to the right
    of the **up** action. An Event Configuration window
    appears (see Figure 14-8).

4.  Press the W key and click OK. The Event
    Configuration window displays the W (Physical) key
    under the **up** action.

5.  Click the + (Add Event) icon that appears to the right
    of the **down** action. An Event Configuration window
    appears (see Figure 14-8).

6. Press the down arrow key and click OK. The Event Configuration window displays the Down (Physical) key under the down action.

7. Click the + (Add Event) icon that appears to the right of the **down** action. An Event Configuration window appears (see Figure 14-8).

8. Press the S key and click OK. The Event Configuration window displays the S (Physical) key under the **down** action.

9. Click the + (Add Event) icon that appears to the right of the **left** action. An Event Configuration window appears (see Figure 14-8).

10. Press the left arrow key and click OK. The Event Configuration window displays the Left (Physical) key under the down action.

11. Click the + (Add Event) icon that appears to the right of the **left** action. An Event Configuration window appears (see Figure 14-8).

12. Press the A key and click OK. The Event Configuration window displays the A (Physical) key under the **left** action.

13. Click the + (Add Event) icon that appears to the right of the **right** action. An Event Configuration window appears (see Figure 14-8).

14. Press the right arrow key and click OK. The Event Configuration window displays the Right (Physical) key under the down action.

15. Click the + (Add Event) icon that appears to the right of the **right** action. An Event Configuration window appears (see Figure 14-8).

16. Press the D key and click OK. The Event Configuration window displays the D (Physical) key under the **right** action.

These steps let you move the player up/down and left/right using either the arrow keys or the WASD keys. Now the final steps involve defining keys to rotate the player left and right and shoot the projectile.

To define keys to rotate left, rotate right, and shoot the projectile, follow these steps:

1. Click the + (Add Event) icon that appears to the right of the **rotate_left** action. An Event Configuration window appears (see Figure 14-8).

2. Press the comma key and click OK. The Event Configuration window displays the Comma (Physical) key under the **rotate_left** action.

3. Click the + (Add Event) icon that appears to the right of the **rotate_right** action. An Event Configuration window appears (see Figure 14-8).

4. Press the period key and click OK. The Event Configuration window displays the Period (Physical) key under the **rotate_right** action.

5. Click the + (Add Event) icon that appears to the right of the **shoot** action. An Event Configuration window appears (see Figure 14-8).

6. Press the space bar and click OK. The Event
   Configuration window displays the Space (Physical)
   key under the **shoot** action. The entire Input Map
   should look like Figure 14-9.

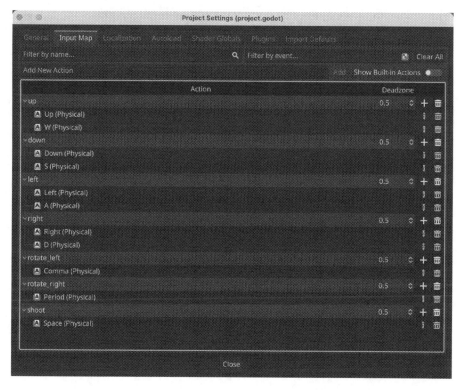

*Figure 14-9. Physical keys assigned to every action on the Input Map*

7. Click Close to make the Project Settings window
   go away.

# Writing GDScript Code to Control the Player

The Input Map defines actions to detect and specific keys to trigger those actions. The next step is to write GDScript to detect when the user presses specific keys associated with specific actions. This involves attaching scripts to different nodes and then writing GDScript code within each script file that ends with a .gd file extension.

To see how to create a script and write GDScript code, follow these steps:

1. Double-click the player.tscn file in the FileSystem dock to select it. This should display the Player, Sprite2D, Marker2D, and CollisionShape2D nodes that make up the player scene.

2. Click Sprite2D in the Scene dock and click the Attach Script icon. An Attach Node Script window appears as shown in Figure 14-10.

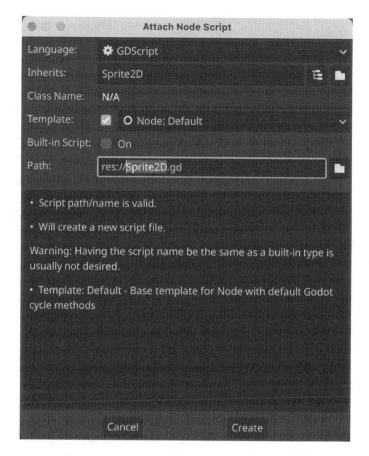

***Figure 14-10.***  *The Attach Node Script window*

3.  Click Create. Godot displays the GDScript editor.

4.  Edit the GDScript code as follows:

```
extends Sprite2D
var spin = 5
func _process(delta):
    spin = 0
    if Input.is_action_pressed("rotate_left"):
        spin = -5
```

303

```
        if Input.is_action_pressed("rotate_right"):
                spin = 5
        rotation += spin * delta
```

5.   Press Ctrl/Command+S to save your changes.

This code constantly checks if the user has pressed any of the keys associated with the "rotate_left" or "rotate_right" actions defined in the Input Map. To test this script out, we need to first make this player.tscn the main scene.

To define the player.tscn file as the main scene, follow these steps:

1.   Choose Project ➤ Project Settings. The Project Settings window appears.

2.   Click the General tab.

3.   Click Run under the Application category. The Main Scene option appears.

4.   Click the folder icon that appears on the far right of the Main Scene option. An Open File dialog box appears.

5.   Click player.tscn and click Open. The Main Scene option should now display player.tscn as shown in Figure 14-11.

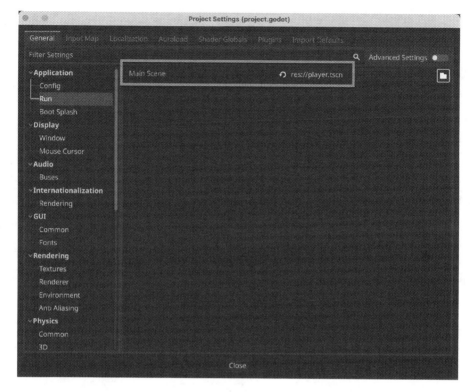

***Figure 14-11.*** *The Main Scene option defines the player.tscn scene to use*

6.  Click Close.

To test if you can rotate the player using the comma and period keys, follow these steps:

1.  Click the Player node in the Scene dock and click 2D near the top middle of the screen. By default, the player node appears in the upper left corner of the Godot game window.

2.   Click the Move Mode icon and drag the icon.svg
     image down and to the right so that it appears
     within the boundary of the Godot game window.

3.   Press Ctrl/Command+S to save the scene.

4.   Click the Run icon. The Godot game window
     appears.

5.   Press the comma and period keys to rotate the icon.
     svg image left and right.

6.   Click the close icon in the (DEBUG) window.

Once you're able to rotate the icon.svg image left and right, the next
step is to move the icon.svg image up/down and left/right along with
shooting a projectile.

To move the player, follow these steps:

1.   Click the Player node in the Scene dock.

2.   Click Player in the Scene dock and click the Attach
     Script icon. An Attach Node Script window appears
     (see Figure 14-10).

3.   Click Create. Godot displays the GDScript editor.

4.   Edit the GDScript code as follows:

```
extends CharacterBody2D
const SPEED = 300.0
func _physics_process(delta):
        velocity = Vector2.ZERO
        if Input.is_action_pressed("left"):
                velocity = Vector2.LEFT * SPEED
        if Input.is_action_pressed("right"):
                velocity = Vector2.RIGHT * SPEED
```

```
if Input.is_action_pressed("up"):
        velocity = Vector2.UP * SPEED
if Input.is_action_pressed("down"):
        velocity = Vector2.DOWN * SPEED
position += velocity * delta
```

5.  Press Ctrl/Command+S to save your changes.

6.  Click the Run icon. The Godot game window appears.

7.  Press the up/down, left/right arrow keys (or the WASD keys) to move the icon.svg image around the screen.

8.  Press the comma and period keys to rotate the icon. svg image left and right.

9.  Click the close icon in the (DEBUG) window.

# Firing a Projectile

Now that we can control the player (icon.svg image) by pressing the arrow keys and the comma/period keys to rotate the image, it's time to shoot a projectile. Remember, when we defined different actions in the Input Map, we also defined a "shoot" action that gets triggered by the space bar.

Firing a projectile involves several steps. The first and most important step is to link the bullet.tscn within the player.tscn file. This involves defining a variable using the @export keyword and declaring it to hold a PackedScene data type like this:

```
@export var bullet_scene : PackedScene
```

The @export keyword lets the variable appear within the Inspector dock where we need to drag and drop the bullet.tscn file. This allows us to access the bullet.tscn file through the bullet_scene variable.

The second step is to detect when the user presses the space bar to trigger the "shoot" action using the Input.is_action_just_pressed command like this:

```
if Input.is_action_just_pressed("shoot"):
```

Notice that this is different from the Input.is_action_pressed() command (note the word "just"). The Input.is_action_just_pressed command will run once, while the Input.is_action_pressed can run multiple times. When firing a projectile, we just want to fire it once each time we press the space bar.

Finally, we need to create a function to fire a projectile. This code looks like this:

```
func shoot():
    var b = bullet_scene.instantiate()
    get_tree().root.add_child(b)
    b.transform = $Sprite2D/Marker2D.global_transform
```

This code creates (instantiates) the bullet_scene variable, which links to the bullet.tscn file. Then it adds that bullet_scene to the root (parent) node, which is Player. Finally, it places the bullet_scene at the location of the Marker2D node, which is a child of Sprite2D.

To see how to link the bullet.tscn file to the player.tscn file, follow these steps:

1. Make sure the Godot project that you edited previously is open.

2. Click the Player node in the Scene dock.

3. Double-click the script icon that appears to the right of the Player node. Godot displays the GDScript code.

4. Add the following above const SPEED = 300.0:

    `@export var bullet_scene : PackedScene`

5. Click Player in the Scene dock. Notice that the Inspector dock now displays an <empty> Bullet Scene property as shown in Figure 14-12.

*Figure 14-12.* The @export keyword displays the bullet_scene variable in the Inspector dock

6. Drag and drop the bullet.tscn file from the FileSystem dock to the Bullet Scene property in the Inspector dock as shown in Figure 14-13. (As an alternative, you can also click the downward-pointing arrow that appears to the right of the Bullet Scene property to display a pull-down menu. Then choose Load and when an Open a File dialog box appears, click bullet.tscn and click Open.)

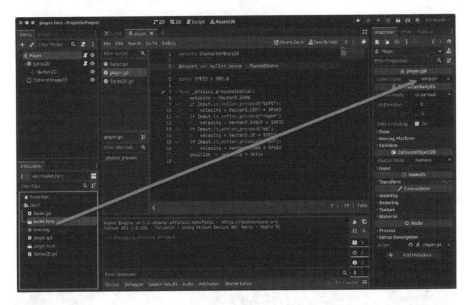

***Figure 14-13.*** *The @export keyword displays the bullet_scene variable in the Inspector dock*

Once we've linked the bullet.tscn file to the player.tscn through the Inspector dock, we now need to write GDScript code to detect when the user presses the space bar to trigger the "shoot" action. We need to write a function to create the bullet.tscn file.

To write GDScript code to create a projectile from the bullet.tscn file, follow these steps:

1. Make sure the Godot project that you edited previously is open.

2. Click the Player node in the Scene dock.

3. Double-click the script icon that appears to the right of the Player node. Godot displays the GDScript code.

4.  Add the following code to the end of the func
    _physics_process(delta) function:

```
if Input.is_action_just_pressed("shoot"):
        shoot()
```

5.  Add the following code at the end and indent all the
    way to the left:

```
func shoot():
        var bullet = bullet_scene.instantiate()
        get_tree().root.add_child(bullet)
        bullet.transform = $Sprite2D/Marker2D.global_
        transform
```

The entire player.gd file should look like this:

```
extends CharacterBody2D
@export var bullet_scene : PackedScene
const SPEED = 300.0
func _physics_process(delta):
        velocity = Vector2.ZERO
        if Input.is_action_pressed("left"):
                velocity = Vector2.LEFT * SPEED
        if Input.is_action_pressed("right"):
                velocity = Vector2.RIGHT * SPEED
        if Input.is_action_pressed("up"):
                velocity = Vector2.UP * SPEED
        if Input.is_action_pressed("down"):
                velocity = Vector2.DOWN * SPEED
        position += velocity * delta
        if Input.is_action_just_pressed("shoot"):
                shoot()
```

```
func shoot():
    var bullet = bullet_scene.instantiate()
    get_tree().root.add_child(bullet)
    bullet.transform = $Sprite2D/Marker2D.global_
    transform
```

6. Press Ctrl/Command+S to save your changes.

7. Click the Run icon.

8. Press the up/down, left/right arrow keys to move the icon.svg image around.

9. Press the space bar. Notice that tiny versions of the icon.svg image shoot out from the top of the player node, which is where the Marker2D node is located.

10. Press the comma and period keys to rotate the icon. svg image.

11. Press the space bar. Notice that the icon.svg image shoots out from the top of the player node no matter which way it's rotated.

12. Click the close icon in the (DEBUG) window.

If you have your own images, add them to the FileSystem dock and substitute those images for the player and bullet. Depending on the size of your images, you may need to adjust the collision boundaries around the player and projectile. Then run your project again to make sure you can still move, rotate, and shoot projectiles.

# Removing Projectiles

One problem with creating and shooting a projectile is that it still exists even after it exits off the edge of the game window and can no longer be seen. Each projectile takes up memory and processing resources, so the more projectiles created, the greater the load on the computer. Create too many projectiles, and you risk slowing down the entire game.

The solution is to remove a projectile the moment it exits the game window. To do this requires several steps:

- Attach a VisibleOnScreenNotifier node to a projectile.

- Create a screen_exited signal to detect when the projectile exits the game window.

- Use the queue_free() function to remove the projectile.

To see the problem with not removing a projectile after creating it, even after it's no longer visible, follow these steps:

1. Make sure the previous Godot project is loaded, which lets you shoot projectiles by pressing the space bar.

2. Double-click player.tscn in the FileSystem dock to display the player.tscn node hierarchy in the Scene dock.

3. Click the Run icon. Notice that a Remote tab appears in the Scene dock.

4. Click the Remote tab.

5. Press the space bar multiple times. Each time you press the space bar to fire a projectile, that projectile disappears from view but remains displayed within the Scene dock under the Remote tab as shown in Figure 14-14.

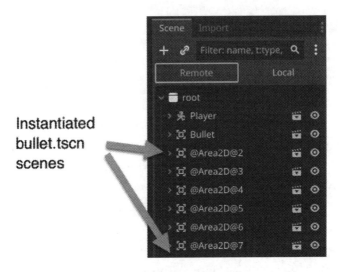

Instantiated
bullet.tscn
scenes

*Figure 14-14.* *The Remote tab lets you view when scenes get created (instantiated)*

6. Click the close icon in the (DEBUG) window.

To remove a projectile when it exits the game window, we need to attach a VisibleOnScreenNotifier node to the projectile's parent node. To detect when the projectile exits the game window, we just need to create an on_exit() function, and within that function, write GDScript code to remove the projectile completely using the queue_free() function.

To make a projectile disappear when it exits the game window, follow these steps:

1. Make sure the previous Godot project is loaded.

2. Double-click bullet.tscn in the FileSystem dock to make it appear in the Scene dock.

3. Click bullet (the parent node of the bullet.tscn scene) to select it.

4. Click the + (Attach Child Node) icon in the Scene
   dock. A Create New Node dialog box appears.

5. Click the Search text field, type
   **VisibleOnScreenNotifier2D**, and click
   Create. (Be careful since there is also a
   VisibleOnScreenEnabler2D node that
   looks nearly the same.) Godot makes the
   VisibleOnScreenNotifier2D node the child node of
   the Bullet parent node.

6. Click the Node tab in the Inspector dock and then
   click Signals.

7. Double-click screen_exited() as shown in
   Figure 14-15. Godot displays a Connect a Signal to a
   Method dialog box.

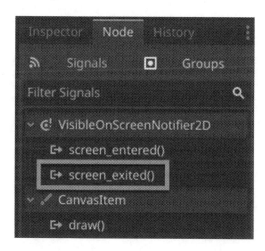

*Figure 14-15.* The screen_exited() function can detect when a scene
exits the game window

8. Make sure Bullet is selected and click Connect. Godot creates an _on_visible_on_screen_ notifier_2d_screen_exited() function in the bullet. gd file.

9. Edit the bullet.gd file as follows:

```
extends Area2D

@export var speed = 700

func _process(delta):
        position += transform.x * speed * delta

func _on_visible_on_screen_notifier_2d_screen_exited():
        queue_free()
```

10. Click the Run icon.

11. Click the Remote tab in the Scene dock.

12. Press the space bar to fire a projectile. Notice that the projectile appears briefly in the Scene dock until it exits the game window. Then it's removed from the Scene dock to show it's no longer taking up memory or processing resources.

13. Click the close icon in the (DEBUG) window.

## Summary

Creating a player involves several nodes: a CharacterBody2D parent node, a Sprite2D node for defining an image to display, and a CollisionShape2D to define the collision boundaries of the player. To fire projectiles, the Sprite2D node also needs a child node defined by the Marker2D node. This Marker2D node defines where a projectile appears and the direction it travels.

You must define a projectile in a separate scene and then link it into the scene that defines the player using GDScript code. To do this, you need to use the @export keyword to define a variable that can hold a PackedScene data type like this:

```
@export var bullet_scene : PackedScene
```

The @export keyword displays the variable name in the Inspector dock. Through the Inspector dock, you must load the .tscn file that represents the projectile you want to display.

Once you've defined a variable that represents a projectile scene, you need to detect when the user presses a key to trigger an action to create and fire a projectile. Creating and firing a projectile involves instantiating that scene, adding it as a child of the parent node, and placing it at the location of the Marker2D node.

The GDScript code of the projectile then makes it move on its own in the direction it's aimed at. Adding a projectile to a game involves building separate scenes for the projectile and player. Once the player and projectile scenes are created, you are now ready to build your 2D shooter game.

# CHAPTER 15

# Hitting Enemies with Projectiles

Once you have a player you can control and a way to fire projectiles, the next step involves hitting enemies with a projectile. This involves creating an enemy, detecting when a collision occurs between a projectile and an enemy, and then removing both the projectile and the enemy afterward. By removing the enemy, the enemy is eliminated in the game.

First, you must create an enemy as a separate scene, which consists of multiple nodes. One node defines the collision boundaries of the enemy, while a second node defines the image used to represent the enemy.

Second, you must write GDScript code to detect when the projectile hits an enemy and what to do when it detects a collision between a projectile and an enemy. Typically, the game needs to remove the projectile from the screen after a collision and then determine how much damage the projectile caused on the enemy. In the simplest case, the projectile removes the enemy after one hit, but in some games, you might want to keep track of how many times an enemy gets hit before the game finally removes it from the screen.

© Wallace Wang, Tonnetta Walcott 2024
W. Wang and T. Walcott, *Programming for Game Design*,
https://doi.org/10.1007/979-8-8688-0190-7_15

# Creating an Enemy Scene

Before you can shoot a projectile at an enemy, you need to create an enemy as a separate scene. That way you can add that enemy scene within another scene later. An enemy scene can consist of the following nodes as shown in Figure 15-1:

- CharacterBody2D (parent)

- Sprite2D (child) – Defines the visual appearance of the enemy

- CollisionObject2D (child) – Defines the physical boundaries of the enemy to detect when a collision occurs

***Figure 15-1.***  *The scene structure of a player*

To see how to create an enemy, follow these steps:

1. Make sure you have opened the previous Godot project where you could move and rotate a player while also shooting a projectile.

2. Choose Scene ➤ New Scene. Godot creates a new scene.

3.  Click 2D at the top of the Godot window to view your newly created scene.

4.  Click Other Node in the Scene dock. A Create New Node dialog box appears.

5.  Click the Search text field, type **CharacterBody2D**, and click Create. Godot makes the CharacterBody2D node the parent node of the newly created scene.

6.  Click the + (Attach Child Node) icon in the Scene dock. A Create New Node dialog box appears.

7.  Click the Search text field, type **Sprite2D**, and click Create. Godot makes the Sprite2D node the child node of the CharacterBody2D parent node.

8.  Click CharacterBody2D in the Scene dock and click the + (Attach Child Node) icon. A Create New Node dialog box appears.

9.  Click the Search text field, type **CollisionShape2D**, and click Create. Godot makes the CollisionShape2D node the child node of the CharacterBody2D node (see Figure 15-1).

# Changing the Name of a Node

When we created the projectile scene, the parent node was Area2D. We changed this name to "Bullet" to make it more descriptive of what that scene actually represents. Likewise, our current enemy scene displays a CharacterBody2D node as its parent node, so we'll need to rename this node to something more descriptive such as "Enemy."

To see how to rename a node, follow these steps:

1. Make sure you have created a Godot project where a scene consists of a CharacterBody2D node with two child nodes: Sprite2D and CollisionShape2D (see Figure 15-1).

2. Double-click CharacterBody2D in the Scene dock. Godot highlights the entire node name.

3. Edit the CharacterBody2D name to **Enemy** as shown in Figure 15-2.

*Figure 15-2. Changing the name of CharacterBody2D to Player*

4. Press Enter.

5. Press Ctrl/Command+S to save your scene. A Save Scene As dialog box appears. Since you changed the root node to Enemy, Godot assumes you want to save your scene using that root node name such as Enemy.tscn.

6. Click Save. Godot saves your scene using the .tscn file extension in the FileSystem dock as shown in Figure 15-3.

***Figure 15-3.*** *A saved scene's file name appears in the FileSystem dock*

# Adding an Enemy Image and Collision Shape

The Sprite2D node contains a Texture property where you can add an image that represents the player in a game. We've used the same icon. svg image to represent both the player and the projectile by making the projectile smaller. Now we're going to use the same icon.svg image to represent an enemy except we'll make it appear visually different and smaller than the player.

To see how to create and scale an image for an enemy, follow these steps:

1. Double-click the enemy.tscn in the FileSystem and click 2D near the top of the Godot window to select and display the enemy.tscn scene.

2. Click Sprite2D in the Scene dock to select it.

3. Drag and drop the icon.svg image into the Texture property of Sprite2D.

4. Click the disclosure triangle that appears to the left of Transform, under Node2D, in the Inspector dock. A list of different transform options appears.

5. Click the X field underneath the Scale category and type 0.75. Godot changes both the X and Y fields to 0.75. This shrinks the enemy image slightly.

6. Click the disclosure triangle that appears to the left of Visibility, under CanvasItem, in the Inspector dock.

7. Click the white rectangle that appears to the right of Modulate as shown in Figure 15-4. A color dialog box appears.

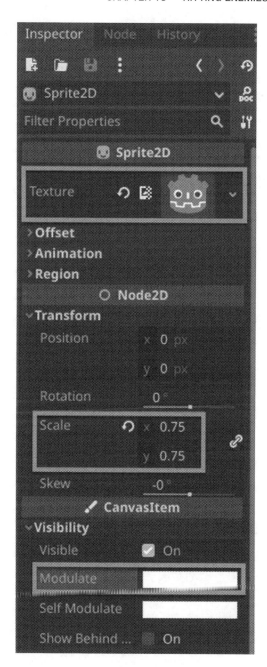

***Figure 15-4.*** *The Inspector dock for the Enemy.tscn scene*

8.  Click a color. Then click away from the color dialog
    box to make it go away. At this point, you've added
    a color to the enemy and scaled it to make it slightly
    smaller.

9.  Click CollisionShape2D in the Scene dock to
    select it.

10. Click the <empty> field that appears in the Shape
    property. A list of options appears in a pull-
    down menu.

11. Click New RectangleShape2D. Godot displays a
    rectangular box with orange handles around the
    sides and corners.

12. Drag the orange handles until the collision
    boundary rectangle covers the icon.svg image.

13. Press Ctrl/Command+S to save your scene.

# Creating a Main Scene

When building a game in Godot, you have to create scenes. In our previous
project, we created a scene to represent a player we could control (player.
tscn), and then we created a second scene to represent a projectile (bullet.
tscn) we could shoot from the player.

Now we've created an enemy scene (enemy.tscn), so we need to
display all of these separate scenes within a main scene. That means we
need to create a main scene and also make sure this main scene appears
first when the project runs.

To create a main scene, follow these steps:

1. Make sure the Godot project you created earlier is open.

2. Choose Scene ➤ New Scene.

3. Click 2D Scene in the Scene dock. Godot creates a Node2D parent node in the Scene dock.

4. Double-click Node2D and change the name of the node to MainScene. Then press Enter.

5. Press Ctrl/Command+S to save the scene. A Save Scene As window appears.

6. Click Save. This saves the scene using the name of the parent node, which is MainScene, so Godot saves this scene as main_scene.tscn. Now we need to fill it with other scenes.

7. Drag the player.tscn scene from the FileSystem dock into the viewport of the main_scene.tscn.

8. Drag the enemy.tscn scene three times from the FileSystem dock into the viewport of the main_ scene.tscn. This should display the player.tscn and three enemy.tscn scenes in the viewport as shown in Figure 15-5.

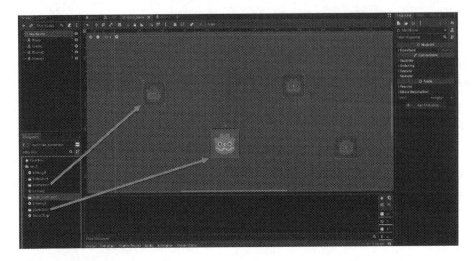

**Figure 15-5.** *Adding the player.tscn and enemy.tscn scenes into the main_scene.tscn*

Once we've created a main scene to represent the game's playing field and filled it with both the player and enemy scenes, the last step is to define this main scene as the scene to appear when the project runs.

To define the scene to run, follow these steps:

1.  Choose Project ➤ Project Settings. A Project Settings window appears.

2.  Click the General tab and then click Run under the Application category. The Main Scene option appears as shown in Figure 15-6.

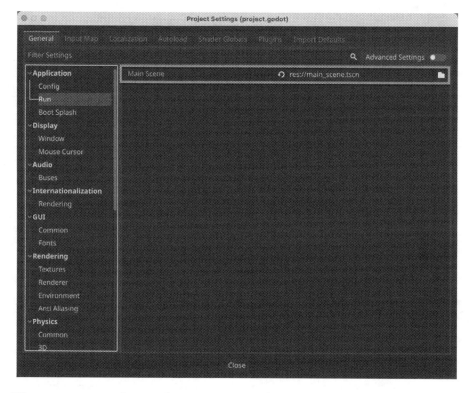

*Figure 15-6.* *Defining the Main Scene for a project*

3. Click the folder icon that appears on the far right of Main Scene. An Open a File dialog box appears.

4. Click main_scene.tscn and click Open.

5. Click Close to make the Project Settings window go away.

6. Click the Run icon. Godot displays the main_scene. tscn file that contains the player.tscn and the three enemy.tscn scenes in a window.

You should be able to use the arrow keys (left/right, up/down) to move the player around and press the comma and period keys to rotate the player. If you press the space bar, you should also be able to shoot a projectile from the player.

However, the projectile simply flies through each enemy, so the next step is to write GDScript code to make the projectile detect a collision with an enemy and make both the projectile and enemy disappear when such a collision occurs.

7.   Click the close icon in the (DEBUG) window.

# Detecting Collisions

To detect collisions, both the projectile and enemy scenes have a CollisionShape2D node that defines the boundaries of each object. Once we've defined a CollisionShape2D node on every object that can collide with the projectile, the next step is to take action when a projectile does collide with an enemy.

Since our game will display multiple enemies, we need to detect when a projectile hits any of those enemies. The simplest way to do this is to first assign the enemy.tscn scene to a specific group name. Then we can use GDScript code to detect whenever the projectile collides with any object within a specific group.

To define the enemy.tscn scene in a group, follow these steps:

1.   Double-click the enemy.tscn scene in the FileSystem dock.

2.   Click 2D near the top of the Godot window to display the contents of the enemy.tscn scene.

3. Click the Enemy parent node in the Scene dock to select it.

4. Click the Node tab and then click the Groups tab.

5. Click the empty text field and type **Enemy**. Then click Add. This assigns the group name "Enemy" to the enemy.tscn scene as shown in Figure 15-7.

***Figure 15-7.*** *Defining a group name for a scene*

By assigning the enemy.tscn scene to a group, we can now use GDScript to detect whenever the projectile collides with this "enemy" group name.

To see how to write GDScript code to detect collisions with an enemy. tscn scene, follow these steps:

1. Double-click the bullet.tscn scene in the FileSystem dock.

2. Click 2D near the top of the Godot window to display the contents of the bullet.tscn scene.

3. Click the Bullet parent node in the Scene dock.

4. Click the Node tab in the Inspector dock and then click Signals as shown in Figure 15-8.

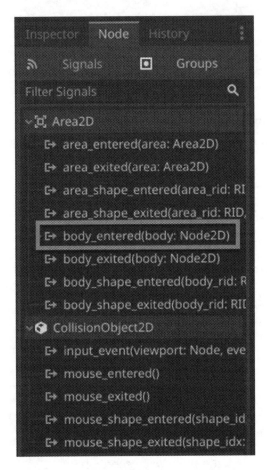

*Figure 15-8.* *The Node tab in the Inspector dock*

5.  Double-click **body_entered(body: Node2D)**.
    A Connect a Signal to a Method window appears as
    shown in Figure 15-9.

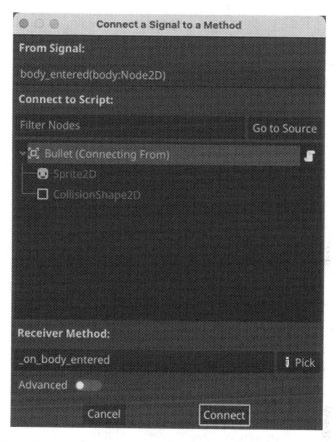

**Figure 15-9.** *The Connect a Signal to a Method window*

6.  Click Connect. Godot creates an empty function in
    the bullet.gd file like this:

```
func _on_body_entered(body):
    pass # Replace with function body.
```

Edit this function as follows:
```
func _on_body_entered(body):
    if body.is_in_group("Enemy"):
        body.visible = false
        hide()
```

In the preceding GDScript code, the (body) parameter represents the object that the projectile hit. So the if statement checks if body.is_in_ group("Enemy"). If so, that means the projectile hit an enemy.

The first line within this if statement sets the visible property of the body to false, which means the enemy.tscn scene no longer is visible. Then the second line, hide(), removes the projectile itself. The entire bullet.gd file should look like this:

```
extends Area2D
@export var speed = 700
func _process(delta):
        position += transform.x * speed * delta
func _on_body_entered(body):
        if body.is_in_group("Enemy"):
                body.visible = false
                hide()
```

7. Press Ctrl/Command+S to save the changes to the bullet.gd file.

8. Click the Run icon to run your project.

9. Move and/or rotate the player and press the space bar to aim at the enemy.tscn scenes. Notice that each time the projectile hits an enemy, both the enemy and the projectile disappear.

10. Click the close icon of the (DEBUG) window to stop the project.

# Summary

The first step to detecting collisions is to add a CollisionShape2D node to every scene that might collide with another scene. The CollisionShape2D node lets you define the physical boundaries that trigger a collision around an object.

Once you've added a Collisionshape2D boundary around an object, the second step is to include one or more scenes to a group. A group is simply an arbitrary name that you can define for one or more scenes. Once you've defined a scene as part of a group, you can later detect if a collision between two scenes includes a scene defined within a particular group.

The third step is to define an _on_body_entered(body) signal that creates a function within the GDScript file of a scene to detect when it collides with another scene.

Finally, within the _on_body_entered(body) function, you can define what action to take when a collision occurs between a specific scene. The most common action to take includes hiding both objects that collide.

# CHAPTER 16

# Displaying a User Interface

One of the most important features of any project is the user interface. The user interface is the visual display of a game. Every user interface serves two purposes, depending on the needs of the program at the time:

- Accept data from the user

- Display data to the user

To accept data, a user interface can let the user type in data such as text or numbers or manipulate user interface controls that represent choices such as sliders or lists of items. To display information back to the user, the user interface can display text (either words or numbers) or other visual images such as a health bar that lists a player's current strength.

The main purpose of a user interface is to let users control a program by giving it new data to accept and manipulate. After using this new data to calculate a different result, the user interface then displays new information to help the user determine what to do next.

© Wallace Wang, Tonnetta Walcott 2024
W. Wang and T. Walcott, *Programming for Game Design*,
https://doi.org/10.1007/979-8-8688-0190-7_16

# Inputting and Displaying Text

Godot offers two ways to input text:

- LineEdit

- TextEdit

The LineEdit control is designed for entering a single line of text, such as a name. The TextEdit control works more like a text editor or word processor, letting you type and edit multiple lines of text.

If you just want to display text without the ability to edit text, Godot offers a Label control. By using a LineEdit or TextEdit to edit text and a Label to display text, you can create a simple user interface to edit and view text. You may want to use either LineEdit, TextEdit, or Label in Godot if you would like to create something like a main menu or to display the player's name above a health bar.

To see how to store and display text using the LineEdit and Label controls, follow these steps:

1. Create a new Godot project.

2. Click Other Node in the Scene dock. A Create New Node dialog box appears.

3. Click the text field and type **control** as shown in Figure 16-1.

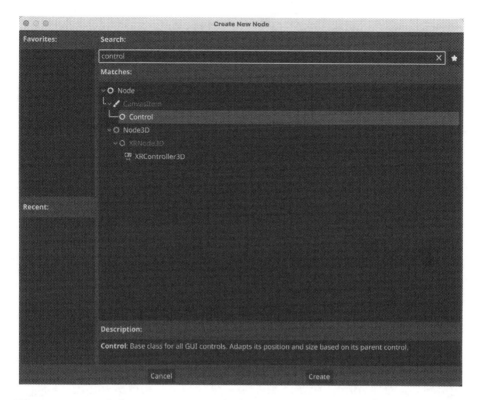

***Figure 16-1.*** *Selecting a Control node*

4.  Click Create. Godot creates a Control node in the
    Scene dock and displays the boundaries of the
    Control in the viewport as shown in Figure 16-2.

***Figure 16-2.*** *The boundaries of the Control node*

5.  Drag the handles of the Control node boundaries
    to make it match the size of the project window as
    shown in Figure 16-3.

**Figure 16-3.**  *Expanding the boundaries of the Control node*

6.  Click the + (Attach Child Node) icon in the Scene
    dock. A Create New Node dialog box appears.

7.  Click the Search text field, type **LineEdit**, and click
    Create. Godot makes the LineEdit node the child
    node of the Control parent node.

8.  Drag and resize the LineEdit control so it appears
    near the top middle of the window.

9.  Click Control in the Scene dock and click the +
    (Attach Child Node) icon. A Create New Node dialog
    box appears.

10.  Click the Search text field, type **Label**, and click
     Create. Drag and resize the Label near the bottom
     middle of the window as shown in Figure 16-4.

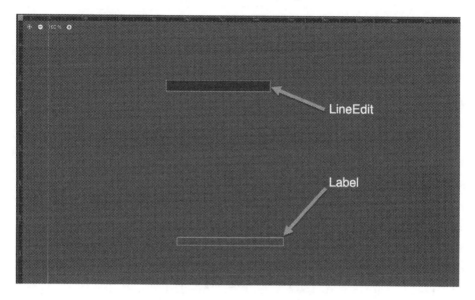

*Figure 16-4.*  *The LineEdit and Label controls*

11.  Press Ctrl/Command+S to save your scene. A Save
     Scene As dialog box appears and uses the parent
     node name for the scene name (control.tscn).

12.  Click Save.

13.  Click the Run icon. A dialog box appears, asking you
     to choose a scene to display.

14.  Click Select Current. The (DEBUG) window appears.
     Notice that the LineEdit control appears visible
     as a rectangle but that the Label control appears
     invisible (even though it's there but empty).

15. Click the LineEdit control and type some text. Notice that you can type and edit text in the LineEdit control but nothing appears in the Label control.

16. Click the close icon of the (DEBUG) window to make it go away.

# Using Signals

Even though we can type and edit text in the LineEdit control, none of that text appears in the Label control. Both the LineEdit and Label controls store data in a text property, so we need to send the data stored in the LineEdit's text property into the Label's text property.

One way to send data from the LineEdit to the Label is through a signal where a signal detects when something happens within the LineEdit. In this example, we're going to use the text_changed signal that detects whenever the text inside the LineEdit control changes. Each time the LineEdit text property changes, it will send the contents of the LineEdit control to the Label control.

A signal detects an event that occurs from a user interface control (such as LineEdit) and creates a GDScript function to handle that event, stored in a separate .gd file. That means before we can create a signal, we must create at least one .gd file to store that Signal function.

To see how to use a signal to run each time the contents of the LineEdit control changes, follow these steps:

1. Make sure you have created a Godot project from the previous section that displays a LineEdit and a Label control on the user interface.

2. Click Control in the Scene dock.

3. Click the Attach Script icon. An Attach Node Script dialog box appears as shown in Figure 16-5.

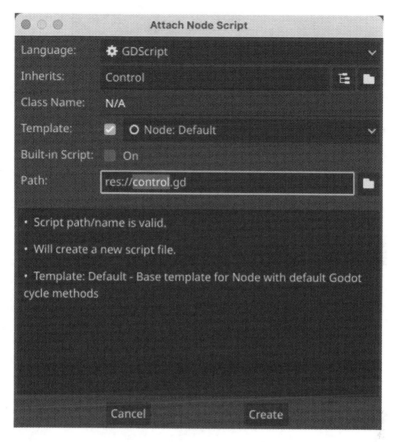

***Figure 16-5.*** *The Attach Node Script dialog box*

4. Click Create. Godot creates a file called control.gd.

5. Click LineEdit in the Scene dock to select it.

6. Click the Node tab in the Inspector dock, and then click Signals. Godot displays a list of signals as shown in Figure 16-6.

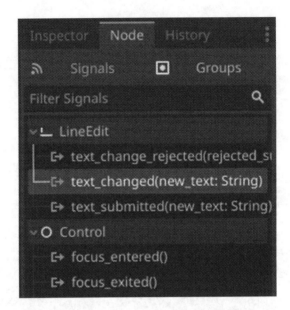

*Figure 16-6.* *The list of signals available in the Node tab of the LineEdit control*

7. Double-click **text_changed(new_text: String)**. A Connect a Signal to a Method dialog box appears as shown in Figure 16-7.

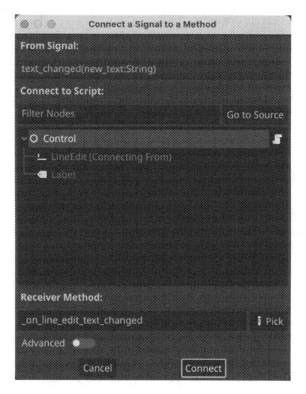

***Figure 16-7.*** *The Connect a Signal to a Method dialog box*

8.  Click Connect. Godot creates the following function
    inside the control.gd file:

    ```
    func _on_line_edit_text_changed(new_text):
        pass # Replace with function body.
    ```

9.  Edit the function so that it looks like this:

    ```
    func _on_line_edit_text_changed(new_text):
        $Label.text = new_text
    ```

This code says that each time the contents of the
LineEdit control changes, send the changed text as
the new_text parameter. Then store this changed
text into the text property of the Label control. (Note
that if you change the name of the Label control, you
would use the changed name of the Label and not
use $Label.)

10.    Press Ctrl/Command+S to save your GDScript file.

11.    Click the Run icon. The user interface window
        appears displaying the LineEdit control at the top
        and the Label at the bottom.

12.    Click the LineEdit control and type text. Notice that
        as you type, those changes automatically appear in
        the Label control.

13.    Press the Backspace key. Notice that each time you
        delete text, the changed contents of the LineEdit
        control also get sent to the Label control.

14.    Click the close icon of the (DEBUG) window to
        make it go away.

A signal works in three steps as shown in Figure 16-8:

•    Detect an event within a node such as a user interface
     control.

•    Create a link to a function stored in a separate .gd file.

•    Run GDScript code stored in that Signal function.

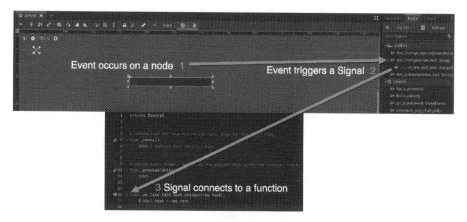

*Figure 16-8.* *The three steps for triggering a signal*

# Working with TextEdit and Buttons

In the previous example, we created a LineEdit control that would trigger a signal every time its contents changed. While Signals can work automatically, you can also use GDScript code to transfer data into a Label control. In addition, the LineEdit control only let us view and edit a single line of text. The TextEdit control lets us view and edit multiple lines of text.

Signals can work automatically, but we want to change text manually. To do that, we can use another user interface control known as a Button. A Button simply represents a single command, so clicking this Button runs one or more lines of GDScript code.

For this simple project, we'll create a TextEdit control, add and edit text, and then use a Button to transfer the contents of the TextEdit control into the Label control.

347

To see how to create and use both a TextEdit and Button control, follow these steps:

1.  Make sure you have the Godot project you created in the previous section that contains a LineEdit and Label control.

2.  Click 2D near the top of the Godot window to view the user interface that contains the LineEdit and Label controls.

3.  Click Control in the Scene dock.

4.  Click the + (Attach Child Node) icon in the Scene dock. A Create New Node dialog box appears.

5.  Click the Search text field, type **TextEdit**, and click Create. Godot makes the TextEdit node the child node of the Control parent node.

6.  Drag and resize the TextEdit control so it appears underneath the LineEdit control.

7.  Click Control in the Scene dock.

8.  Click the + (Attach Child Node) icon in the Scene dock. A Create New Node dialog box appears.

9.  Click the Search text field, type **Button**, and click Create. Godot makes the Button node the child node of the Control parent node.

10. Drag and resize the Button control so it appears above the Label control as shown in Figure 16-9.

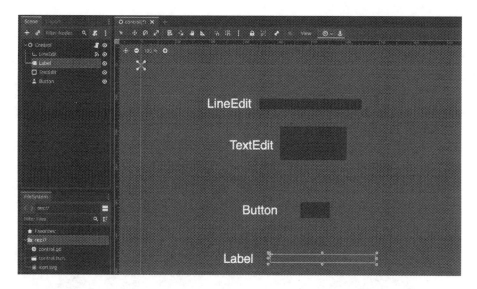

***Figure 16-9.*** *The appearance of the user interface controls*

11.  Click Button in the Scene dock.

12.  Click the Inspector tab in the Inspector dock.

13.  Click the Text property and type ***Send Text*** as shown
     in Figure 16-10.

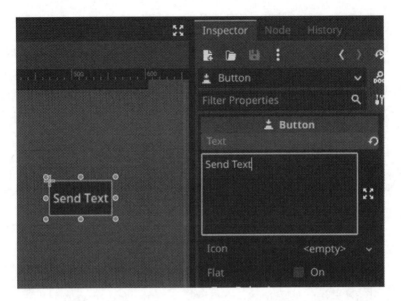

***Figure 16-10.*** *The Text property lets you display text on a Button*

14.  Click the Button in the Scene dock to select it,
     click the Node tab in the Inspector dock, and then
     click Signals to view a list of Signals available for
     the Button.

15.  Double-click **pressed()**. A Connect a Signal to a
     Method dialog box appears.

16.  Make sure Control is selected and click Connect.
     Godot creates an on_button_pressed() function
     inside the control.gd file like this:

```
func _on_button_pressed():
     pass # Replace with function body.
```

17.  Edit the on_button_pressed() function as follows:

```
func _on_button_pressed():
     $Label.text = $TextEdit.text
```

18.  Press Ctrl/Command+S to save your GDScript code changes.

19.  Click the Run icon.

20.  Click the TextEdit control and type some text. Notice that unlike the LineEdit control, changes do not automatically appear in the Label control.

21.  Click the Send Text Button. Notice that the contents of the TextEdit control now appear in the Label control.

22.  Click the close icon in the (DEBUG) window to make it go away.

Where the LineEdit control used a text_changed(new_text) Signal to send the contents of the LineEdit control to the Label control, the TextEdit control does not use any Signals. Instead, a Button uses a signal to detect whenever the user clicks on it. This pressed() Signal then allows us to transfer the contents of the TextEdit control to the Label control.

The main idea is that if you create a signal directly to a control, any changes can occur automatically, while if you create a signal to a separate control like a Button, changes won't occur until the user triggers the signal on another control like clicking on a Button.

# Using Option Buttons and Item Lists

A LineEdit or TextEdit control lets users type text into a program. However, this means that the user can type anything into a LineEdit or TextEdit control. If you want to give users an option of valid choices to select, you can use either Option Buttons or Item Lists.

An Option Button displays a downward-pointing arrow as shown in Figure 16-11.

***Figure 16-11.*** *The appearance of an Option Button*

Clicking an Option Button displays a list of options as shown in Figure 16-12. No matter how many options an Option Button shows, its initial appearance always remains the same size. For that reason, Option Buttons are useful to display a large number of choices to the user without taking up much space.

***Figure 16-12.*** *A list of options appears only if the user selects the Option Button*

One problem with the Option Button is that you can't see the list of available choices until you first select the Option Button. To get around this problem, an Item List displays all choices at all times as shown in Figure 16-13.

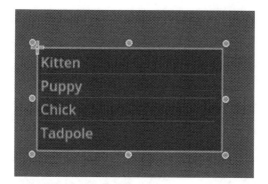

***Figure 16-13.*** *An Item List displays all choices at once*

This makes it easy to see all possible choices, but the size of the Item List expands to display every possible choice. If an Item List contains too many choices, it will take up too much space.

To see how to use an Option Button, follow these steps:

1. Make sure the Godot project you created earlier is open.

2. Click Control in the Scene dock.

3. Click the + (Attach Child Node) icon in the Scene dock. A Create New Node dialog box appears.

4. Click the Search text field, type **OptionButton**, and click Create. Godot makes the OptionButton node the child node of the Control parent node.

5. Drag and resize the OptionButton control so it appears near the left edge of the window.

6. Click OptionButton in the Scene dock to select it. The Inspector dock should display all the properties available for the OptionButton.

7. Click the disclosure triangle that appears to the left of Items. An Add Element button appears as shown in Figure 16-14. Initially, the OptionButton is empty, so you need to click the Add Element button for each item you want to display in the OptionButton.

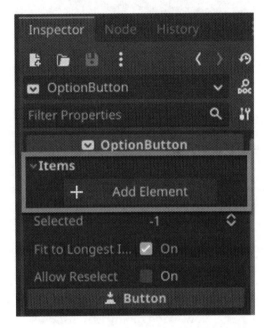

***Figure 16-14.*** *The Add Item in the OptionButton Inspector dock*

8. Click the Add Element. A list of additional properties appears as shown in Figure 16-15. The most important one is the Text property, which defines each item that appears in the OptionButton.

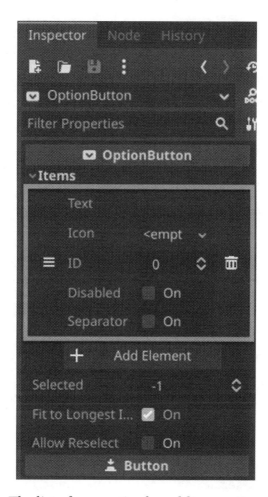

***Figure 16-15.*** *The list of properties for adding an item to an OptionButton*

9.  Click the Text property, type some text such as **Kitten**, and then click the Add Element button again.

10. Click the Text property, type some text such as **Puppy**, and then click the Add Element button again.

355

11.  Click the Text property, type some text such as
     **Chick**, and then click the Add Element button again.

12.  Click the Text property and type some text such as
     **Tadpole**.

13.  Click the Run icon.

14.  Click the downward-pointing arrow of the
     OptionButton. The list of your choices appears.

15.  Click the close icon of the (DEBUG) window to
     make it go away.

At this point, we've just added choices to appear in the OptionButton.
Now we need to detect which option the user selects so it can appear in the
Label control.

To make the OptionButton work, follow these steps:

1.  Click OptionButton in the Scene dock.

2.  Click the Node tab in the Inspector dock and click
    Signals.

3.  Double-click **item_selected(index: int)**. A Connect
    a Signal to a Method dialog box appears.

4.  Click Connect. Godot creates an on_option_button_
    selected(index) function in the control.gd file.

5.  Edit the on_option_button_selected(index) function
    as follows:

```
func _on_option_button_item_selected(index):
        $Label.text = $OptionButton.get_item_text(index)
```

An OptionButton stores a list of choices where the topmost choice is represented as index position 0, the second topmost choice is at index position 1, and so on. So whatever choice the user selects in the OptionButton, the index value of that item gets stored in the index parameter.

Then the code uses this index parameter to retrieve the actual text of each choice using .get_item_text(index). This retrieves the choice the user selected and sends this text to the Label control's text property.

6.   Press Ctrl/Command+S to save your GDScript code.

7.   Click the Run icon. Godot displays the user interface in a window.

8.   Click the OptionButton. A list of choices appears.

9.   Click any option. Notice that whatever option you choose, that option appears in the Label control.

10.   Click the close icon of the (DEBUG) window to make it go away.

The main advantage of an OptionButton is that it takes up a minimal amount of space no matter how many choices it may display. The drawback is that the user must go through a two-step process to use an OptionButton. First, the user must click the OptionButton to display a list of choices. Second, the user must then select one of the available choices.

To provide a list of choices that the user can select in one step, you can display a list of choices in an ItemList instead. The drawback is that the more choices stored in the ItemList, the more space it takes up on the screen.

To see how to use an ItemList, follow these steps:

1. Make sure the previous Godot project is open, which contains the OptionButton, LineEdit, and TextEdit controls.

2. Click Control in the Scene dock.

3. Click the + (Attach Child Node) icon in the Scene dock. A Create New Node dialog box appears.

4. Click the Search text field, type **ItemList**, and click Create. Godot makes the ItemList node the child node of the Control parent node.

5. Drag and resize the ItemList control so it appears near the right edge of the window.

6. Click ItemList in the Scene dock to select it. The Inspector dock should display all the properties available for the ItemList.

7. Click the disclosure triangle that appears to the left of Items. An Add Element button appears. Initially, the ItemList is empty, so you need to click the Add Element button for each item you want to display in the ItemList.

8. Click the Add Element button. The Inspector dock displays multiple properties including a Text property.

9. Click the Text property and type an option such as **Cat**.

10. Click the Add Element button to create another choice.

11. Click the Text property and type an option such as **Dog**.

12. Click the Add Element button to create another choice.

13. Click the Text property and type an option such as **Parrot**.

14. Click the Add Element button to create another choice.

15. Click the Text property and type an option such as **Frog**.

16. Press Ctrl/Command+S to save your scene.

17. Click the Run icon. The user interface window appears. Notice that the ItemList displays the four items you added in a list.

At this point, we've just added choices to appear in the ItemList. Now we need to detect which option the user selects so it can appear in the Label control.

To make the ItemList work, follow these steps:

1. Click ItemList in the Scene dock.

2. Click the Node tab in the Inspector dock and click Signals.

3. Double-click **item_clicked(index: int, at_position: Vector2, mouse_button_index: int)**. A Connect a Signal to a Method dialog box appears.

4. Click Connect. Godot creates an on_item_list_item_clicked(index, at_position, mouse_button_index) function in the control.gd file.

5.  Edit the on_item_list_item_clicked(index, at_
    position, mouse_button_index) function as follows:

```
func _on_item_list_item_clicked(index, at_position,
mouse_button_index):
        $Label.text = $ItemList.get_item_text(index)
```

An ItemList stores a list of choices where the
topmost choice is represented as index position 0,
the second topmost choice is at index position 1,
and so on. So whatever choice the user selects in the
ItemList, the index value of that item gets stored in
the index parameter.
Then the code uses this index parameter to retrieve
the actual text of each choice using .get_item_
text(index). This retrieves the choice the user
selected and sends this text to the Label control's
text property.

6.  Press Ctrl/Command+S to save your GDScript code.

7.  Click the Run icon. Godot displays the user interface
    in a window.

8.  Click any option displayed in the ItemList as shown
    in Figure 16-16. Notice that whatever option you
    choose, that option appears in the Label control.

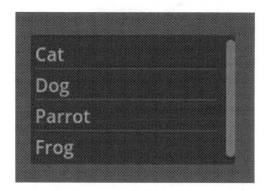

***Figure 16-16.*** *The ItemList displays all choices at once*

9.  Click the close icon of the (DEBUG) window to make it go away.

# Working with CheckButtons

OptionButtons let you display a list of valid choices, but you can only select one option at a time. If you want to display exactly two options, you can use a CheckButton instead.

A CheckButton has two states: toggled or not toggled as shown in Figure 16-17.

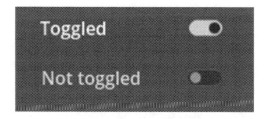

***Figure 16-17.*** *The two states of a CheckButton*

When a CheckButton appears toggled, its button_pressed property is set to true. When a CheckButton is not toggled, its button_pressed property is false. By checking a CheckButton's button_pressed property, we can determine whether the CheckButton is toggled or not.

To see how CheckButtons work, follow these steps:

1. Make sure the previous Godot project is open, which contains the OptionButton, LineEdit, ItemList, and TextEdit controls.

2. Click Control in the Scene dock.

3. Click the + (Attach Child Node) icon in the Scene dock. A Create New Node dialog box appears.

4. Click the Search text field, type **CheckButton**, and click Create. Godot makes the CheckButton node the child node of the Control parent node.

5. Drag and resize the CheckButton control so it appears near the bottom right corner of the window.

6. Click the CheckButton in the Scene dock to display its properties in the Inspector dock.

7. Click the Text property in the Inspector dock and type **First Check Button**.

8. Click Control in the Scene dock.

9. Click the + (Attach Child Node) icon in the Scene dock. A Create New Node dialog box appears.

10. Click the Search text field, type **CheckButton**, and click Create. Godot makes the CheckButton2 node the child node of the Control parent node.

11. Drag and resize the CheckButton2 control so it appears near the bottom right corner of the window.

12. Click the CheckButton2 in the Scene dock to display its properties in the Inspector dock.

13. Click the Text property in the Inspector dock and type **Second Check Button**.

At this point, we've created two CheckButtons. If you run this project, you'll be able to click each CheckButton to toggle it from an off to an on state. However, we still need to write GDScript code to make both of these CheckButtons actually do something.

To see how to write GDScript code to make the CheckButtons work, follow these steps:

1. Make sure you have the Godot project open that contains the two CheckButtons.

2. Click CheckButton in the Scene dock.

3. Click the Node tab and then Signals in the Inspector dock.

4. Double-click **toggled(toggled_on: bool)**. A Connect a Signal to a Method dialog box appears.

5. Click Connect. Godot creates an on_check_button_ toggled(toggled_on) function.

6. Edit this function as follows:

```
func _on_check_button_toggled(toggled on):
    if toggled_on:
        $Label.text = "First check button selected"
    else:
        $Label.text = ""
```

7. Click CheckButton2 in the Scene dock.

8. Click the Node tab and then Signals in the Inspector dock.

9. Double-click **toggled(toggled_on: bool)**. A Connect a Signal to a Method dialog box appears.

10. Click Connect. Godot creates an on_check_ button_2_toggled(toggled_on) function.

11. Edit this function as follows:

```
func _on_check_button_2_toggled(toggled_on):
        if toggled_on:
                $Label.text = "Second check button
                selected"
        else:
                $Label.text = ""
```

12. Press Ctrl/Command+S to save the changes to the control.gd file.

13. Click the Run icon to run your project.

14. Click the first check button. Notice that "First check button selected" appears in the Label control.

15. Click the first check button again to toggle it off. Notice that the Label control now appears empty.

16. Click the second check button. Notice that "Second check button selected" appears in the Label control.

17. Click the second check button again to toggle it off. Notice that the Label control now appears empty.

18. Click the close icon of the (DEBUG) window to stop the project.

# Working with Sliders

If a game needs the user to input numeric data, it could display a LineEdit control for the user to type in a number. Unfortunately, the LineEdit control would store any number as text, which is a String data type. Even worse, users could type in "twenty" instead of 20 or type in a completely outrageous number such as -937 for someone's strength.

To restrict users to a valid range of numbers, use an HSlider or VSlider, which lets you define the following properties:

- The minimum value the slider can represent (Min Value)

- The maximum value the slider can represent (Max Value)

- The current value that the slider represents (Value)

The HSlider creates a horizontal slider, while the VSlider creates a vertical slider. Other than the orientation, both sliders work identically.

To see how sliders work, follow these steps:

1. Make sure the previous Godot project is open, which contains the OptionButton, LineEdit, CheckButtons, ItemList, and TextEdit controls.

2. Click Control in the Scene dock.

3. Click the + (Attach Child Node) icon in the Scene dock. A Create New Node dialog box appears.

4. Click the Search text field, type **HSlider**, and click Create. Godot makes the HSlider node the child node of the Control parent node.

5. Drag and resize the HSlider control so it appears near the bottom left corner of the window.

6.   Click the HSlider in the Scene dock to display its properties in the Inspector dock.

7.   Click the Node tab and Signals in the Inspector dock.

8.   Double-click **value_changed(value: float)**. A Connect a Signal to a Method dialog box appears.

9.   Click Connect. Godot creates an on_h_slider_value_ changed(value) function in the control.gd file.

10.   Edit the on_h_slider_value_changed(value) function as follows:

```
func _on_h_slider_value_changed(value):
     $Label.text = "The value of the slider = " +
     str($HSlider.value)
```

The value parameter represents the current value that the slider represents, defined by the Min Value and Max Value properties. Since the value property of a slider represents a float data type (decimal number), we need to convert this float data type into a string by using the str() command. Then this converted string gets stored in the text property of the Label control.

11.   Press Ctrl/Command+S to save the changes to the control.gd file.

12.   Click the Run icon to run your project.

13.   Drag the slider left and right. Notice that as you drag the slider, the text in the Label control displays the current value of the slider.

14.   Click the close icon of the (DEBUG) window to stop the project.

# Summary

A user interface can accept data from the user and display information to the user. The LineEdit and TextEdit controls can accept text data where the LineEdit control is meant for short amounts of text and the TextEdit control is meant for multiple lines of text.

Since users can type anything into a LineEdit or TextEdit control, Godot offers two ways to offer choices for the user to select. An OptionButton displays a pull-down menu of items the user can select, while an ItemList displays all options in a list. The OptionButton takes up the same amount of space no matter how many options it may contain, while the ItemList expands in size the more options it displays.

A CheckButton can be toggled or not toggled. By using multiple CheckButtons, users can select one or more options.

For inputting numeric data, Godot offers a slider. An HSlider appears horizontally, while a VSlider appears vertically. Both types of sliders let you define a minimum value and a maximum value. By dragging the slider, users can define a numeric value that falls within the range of the minimum and maximum values.

User interface controls rely on GDScript code to make them actually work. By creating Signals for each user interface control, you can create functions that respond to specific events that occur.

# CHAPTER 17

# Adding Physics

Physics in a video game lets objects collide, bounce, slide, or ricochet off each other. In addition, physics lets objects work with gravity that forces objects to fall down or even fall upward if you reverse gravity as a negative number. By learning how to add physics to a game, you can create barriers, platforms, walls, and collisions between different objects.

Physics can make any game more interactive and realistic. Gravity creates downward (or upward) movement automatically, so there's no code needed to define this behavior. Collisions allow obstacles that force players to avoid and move around to achieve their goals. Physics simply makes objects on a screen behave as if they were physical objects in the real world.

## Playing with Gravity

In Godot, each node serves a specific purpose. A Sprite2D node lets you display an image, while a CollisionBody2D node lets you define the physical boundaries of an object. To create an object that's affected by gravity, you need to use the RigidBody2D node.

One of the RigidBody2D node's properties is the Gravity Scale, which lets you define the strength of gravity as an integer as shown in Figure 17-1. Positive values represent gravity pulling an object down. Negative values

© Wallace Wang, Tonnetta Walcott 2024
W. Wang and T. Walcott, *Programming for Game Design*,
https://doi.org/10.1007/979-8-8688-0190-7_17

represent gravity pushing an object up. The Gravity Scale can range from -128 to 128 where you can either choose a value by dragging the slider left or right or by typing in a value.

*Figure 17-1.* *The Gravity Scale in the Inspector dock of a RigidBody2D node*

To see how gravity can affect an object, follow these steps:

1. Create a new Godot project.

2. Click 2D Scene in the Scene dock. Godot creates a Node2D in the Scene dock.

3.  Click the Add Child Node (+) icon. A Create New Node window appears.

4.  Click the Search text field, type RigidBody2D, and then click Create. Godot creates a RigidBody2D node as a child of Node2D.

5.  Click RigidBody2D in the Scene dock and click the Add Child Node (+) icon. A Create New Node window appears again.

6.  Click the Search text field, type Sprite2D, and then click Create. Godot creates a Sprite2D node as a child of RigidBody2D.

7.  Drag the icon.svg image from the FileSystem dock into the Texture property in the Inspector dock.

8.  Drag the Sprite2D node (displaying the icon.svg image) from the upper left corner of the Godot window outline to the middle of the window outline.

9.  Click Rigidbody2D in the Scene dock to select it.

10. Click the Add Child Node (+) icon. A Create New Node window appears.

11. Click the Search text field, type CollisionBody2D, and then click Create. Godot creates a CollisionShape2D node as a child of RigidBody2D.

12. Click CollisionShape2D in the Scene dock.

13. Click Shape in the Inspector dock. A pull-down menu appears.

14. Choose New RectangleShape2D. Godot displays an orange rectangle to define the boundaries of the collision shape.

15. Move and resize the collision body shape to cover the Sprite2D node that displays the icon.svg image. The Scene dock should look like Figure 17-2.

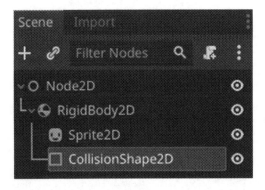

**Figure 17-2.** *The structure of nodes in the Scene dock*

16. Click RigidBody2D in the Scene dock to select it. Notice that the Gravity Scale property in the Inspector dock displays a default value of 1.

17. Click the Run icon at the top of the window. The (DEBUG) window appears. Notice that the icon.svg image drops down because of gravity.

18. Click the close icon of the (DEBUG) window to make it go away.

19. Click RigidBody2D in the Scene dock to select it. Change the Gravity Scale property in the Inspector dock to -1.

20. Click the Run icon at the top of the window. The (DEBUG) window appears. Notice that the icon.svg image now rises up because of negative gravity.

21. Click the close icon of the (DEBUG) window to make it go away.

22. Click RigidBody2D in the Scene dock to select it. Change the Gravity Scale property in the Inspector dock to 0.

23. Click the Run icon at the top of the window. The (DEBUG) window appears. Notice that the icon. svg image now remains stationary because a Gravity Scale property of 0 means there is no gravity affecting the object.

24. Click the close icon of the (DEBUG) window to make it go away.

25. Change the Gravity Scale property back to 1 again.

When the Gravity Scale is a positive number, objects fall downward like in the real world. When the Gravity Scale is a negative number, objects fall upward. This can be useful for creating floating objects such as balloons, clouds, or birds. Objects falling downward can apply to a ball or items needed for a game inventory.

Experiment with different values for the Gravity Scale, both positive and negative numbers, so you can see how it affects the way an object falls or rises. The greater the Gravity Scale value, the faster the object will move downward (for large positive numbers) or upward (for small negative numbers).

You can also define the strength of gravity and its direction as well. By default, the strength of gravity is defined as 980 that pulls in the positive y axis direction (down). However, you can change both the strength and direction of gravity if you wish.

To change gravity's settings, follow these steps:

1. Make sure the previous Godot project is loaded, which displays an icon.svg image that falls downward under the influence of gravity.

2. Choose Project ➤ Project Settings. A Project Settings window appears.

3. Click 2D under the Physics category. The Project Settings window displays a Default Gravity and Default Gravity Vector properties as shown in Figure 17-3.

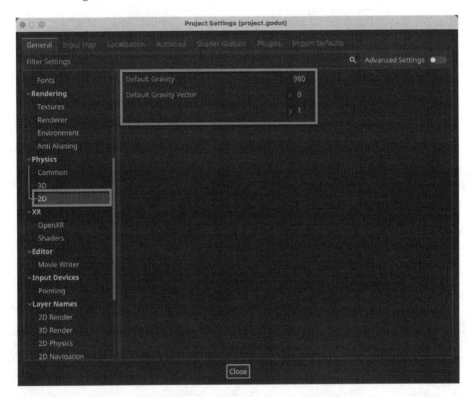

***Figure 17-3.*** *Default gravity settings*

4. Change the Default Gravity value to 100, which will create weaker gravity.

5. Change the x value of the Default Gravity Vector to 1. This will make gravity affect objects horizontally. Because the value is a positive number, gravity will pull objects to the right.

6. Change the y value of the Default Gravity Vector to 0.

7. Click Close.

8. Click the Run icon at the top of the window. The (DEBUG) window appears. Notice that the icon. svg image now moves slowly to the right because the Default Gravity value is 100 (much less than the default value of 980) and because the Default Gravity Vector x value is 1 while the y value is 0.

9. Click the close icon of the (DEBUG) window to make it go away.

10. Choose Project ➤ Project Settings, change the Default Gravity property back to 980 again, and change the x value of the Default Gravity Vector to 0 and the y value of the Default Gravity Vector to 1.

By changing the default gravity settings, you can create unique ways individual objects interact within your game. Changing gravity settings can be perfect for settings in outer space where gravity might be weaker or different, but in most cases, you'll probably never need to modify the default gravity settings.

# Adding Damping

When the Gravity Scale value is extremely high or low for an object, that object will move much faster up or down. To alter the speed that an object moves under the effect of gravity, you can change its Damp property. By default, the Damp property is set to 0, which means there's no effect on an object moving under gravity.

The Damp property can vary from -1 to 100. When set to -1, any object moves rapidly up or down under the influence of gravity. When the Damp property is a nonzero positive number, the greater the value, the slower an object will move.

To see how to damp the way an object moves under the influence of gravity, follow these steps:

1.  Make sure you have created a Godot project from the previous section that displays the icon.svg image that falls under gravity.

2.  Click RigidBody2D in the Scene dock to select it.

3.  Make sure the Gravity Scale property value is 1 in the Inspector dock.

4.  Drag the horizontal slider in the Damp property under the Linear category all the way to the left so that it displays a value of -1 as shown in Figure 17-4.

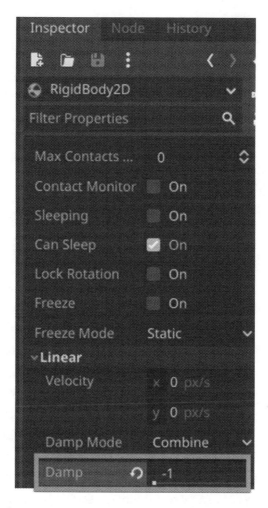

***Figure 17-4.*** *The Damp property in the Inspector dock*

5. Click the Run icon. The (DEBUG) window appears. The icon svg image should drop rapidly downward.

6. Click the close icon of the (DEBUG) window to make it go away.

7. Drag the horizontal slider in the Damp property to the right so a large positive number (such as 30) appears as the Damp property value.

8. Click the Run icon. The (DEBUG) window appears. Notice that the icon.svg image now drops much slower.

9. Click the close icon of the (DEBUG) window to make it go away.

# Working with Static and Rigid Bodies

Gravity affects RigidBody2D nodes where we can change the Gravity Scale value from -128 to 128. If you set the Gravity Scale of a RigidBody2D node to 0, then that object will simply float on the screen. However, if bumped by another RigidBody2D node, it will move. With its Gravity Scale value set to 0, such a node will float around the screen.

Setting a RigidBody2D node to a Gravity Scale value of 0 makes it initially motionless until hit. If you want an object to stay motionless even after being hit, you can use a StaticBody2D node instead. The StaticBody2D node can be used to create barriers and obstacles within a game that do not move but allow other objects to bounce off them.

To see how to create and use a RigidBody2D without gravity, follow these steps:

1. Make sure you have the Godot project you created in the previous section that contains the icon.svg that falls down under the influence of gravity.

2. Click Node2D at the top of the Scene dock to select it.

3.  Click the + (Attach Child Node) icon in the Scene dock. A Create New Node dialog box appears.

4.  Click the Search text field, type **RigidBody2D**, and click Create. Godot makes the RigidBody2D node the child node of the Node2D parent node.

5.  Click this newly added RigidBody2D in the Scene dock.

6.  Click the + (Attach Child Node) icon in the Scene dock. A Create New Node dialog box appears.

7.  Click the Search text field, type **Sprite2D**, and click Create. Godot makes the Sprite2D node the child node of the newly added RigidBody2D node.

8.  Drag the icon.svg image into the Texture property of the Sprite2D node in the Inspector dock.

9.  Click the Modulate property under the Visibility category as shown in Figure 17-5. A Color wheel appears.

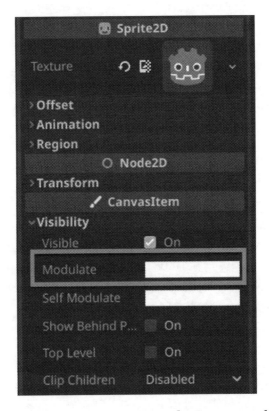

*Figure 17-5.* *The Modulate property in the Inspector dock*

10. Click a color to make the icon.svg image look unique.

11. Resize the Sprite2D node so it's smaller and move it underneath the other RigidBody2D object.

12. Click the newly added RigidBody2D in the Scene dock to select it again.

13. Click the + (Attach Child Node) icon in the Scene dock. A Create New Node dialog box appears.

14.  Click the Search text field, type **CollisionShape2D**, and click Create. Godot makes the CollisionShape2D node the child node of the newly added RigidBody2D node.

15.  Click the Shape property in the Inspector dock. A pull-down menu appears.

16.  Click New RectangleShape2D. Godot displays the orange outline of the rectangle shape.

17.  Drag and resize this orange rectangle shape so it appears around the second icon.svg object that already appears as shown in Figure 17-6.

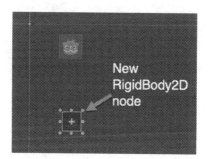

*Figure 17-6.* The second RigidBody2D object should appear underneath the first RigidBody2D object

18.  Click the recently added RigidBody2D in the Scene dock to select it. This should select the RigidBody2D node that appears underneath the other RigidBody2D node.

19.  Change the Gravity Scale property to 0. By making this Gravity Scale value 0, the RigidBody2D node won't move until hit by another RigidBody2D node.

20. Click the Run icon. Notice that the top icon.svg image drops because its Gravity Scale property is 1, but the second icon.svg image remains stationary because its Gravity Scale property is 0. The moment the two icon.svg images collide, the top one keeps falling, while the second one ricochets away depending on the angle that they collide.

21. Click the close icon in the (DEBUG) window to make it go away.

Experiment with moving the second icon.svg image in different positions underneath the top icon.svg image to change the way they collide and how the second icon.svg image bounces away after being hit.

A RigidBody2D node can be affected by gravity, but if its Gravity Scale property is set to 0, then it will appear stationary until hit. After a collision, it will then move around. If you want an object to remain stationary after being hit, then you need to use a StaticBody2D node instead.

To see how to create and use a StaticBody2D node, follow these steps:

1. Make sure you have the Godot project you created in the previous section that contains the icon.svg that falls down under the influence of gravity and hits another icon.svg image.

2. Click Node2D at the top of the Scene dock to select it.

3. Click the + (Attach Child Node) icon in the Scene dock. A Create New Node dialog box appears.

4. Click the Search text field, type **StaticBody2D**, and click Create. Godot makes the StaticBody2D node the child node of the Node2D parent node.

5. Click StaticBody2D at the top of the Scene dock to select it.

6. Click the + (Attach Child Node) icon in the Scene dock. A Create New Node dialog box appears.

7. Click the Search text field, type **Sprite2D**, and click Create. Godot makes the Sprite2D node the child node of the StaticBody2D node.

8. Drag the icon.svg image into the Texture property in the Inspector dock.

9. Resize the Sprite2D node and move it underneath the two previous icon.svg images.

10. Click the Modulate property in the Inspector dock. A color dialog box appears.

11. Click a color to change the appearance of the icon. svg image.

12. Click StaticBody2D in the Scene dock to select it.

13. Click the + (Attach Child Node) icon in the Scene dock. A Create New Node dialog box appears.

14. Click the Search text field, type **CollisionShape2D**, and click Create. Godot makes the CollisionShape2D node the child node of the StaticBody2D node.

15. Click the Shape property in the Inspector dock. A pull-down menu appears.

16. Click New RectangleShape2D. Godot displays the orange outline of the rectangle shape.

17. Drag and resize this orange rectangle shape so it
appears around the bottom icon.svg object so that
it looks like Figure 17-7. Make sure all three objects
appear in a nearly vertical line so that way when the
top object falls, it will hit the other two objects.

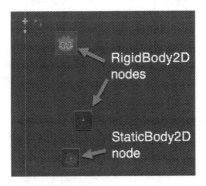

***Figure 17-7.*** *Two RigidBody2D nodes appear above a
StaticBody2D node*

18. Click the Run icon. Notice that the bottom icon.svg
image in the StaticBody2D node remains stationary
even after other objects collide with it.

19. Click the close icon in the (DEBUG) window to
make it go away.

When a RigidBody2D node has a nonzero Gravity Scale value, it will
automatically move up or down. When a RigidBody2D node has a zero
Gravity Scale value, it will remain stationary until hit by another object.
Then it will bounce away. However, when a StaticBody2D node appears, it
always remains stationary no matter how many objects hit it.

# Working with Polygons

If you create a RigidBody2D node and set its Gravity Scale to 0, that object won't move. If you use a StaticBody2D node, that object also won't move. However, both the RigidBody2D and StaticBody2D node creates a single object. If you need to create larger barriers such as walls, you'll need to use polygons instead.

Polygons let you draw lines to create an object. The Polygon2D node lets you draw a polygon, and the CollisionPolygon2D node lets you draw the physical boundaries so other nodes (such as the RigidBody2D) will bounce off.

To see how to use polygons, follow these steps:

1. Make sure the Godot project you created earlier is open.

2. Click Node2D (the parent node) in the Scene dock to select it.

3. Click the + (Attach Child Node) icon in the Scene dock. A Create New Node dialog box appears.

4. Click the Search text field, type **StaticBody2D**, and click Create. Godot makes the StaticBody2D node the child node of the Node2D parent node.

5. Click this newly created StaticBody2D node to select it.

6. Click the + (Attach Child Node) icon in the Scene dock. A Create New Node dialog box appears.

7.  Click the Search text field, type
    **CollisionPolygon2D**, and click Create. Godot makes
    the CollisionPolygon2D node the child node of the
    StaticBody2D parent node.

8.  Click the Select icon on the far left (it looks like an
    arrow) or press Q to select it.

9.  Click the Create Points icon that appears near
    the top middle of the Godot screen as shown in
    Figure 17-8.

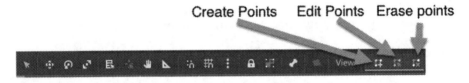

*Figure 17-8.* *The Create Points icon*

10. Click underneath the existing icon.svg images that
    already appear. Each time you click, Godot draws
    a point and connects it with a line. Draw multiple
    lines and double-click the first point you created to
    finish defining a polygon collision shape as shown
    in Figure 17-9.

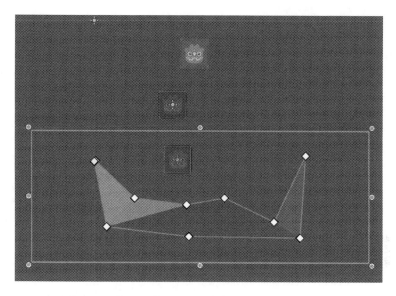

*Figure 17-9.* *Creating a CollisionPolygon2D shape*

11. Click the Run icon. Notice that the icon.svg images fall downward under the influence of gravity and then bounce off the boundaries of the CollisionPolygon2D node. However, we can't see these boundaries.

12. Click the close icon of the (DEBUG) window to make it go away.

The boundaries of a CollisionPolygon2D node are invisible but still affect other nodes such as RigidBody2D nodes. Ideally, you should create a Polygon2D node that matches the boundaries of the CollisionPolygon2D node. Creating a shape for a Polygon2D node is identical to defining the boundaries of a CollisionPolygon2D node.

To add a Polygon2D node, follow these steps:

1. Click the StaticBody2D node that has the CollisionPolygon2D node as its child node.

2. Click the + (Attach Child Node) icon in the Scene dock. A Create New Node dialog box appears.

3. Click the Search text field, type **Polygon2D**, and click Create. Godot makes the Polygon2D node the child node of the StaticBody2D parent node.

4. Click the Select icon on the far left (it looks like an arrow) or press Q to select it.

5. Click the Create Points icon that appears near the top middle of the Godot screen (see Figure 17-8).

6. Click the points that match the shape of the boundaries defined by the CollisionPolygon2D node. Double-click the last point to complete creating the polygon.

7. Click the Color property in the Inspector dock. A color dialog box appears. By default, the color of a polygon is white.

8. Click a different color for your newly created polygon.

9. Click the Run icon. Notice that the Polygon2D node makes it easy to see the boundaries of the CollisionPolygon2D node as shown in Figure 17-10.

***Figure 17-10.*** *A Polygon2D shape makes the boundaries of the CollisionPolygon2D node easy to see*

10.  Click the close icon of the (DEBUG) window to
     make it go away.

# Using Layers and Masks

Having objects collide and bounce off each other can be useful in most
cases. However, sometimes you may not want certain objects to collide
with other objects. For example, a swarm of enemies charging toward a
player shouldn't bump and interfere with each other so enemy objects
should ignore collisions with each other.

Another example might be a treasure that the player can pick up.
However, you wouldn't want enemy objects to pick up the treasure if they
bump into it. So to define which objects can collide with one another,
Godot offers layers and masks, which is another way to detect collisions
between objects instead of using group names (described in Chapter 15)

Godot offers up to 32 different layers. The main idea is that you can
assign objects to different layers. Then you can use masks to define which
layers an object can recognize. For example, a game might put a player
object on Layer 1, a treasure object on Layer 2, and an enemy object on
Layer 3.

Thus you would want the player object (on Layer 1) to interact with a treasure object and an enemy, so its mask would include Layers 2 and 3. On the other hand, an enemy object (on Layer 3) would never interact with a treasure object, so its mask would include only Layer 1. The Inspector dock, under the CollisionObject2D category, defines the Layer and Masks for an object as shown in Figure 17-11.

***Figure 17-11.*** *The Layers and Masks under the CollisionObject2D category in the Inspector dock*

A node can appear on more than one Layer but often only appears on a single layer. Nodes can list multiple numbers in the Mask category to define all the different objects (Layers) it can interact with in a collision.

By default, Godot puts every node on Layer 1 with Mask 1. This means that every node appears on Layer 1 and can interact with every node that also appears on Layer 1. Since Godot offers up to 32 Layers and identifying Layers by number can confusing, you can also give Layers a more descriptive name such as "Player" or "Walls."

To see how to use layers and masks, follow these steps:

1. Make sure the Godot project you created earlier is open.

2. Move the two RigidBody2D nodes above and over the two StaticBody2D nodes as shown in Figure 17-12. You want each RigidBody2D node to fall and hit the StaticBody2D node and then fall to hit the polygon that represents the ground at the bottom of the screen.

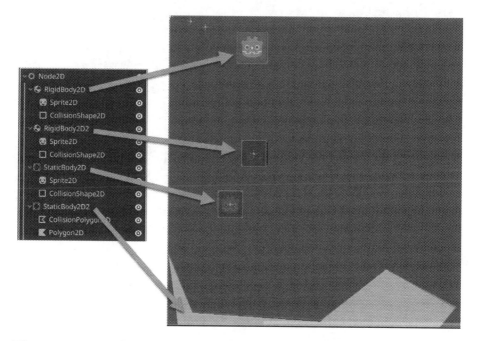

***Figure 17-12.*** *The RigidBody2D nodes should appear above the two StaticBody2D nodes*

3. Click the Run icon. Notice that the two RigidBody2D nodes fall, bounce off the StaticBody2D node, and then land on the second StaticBody2D node.

391

4.  Click the close icon of the (DEBUG) window to make it go away.

5.  Click the StaticBody2D node that represents the stationary icon.svg image as shown in Figure 17-13.

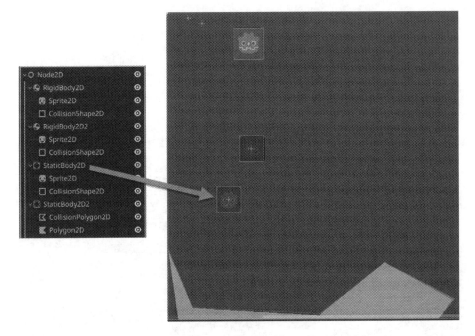

*Figure 17-13. Selecting the StaticBody2D node that represents the stationary icon.svg image*

6.  Click Layer 1 (to clear it) under the Collision category in the Inspector dock.

7.  Click Layer 2 under the Collision category in the Inspector dock. This puts the StaticBody2D node only on Layer 2. That means the two RigidBody2D nodes can only interact with nodes on Layer 1, so they won't recognize the StaticBody2D node on Layer 2.

8.  Click the Run icon. Notice that the two RigidBody2D nodes fall through the StaticBody2D node (on Layer 2) and then land on the second StaticBody2D node (still on Layer 1).

9.  Click the close icon of the (DEBUG) window to make it go away.

10. Click the top RigidBody2D node to select it.

11. Click Mask 2 under the Collision category in the Inspector dock. Both Mask 1 and Mask 2 should be highlighted as shown in Figure 17-14. This means that the top RigidBody2D node can now interact with nodes on Layer 2 (the StaticBody2D node representing the stationary icon.svg image).

*Figure 17-14*   *Mask 1 and 2 selected*

12.   Click the Run icon. Notice that the top RigidBody2D
      nodes bounce off the StaticBody2D node (on Layer
      2) and then land on the second StaticBody2D node
      (still on Layer 1). However, the middle RigidBody2D
      node falls through the StaticBody2D node (on
      Layer 2).

13.   Click the close icon of the (DEBUG) window to
      make it go away.

Placing nodes on separate Layers can make it easy to define how
different objects interact. However, using generic Layer 1 or Layer 3 can
be confusing. That's why Godot also lets you create descriptive names for
each Layer. These descriptive names are for your benefit only. Godot still
treats each Layer as a number such as Layer 2.

To see how to give descriptive names to Layers, follow these steps:

1.   Make sure the previous Godot project is loaded.

2.   Choose Project ➤ Project Settings. A Project Settings
     window appears.

3.   Click the General tab.

4.   Select 2D Physics under the Layer Names category.
     The Project Settings window displays all the
     different layers as shown in Figure 17-15.

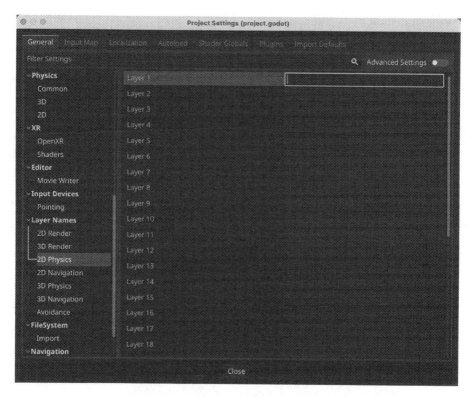

***Figure 17-15.*** *Creating descriptive layer names in the Project Settings window*

5.  Click the text field that appears to the right of Layer 1 and type **FallingNodes**.

6.  Click the text field that appears to the right of Layer 1 and type **StaticNodes**.

7.  Click Close.

To see another way to give a Layer a descriptive name, follow these steps:

1. Make sure the previous Godot project is loaded.

2. Click RigidBody2D to select it. (It doesn't matter which one you select.)

3. Right-click Layer 1 under the Collision category in the Inspector dock. A Rename layer pop-up menu appears as shown in Figure 17-16.

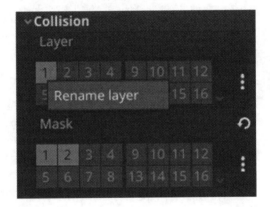

**Figure 17-16.** *Right-clicking a Layer number displays a Rename layer option*

4. Click Rename layer. A Renaming layer dialog box appears as shown in Figure 17-17.

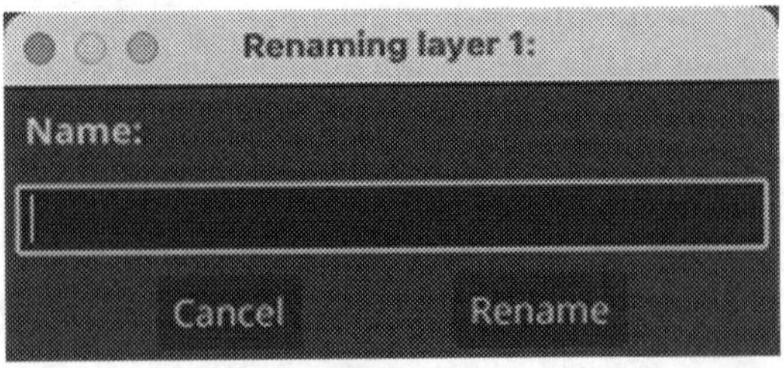

**Figure 17-17.** *The Renaming layer dialog box*

5. Click the Name text field and type a name for your chosen layer.

6. Click Rename.

# Restricting Movement

When creating a video game, you may want to restrict the movement of the player within the boundaries of the game window. Otherwise, the player could move off the screen and disappear. To restrict the movement of any object within specific boundaries, Godot offers the clamp function that looks like this:

```
clamp(position, minimum, maximum)
```

The clamp function accepts the current position of a node and compares it to a minimum and maximum value. This keeps the current position within the range defined by the minimum and maximum values. So if the minimum value is 0 and the maximum value is 500, the position of a node can only be moved within the range of 0–500 in both the x and y axis. If you want to limit the clamp function to float (decimal numbers) or integers, you can use a variation of the clamp function such as follows:

```
clampf(position, minimum, maximum)    # clampf for float values
clampi(position, minimum, maximum)    # clampi for
integer values
```

Godot assigns the origin (0,0) to the upper left corner of the screen where a positive x value moves to the right and a positive y value moves down. Since every computer has different resolutions, you need to identify the total size of a game window by using the following property:

```
get_viewport_rect().size
```

The get_viewport_rect().size property retrieves the size of the game window. You can create a variable to hold this value and then use it in the clamp function like this:

```
var screen_size
screen_size = get_viewport_rect().size

position.x = clamp(position.x, 0, screen_size.x)
position.y = clamp(position.y, 0, screen_size.y)
```

To see how to use the clamp function to restrict movement of a player, follow these steps:

1. Make sure the previous Godot project is loaded.

2. Click Node2D in the Scene dock to select it.

3. Click the Add Child Node (+) icon. A Create New Node window appears.

4. Click the Search text field, type CharacterBody2D, and then click Create. Godot creates a CharacterBody2D node as a child of Node2D.

5. Click CharacterBody2D in the Scene dock to select it.

6. Click the Add Child Node (+) icon. A Create New Node window appears.

7. Click the Search text field, type Sprite2D, and then click Create. Godot creates a Sprite2D node as a child of CharacterBody2D.

8. Drag the icon.svg image into the Texture property of the Sprite2D node in the Inspector dock.

9. Click the Modulate property under the Visibility category (see Figure 17-5). A Color wheel appears.

10. Click a color to modify the Sprite2D node.

11. Click CharcterBody2D in the Scene dock to select it.

12. Click the Add Child Node (+) icon. A Create New Node window appears.

13. Click the Search text field, type CollisionBody2D, and then click Create. Godot creates a CollisionBody2D node as a child of CharacterBody2D.

14. Click the Shape property in the Inspector dock. A pull-down menu appears.

15. Click New RectangleShape2D. Godot displays the orange outline of the rectangle shape.

16. Drag and resize this orange rectangle shape so it appears around the bottom icon.svg object (see Figure 17-7). The CharacterShape2D node should now have two children nodes (Sprite2D and CollisionShape2D) as shown in Figure 17-18.

***Figure 17-18.*** *The CharacterBody2D node with a Sprite2D and CollisionBody2D node as children*

17. Click the CharacterBody2D node in the Scene dock and then click the Add Script icon. An Attach Node Script dialog box appears.

18.  Click Create. Godot creates a GDScript file called CharacterBody2D.gd.

19.  Edit this CharacterBody2D.gd file as follows:

```
extends CharacterBody2D

const SPEED = 300.0
var screen_size

func _ready():
    screen_size = get_viewport_rect().size
    position.x = 400
    position.y = 250

func _physics_process(delta):

    var x_direction = Input.get_axis("ui_left",
    "ui_right")
    if x_direction:
        velocity.x = x_direction * SPEED
    else:
        velocity.x = move_toward(velocity.x, 0,
        SPEED)

    var y_direction = Input.get_axis("ui_up",
    "ui_down")
    if y_direction:
        velocity.y = y_direction * SPEED
    else:
        velocity.y = move_toward(velocity.y, 0,
        SPEED)

    move_and_slide()

    position.x = clampi(position.x, 0, screen_size.x)
    position.y = clampi(position.y, 0, screen_size.y)
```

20. Press Ctrl/Command+S to save your GDScript file.

21. Click the Run icon. The two RigidBody2D nodes should fall and hit the StaticBody2D node that represents a polygon shape.

22. Press the up/down, left/right keys to move the CharacterBody2D node around. Try moving the CharacterBody2D node off the screen. The clampi function should keep it from completely moving out of sight. Also notice that by default, the CharacterBody2D node is on Layer 1 and has Mask 1, which means it can interact with anything on Layer 1.

23. Move the CharacterBody2D node into the StaticBody2D node that represents the stationary icon.svg. This StaticBody2D node is on Layer 2, so the CharacterBody2D node won't collide with it.

24. Click the close icon of the (DEBUG) window to make it go away.

Experiment with changing the Layer and Mask of different items to see how this changes the way the different nodes collide. The clampi function keeps the CharacterBody2D node from exiting the boundaries of the game window, but part of it can still disappear from sight. Play with different values in the clampi function to define the minimum and maximum so no part of the CharacterBody2D node can disappear off the window boundaries.

# Summary

Gravity is one way to move items in a game. When objects hit one another, they need to bounce off each other like in real life, which creates greater realism. In Godot, the RigidBody2D node allows objects to interact with gravity where gravity is defined within the 2D Physics category in the Project Settings window.

Gravity typically pulls objects down, but you can define the strength of gravity to make it stronger or weaker or have it affect objects in other directions besides down. When objects fall, they collide with other objects and bounce off them. If you don't want this behavior, you can adjust a node's Layer and Mask.

Nodes can appear on one or more layers. Masks define the layer that a node can identify. If a node does not recognize a layer and a node appears on that layer, the two nodes will ignore each other. By using Layers and Masks, you can define how different nodes can collide (or ignore) each other.

Godot offers up to 32 Layers and Masks for each node. For your convenience, you can give descriptive names to specific Layers to make it easier to understand what nodes on each Layer represent.

Finally, use the clamp function to restrict movement within a game window. The clamp function defines a minimum and maximum x and y value where a node can move. By restricting movement, you can ensure that a game object can't accidentally disappear off the edge of the screen.

# CHAPTER 18

# Playing Audio

While video games are largely a visual medium, don't overlook the importance that sound can play in your project. Sometimes sound is essential in a video game such as hearing enemies nearby to alert the player or set the tone of a horror game. One type of sound might be background noise such as the wind blowing, rain falling, or background music playing. A second type of sound can give feedback such as when a player picks up a treasure where a beep confirms that the player successfully grabbed the treasure.

There can also be spoken dialogue between characters or explanatory dialogue to help you better understand the game settings. Audio can be music, sound effects, dialogue, or any noise that helps create greater immersion into the game.

Although audio might seem unnecessary in a game, play your favorite game with the sound turned completely off. Even without background sound effects or music, the lack of sound can detract from a game and make playing it less enjoyable.

## Audio Formats in Godot

Godot can use audio stored in one of three audio file formats:

- WAV

- Ogg Vorbis

- MP3

© Wallace Wang, Tonnetta Walcott 2024
W. Wang and T. Walcott, *Programming for Game Design*,
https://doi.org/10.1007/979-8-8688-0190-7_18

The WAV file format offers the greatest sound quality but at the expense of storage space. Because a WAV file does not compress audio in any way, which can reduce sound quality, WAV files are best when you need the best sound quality possible. Just be aware that even simple sounds, stored as a WAV file, can take up a large amount of storage space.

The Ogg Vorbis file format is a completely free and open source standard for compressing audio into smaller files than WAV files. The main drawback with compression is that the greater the compression (and the smaller the audio file), the lower the audio quality.

Although the Ogg Vorbis file format is technically superior to the MP3 audio compression file format, MP3 files are far more common and popular. The main drawback with MP3 files is that the compression standard is a proprietary format. This proprietary format of MP3 audio files is the reason programmers created the alternative Ogg Vorbis file format.

Both the Ogg Vorbis and MP3 file formats are best for compressing audio files to take up less space than a WAV file. The drawback is that the greater the compression, the lower the audio quality.

It's possible to convert sound from one audio file format to another. While there are plenty of commercial audio software available for recording and editing audio, one popular option is Audacity (https://www.audacityteam.org), which runs on Windows, macOS, and Linux. Even better, Audacity is completely free and easy to use, so anyone can record and edit audio in multiple file formats including WAV, Ogg Vorbis, and MP3.

To see how to play an audio file, follow these steps:

1.  Create a new Godot project.

2.  Drag a WAV, Ogg Vorbis, or MP3 file into the FileSystem dock.

3.  Click 2D Scene in the Scene dock. Godot creates a Node2D in the Scene dock.

4.  Click the Add Child Node (+) icon. A Create New
    Node window appears.

5.  Click the Search text field, type AudioStreamPlayer,
    and then click Create. Godot creates an
    AudioStreamPlayer node as a child of Node2D.

6.  Click the Stream property in the Inspector dock.
    A pull-down menu appears so you can choose the
    type of audio to use as shown in Figure 18-1.

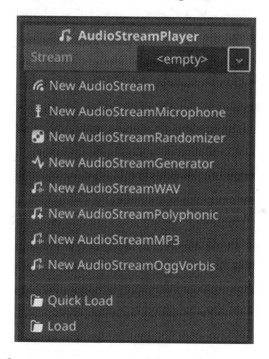

***Figure 18-1.*** *The Stream property of the AudioStreamPlayer node*

7.  Choose New AudioStreamWAV, New
    AudioStreamOggVorbis, or New AudioStreamMP3,
    depending on the type of audio file you placed in
    the FileSystem dock in step 2.

405

8.  Click AudioStreamPlayer in the Scene dock to
    select it.

9.  Drag the audio file from the FileSystem dock into the
    Stream property in the Inspector dock. The Stream
    property displays the name of your audio file as
    shown in Figure 18-2.

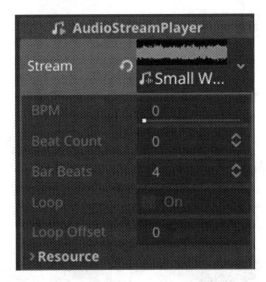

*Figure 18-2.*  *The Stream property displaying an audio file*

10. Click the Autoplay check box as shown in
    Figure 18-3.

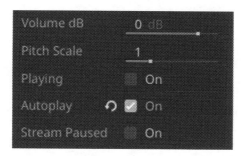

*Figure 18-3.* *The Autoplay check box*

11. Click the Run icon. The (DEBUG) window appears. Because the Autoplay property has been turned on (in step 10), the audio file stored in the Stream property starts playing automatically and stops when the audio has played once.

12. Click the close icon of the (DEBUG) window to make it go away.

13. Click AudioStreamPlayer in the Scene dock to select it

14. Change the Pitch Scale property in the Inspector dock (see Figure 18-3). The Pitch Scale property can range from 0.01 to 4. The lower the Pitch Scale, the slower the audio will play. The higher the Pitch Scale property, the faster the audio will play.

15. Change the Volume dB property in the Inspector dock (see Figure 18-3). The Volume dB property can range from -80 to 24. The lower the value, the quieter the audio. The higher the value, the louder the audio.

407

16.  Click the Run icon. The (DEBUG) window appears and your audio plays based on the settings you chose.

17.  Click the close icon of the (DEBUG) window to make it go away.

Try the preceding steps using all three types of audio files (WAV, Ogg Vorbis, and MP3) so you can see that they work identically. The main difference is the trade-off between higher quality vs. larger storage space. For the best audio quality, use WAV files. For large audio files, use the compressed audio formats Ogg Vorbis or MP3. You may want to experiment with your particular audio files to see whether they sound better and compress more using Ogg Vorbis or MP3.

# Starting and Stopping Audio

When you set the Autoplay property to on for an AudioStreamPlayer node, the audio stored in the Stream property plays as soon as your game starts running. This can be fine for background music, but in some cases, you may want to control when the audio starts and stops.

To start and stop audio, you can write GDScript code. To play audio, you need to identify the AudioStreamPlayer node followed by the .play() method. To stop audio, you also need to identify the AudioStreamPlayer node followed by the .stop() method.

To see how to start and stop audio, follow these steps:

1.  Make sure the previous Godot project is loaded, which plays an audio file when the project runs.

2.  Click AudioStreamPlayer in the Scene dock to select it.

3.  Clear the Autoplay check box in the Inspector dock.

4. Click Node2D in the Scene dock to select it.

5. Click the Add Child Node (+) icon. A Create New Node window appears.

6. Click the Search text field, type Button, and then click Create. Godot creates a Button node as a child of Node2D.

7. Resize and move this Button on the user interface.

8. Press Ctrl/Command+D to duplicate the Button. The Scene dock displays a Button2 node.

9. Move this duplicate Button underneath the first Button.

10. Click the first Button, click the Text property in the Inspector dock, and type **Start**.

11. Click the second Button, click the Text property in the Inspector dock, and type **Stop**. The two Buttons should look like Figure 18-4.

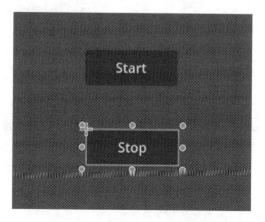

*Figure 18-4. Creating two Buttons on the user interface*

12. Click Node2D in the Scene dock and click the
    Attach Script icon. An Attach Node Script dialog box
    appears.

13. Click Create to create a Node2D.gd file.

14. Click the Button labeled Start in the Scene dock to
    select it.

15. Click the Node tab in the Inspector dock and click
    Signals. A list of different signals appears.

16. Double-click **pressed()**. A Connect a Signal to a
    Method dialog box appears as shown in Figure 18-5.

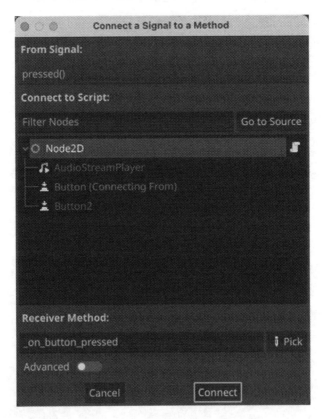

***Figure 18-5.***  *The Connect a Signal to a Method dialog box*

17.  Make sure Node2D is selected and click Connect. Godot adds an _on_button_pressed() function in the Node2D.gd file.

18.  Click the Button labeled Stop in the Scene dock to select it.

19.  Click the Node tab in the Inspector dock and click Signals. A list of different signals appears.

20.  Double-click **pressed()**. A Connect a Signal to a Method dialog box appears (see Figure 18-5).

21.  Make sure Node2D is selected and click Connect. Godot adds an _on_button_2_pressed() function in the Node2D.gd file.

22.  Edit the Node2D.gd file as follows:

```
extends Node2D

func _on_button_pressed():
        $AudioStreamPlayer.play()

func _on_button_2_pressed():
        $AudioStreamPlayer.stop()
```

This code assumes that the AudioStreamPlayer exists. The .play() method starts playing the audio file stored in the Stream property of the AudioStreamPlayer node, and the .stop() function stops playing the audio file.

23.  Click the Run icon. The Godot window appears.

24.  Click the Start Button. This runs the _on_button_ pressed() function to start playing the audio file.

25. Click the Stop Button. This runs the _on_button_
    2_pressed() function to stop playing the audio file.

26. Click the close icon of the (DEBUG) window to
    make it go away.

# Pausing Audio

To start or stop the audio, we can just use the .play() and .stop() methods,
respectively, on the AudioStreamPlayer. However, what if we want to pause
the audio and start playing it again from the location where we last paused,
we need to take additional steps.

First, we need a float variable to store the location where an audio file
has paused. To get this location, we can use the .get_playback_position(),
which returns a decimal number defining the location where the audio
file paused.

After storing the position where the audio paused, we can then play it
back. Instead of using the ordinary .play() method, we need to include the
position in the audio file to start playing from such as .play(paused) where
"paused" represents a decimal value retrieved using the .get_playback_
position() method.

To see how to pause audio, follow these steps:

1. Make sure you have created a Godot project from
   the previous section that displays a Start and Stop
   Button that can start and stop playing an audio file.

2. Click Node2D in the Scene dock to select it.

3. Click the + (Attach Child Node) icon in the Scene
   dock. A Create New Node dialog box appears.

4. Click in the Search text field, type **Button**, and click Create. Godot makes the Button node the child node of the Node2D parent node.

5. Drag and resize the Button so it appears underneath the two existing Buttons (Start and Stop).

6. Change the Text property of this newly created Button to **Pause**. You should now have three Buttons (Start, Stop, and Pause) on the user interface as shown in Figure 18-6.

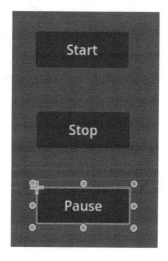

*Figure 18-6.* *The three Buttons on the user interface*

7. Click the Pause Button to select it. Then click Node and Signals in the Inspector dock.

8. Double-click **pressed()**. A Connect a Signal to a Method dialog box appears.

9.  Make sure Node2D is selected and then click Create. Godot creates a func _on_button_3_pressed() function in the Node2D.gd file.

10. Edit the Node2D.gd file as follows:

```
extends Node2D

var save_position: float
var paused: bool = false

func _on_button_pressed():
        if paused == false:
                $AudioStreamPlayer.play()
        else:
                $AudioStreamPlayer.play(save_position)
                paused = false

func _on_button_2_pressed():
        $AudioStreamPlayer.stop()

func _on_button_3_pressed():
        save_position = $AudioStreamPlayer.get_playback_
        position()
        paused = true
        $AudioStreamPlayer.stop()
```

11. Click the Run icon. The (DEBUG) window appears.

12. Click the Start Button. The audio file defined in the Stream property of the AudioStreamPlayer node starts playing.

13. Click the Pause Button. The audio file stops playing.

14.    Click the Start Button again. The audio file should now start playing again where it left off.

15.    Click the close icon of the (DEBUG) window to make it go away.

To better understand this code, start with the two variables. The "paused" variable is defined as a Boolean data type and initially set to false. The "save_position" variable is defined as a float data type and initially has no value:

```
var save_position: float
var paused: bool = false
```

The _on_button_3_pressed() function runs when the user selects the Pause Button on the user interface. This function uses the .get_playback_position() method to get the location in the audio where the user paused the sound. Then the function sets the "paused" variable to true and tells the AudioStreamPlayer to stop playing audio:

```
func _on_button_3_pressed():
        save_position = $AudioStreamPlayer.get_playback_
        position()
        paused = true
        $AudioStreamPlayer.stop()
```

The code for the Start Button uses an if-else statement to determine whether to play from the start of the audio file (.play()) or if the "paused" variable is true to play from the location stored in the "save_position" variable (.play(save_position)):

```
func _on_button_pressed():
        if paused == false:
                $AudioStreamPlayer.play()
```

```
else:
      $AudioStreamPlayer.play(save_position)
      paused = false
```

Essentially, pausing audio must let your code know where the audio paused and if paused, where to start playing the audio again. Notice that once the audio starts playing from the last paused position (save_position), the code resets the "paused" variable to false.

For an even simpler solution, we can just use the stream_paused property, which automatically stores the location of where an audio file paused. The drawback is that we won't know the exact location in the audio file where it paused, but if that's not important, then the stream_paused property is much easier and more straightforward to use.

To see how to use the stream_paused property, follow these steps:

1.  Make sure you have created a Godot project from the previous section that displays a Start and Stop Button that can start and stop playing an audio file.

2.  Double-click the Node2D.gd in the FileSystem dock. Godot opens the Node2D.gd file.

3.  Edit the Node2D.gd file as follows:

```
extends Node2D

func _on_button_pressed():
      $AudioStreamPlayer.play()

func _on_button_2_pressed():
      $AudioStreamPlayer.stop()

func _on_button_3_pressed():
      $AudioStreamPlayer.stream_paused = not
      $AudioStreamPlayer.stream_paused
```

Notice how much simpler the code looks. Also notice that the on_button_3_pressed() function toggles the stream_paused property.

4.  Click the Run icon. The audio file, defined in the Stream property of the AudioStreamPlayer, starts playing automatically.

5.  Click the Pause Button. This pauses the audio.

6.  Click the Pause Button again. This starts the audio playing again starting from the location where it paused.

7.  Click the close icon of the (DEBUG) window to make it go away.

# Looping Audio

Most of the time, you want an audio file to play once such as the sound of a gunshot, a lion roaring, or a glass window shattering. However, in some cases, you want an audio file to keep playing in an endless loop such as background music or background sound effects such as birds chirping. The looping of sounds can indicate the type of environment taking place.

To loop audio, you need to follow three steps:

•  Add an AudioStreamPlayer node to a project.

•  Add an audio file (WAV, Ogg Vorbis, or MP3) to the Stream property of the AudioStreamPlayer.

•  Use the **finished()** signal to create a function to run the .play() method again.

To see how to loop audio, follow these steps:

1.  Create a new Godot project.

2.  Click 2D near the top of the Godot window to create a Node2D node.

3.  Click the + (Attach Child Node) icon in the Scene dock. A Create New Node dialog box appears.

4.  Click the Search text field, type **AudioStreamPlayer,** and click Create. Godot makes the AudioStreamPlayer node the child node of the Node2D parent node.

5.  Drag and drop an audio file (WAV, Ogg Vorbis, or MP3) into the FileSystem dock. Make sure this audio file is fairly short so it will be easy to tell when it ends and starts repeating again.

6.  Drag the audio file into the Stream property of the AudioStreamPlayer in the Inspector dock.

7.  Select the Autoplay check box.

8.  Click Node2D in the Scene dock to select it.

9.  Click the Attach Script icon. An Attach Node Script dialog box appears.

10. Click Create. Godot creates a Node2D.gd file.

11. Click the AudioStreamPlayer in the Scene dock to select it.

12. Click the Node tab and then Signals in the Inspector dock.

13. Double-click **finished()** as shown in Figure 18-7. A Connect a Signal to a Method dialog box appears.

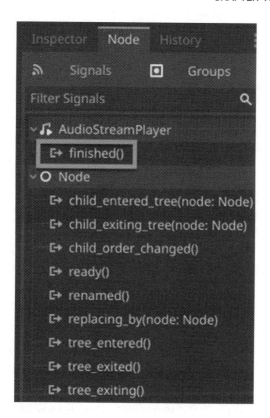

***Figure 18-7.*** *The finished() signal in the Inspector dock*

14.   Make sure Node2D is selected and then click
      Connect. Godot creates a _on_audio_stream_
      player_finished() function in the Node2D.
      gd file. This function will run as soon as the
      audio file, stored in the Stream property of the
      AudioStreamPlayer, ends.

15.  Edit the _on_audio_stream_player_finished()
     function as follows:

```
extends Node2D

func _on_audio_stream_player_finished():
        $AudioStreamPlayer.play()
```

16.  Press Ctrl/Command+S to save your GDScript code
     changes.

17.  Click the Run icon. Notice that as soon as your audio
     file ends, it repeats again.

18.  Click the close icon in the (DEBUG) window to
     make it go away.

# Playing Audio When Detecting a Collision

One common use for audio is to provide feedback when something
happens in a game such as when a player picks up a treasure or hits an
obstacle that causes them to lose health or lose a life altogether. In our
previous examples, we stored audio in an AudioStreamPlayer. However,
when you want audio to play based on the actions of a moving object,
you'll need to attach an AudioStreamPlayer2D node instead.

In this project, we'll create one scene to define an obstacle and a
second scene to define a player that we can move around the screen by
using the cursor keys (up/down and left/right). The main node will be an
Area2D node with a Sprite2D and CollisionShape2D node as child nodes.
The player node will also contain an AudioStreamPlayer2D node that will
hold the audio file to play when the player and a stationary object collide.

To see how to play audio when detecting a collision, follow these steps:

1.  Create a new Godot project.

2.  Drag and drop a WAV, Ogg Vorbis, or MP3 file into the FileSystem dock. Ideally, use an audio file that's short such as a beep or crashing sound because this audio will play when two objects collide, so a long playing audio will feel distracting.

3.  Click Other Node in the Scene dock. A Create New Node dialog box appears.

4.  Click the Search text field, type Area2D, and then click Create. Godot creates an Area2D node as the parent in the Scene dock.

5.  Double-click Area2D and edit the node name to **Player**.

6.  Click the + (Attach Child Node) icon in the Scene dock. A Create New Node dialog box appears.

7.  Click the Search text field, type Sprite2D, and then click Create. Godot creates a Sprite2D node as a child of the Player (Area2D) node.

8.  Drag and drop the icon.svg image into the Texture property in the Inspector dock.

9.  Click Player to select it.

10. Click the + (Attach Child Node) icon in the Scene dock. A Create New Node dialog box appears.

11. Click the Search text field, type CollisionShape2D, and then click Create. Godot creates a CollisionShape2D node as a child of the Player (Area2D) node.

12. Click the Shape property in the Inspector dock. A pull-down menu appears.

13. Choose New RectangleShape2D. Godot displays a collision shape rectangle.

14. Resize this collision shape so it covers the entire icon.svg image.

15. Click Player (Area2D) in the Scene dock to select it.

16. Click the + (Attach Child Node) icon in the Scene dock. A Create New Node dialog box appears.

17. Click the Search text field, type AudioStreamPlayer2D, and then click Create. Godot creates an AudioStreamPlayer2D node as a child of the Player (Area2D) node.

18. Drag and drop the audio file into the Stream property in the Inspector dock.

19. Press Ctrl/Command+S to save your scene. A Save Scene As dialog box appears.

20. Click Save. Godot saves the scene under the name player.tscn.

At this point, we've created a player scene consisting of the following:

- Area2D (parent node)

- Sprite2D (child node that displays the icon.svg image in the Texture property)

- CollisionShape2D (child node that defines the collision boundaries of the scene)

- AudioStreamPlayer2D (child node that holds the audio file)

Now we need to create an obstacle scene so that way when the player scene collides with the obstacle scene, it plays an audio file:

1. Choose Scene ➤ New Scene.

2. Click Other Node in the Scene dock.

3. Click Other Node in the Scene dock. A Create New Node dialog box appears.

4. Click the Search text field, type Area2D, and then click Create. Godot creates an Area2D node as the parent in the Scene dock.

5. Double-click Area2D and edit the node name to **Obstacle**.

6. Click the + (Attach Child Node) icon in the Scene dock. A Create New Node dialog box appears.

7. Click the Search text field, type Sprite2D, and then click Create. Godot creates a Sprite2D node as a child of the Obstacle (Area2D) node.

8. Drag and drop the icon.svg image into the Texture property in the Inspector dock.

9. Click the Modulate property under the Visibility category in the Inspector dock. A color dialog box appears.

10. Click a color to modify the appearance of the icon. svg image.

11. Click Obstacle in the Scene dock to select it.

12. Click the + (Attach Child Node) icon in the Scene dock. A Create New Node dialog box appears.

13.  Click the Search text field, type CollisionShape2D, and then click Create. Godot creates a CollisionShape2D node as a child of the Obstacle (Area2D) node.

14.  Click the Shape property in the Inspector dock. A pull-down menu appears.

15.  Choose New RectangleShape2D. Godot displays a collision shape rectangle.

16.  Resize this collision shape so it covers the entire icon.svg image.

17.  Click Obstacle in the Scene dock to select it.

18.  Click the Node tab in the Inspector dock and then click Groups.

19.  Click the text field under Manage Groups, type **obstacle**, and press Enter. This defines the Obstacle. tscn scene as an "obstacle" group as shown in Figure 18-8.

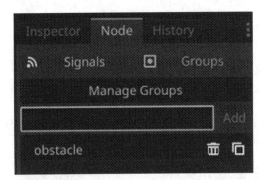

*Figure 18-8.* *Defining the Obstacle.tscn scene as an "obstacle" group*

20. Press Ctrl/Command+S to save your scene. A Save Scene As dialog box appears.

21. Click Save. Godot saves the scene under the name obstacle.tscn.

At this point, we've created a player scene consisting of the following:

- Area2D (parent node)

- Sprite2D (child node that displays the icon.svg image in the Texture property)

- CollisionShape2D (child node that defines the collision boundaries of the scene)

At this point, we have two scenes: player.tscn and obstacle.tscn. Now we need to create a main scene:

1. Choose Scene ➤ New Scene.

2. Click Other Node in the Scene dock. A Create New Node dialog box appears.

3. Click the Search text field, type Node, and then click Create. Godot creates a Node as the parent in the Scene dock.

4. Double-click Node and edit the node name to **Main**.

5. Drag and drop player.tscn from the FileSystem dock into the viewport. Make sure you drop the player. tscn scene inside the boundaries of game window.

6. Drag and drop obstacle.tscn from the FileSystem dock into the viewport. Make sure you drop the obstacle.tscn scene inside the boundaries of game window as shown in Figure 18-9.

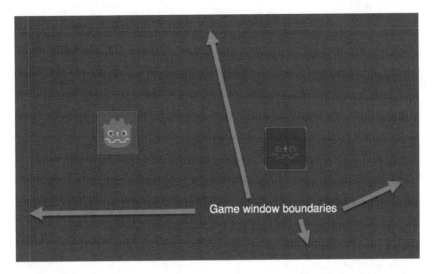

Game window boundaries

*Figure 18-9.* *Placing the Scene.tscn and Obstacle.tscn scene within the game window boundaries*

7.  Press Ctrl/Command+S to save your scene. A Save Scene As dialog box appears.

8.  Click Save. Godot saves the scene under the name main.tscn.

9.  Choose Project ➤ Project Settings. A Project Settings window appears.

10. Click Run under the Application category.

11. Click the folder icon that appears to the right of Main Scene. A dialog box appears.

12. Click main.tscn and click Open.

13. Click Close to make the Project Setting window go away.

This project is almost complete. All we need to do is write GDScript to detect a collision between the Player.tscn scene and the Obstacle.tscn. So we need to write GDScript to move the Player.tscn around and then detect a collision by following these steps:

1. Make sure you have the Godot project open that includes a Player.tscn, Obstacle.tscn, and Main.tscn scene files.

2. Double-click Player.tscn in the FileSystem dock. All the nodes that make up the Player.tscn scene appear in the Scene dock.

3. Click Player in the Scene dock to select it.

4. Click the Attach Script icon. An Attach Node Script dialog box appears.

5. Click Create. Godot creates a GDScript file called player.gd.

6. Edit the Player.gd script as follows:

```
extends Area2D

var speed = 300

func _process(delta):
        var velocity = Vector2.ZERO

        if Input.is_key_pressed(KEY_RIGHT):
                velocity = Vector2.RIGHT * speed

        if Input.is_key_pressed(KEY_LEFT):
                velocity = Vector2.LEFT * speed
```

```
if Input.is_key_pressed(KEY_UP):
        velocity = Vector2.UP * speed

if Input.is_key_pressed(KEY_DOWN):
        velocity = Vector2.DOWN * speed

position += velocity * delta
```

7. Press Ctrl/Command+S to save the player.gd file.

8. Click the Run icon. The game window appears.

9. Press the up/down, left/right arrow keys to move the player.tscn around.

10. Click the close icon in the (DEBUG) window to make it go away.

We can now move the player around the screen, so the final step is to detect a collision between the player and the obstacle. When that collision occurs, we can then play the audio file stored in the Stream property of the AudioStreamPlayer2D node.

To detect collisions and play audio, follow these steps:

1. Double-click player.tscn in the FileSystem dock. Godot displays all the nodes that make up the player.tscn scene in the Scene dock.

2. Click Player in the Scene dock.

3. Click the Node tab in the Inspector dock and then click Signals.

4. Double-click **area_entered(area: Area2D)**. A Connect a Signal to a Method dialog box appears as shown in Figure 18-10.

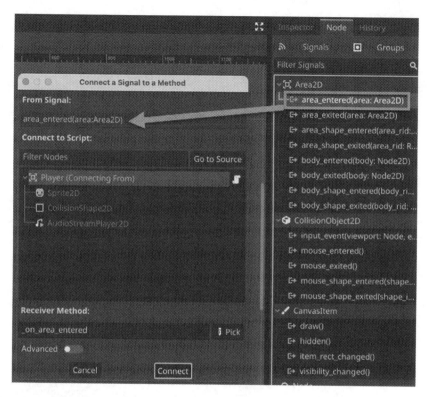

***Figure 18-10.*** *Double-clicking area_entered(area: Area2D) displays a Connect a Signal to a Method dialog box*

5. Click Connect. Godot adds an on_area_ entered(area) function.

6. Edit this on_area_entered(area) function as follows:

```
func _on_area_entered(area):
    if area.is_in_group("obstacle"):
        $AudioStreamPlayer2D.play()
```

The entire player.gd file should look like this:

```
extends Area2D

var speed = 300

func _process(delta):
        var velocity = Vector2.ZERO

        if Input.is_key_pressed(KEY_RIGHT):
                velocity = Vector2.RIGHT * speed

        if Input.is_key_pressed(KEY_LEFT):
                velocity = Vector2.LEFT * speed

        if Input.is_key_pressed(KEY_UP):
                velocity = Vector2.UP * speed

        if Input.is_key_pressed(KEY_DOWN):
                velocity = Vector2.DOWN * speed

        position += velocity * delta

func _on_area_entered(area):
        if area.is_in_group("obstacle"):
                $AudioStreamPlayer2D.play()
```

7.  Press Ctrl/Command+S to save the player.gd file.

8.  Click the Run icon. The game window appears.

9.  Press the up/down, left/right arrow keys to move the player.tscn around. Notice that when the player.tscn touches the obstacle.tscn, the audio stored in the AudioStreamPlayer2D node plays.

10. Click the close icon in the (DEBUG) window to make it go away.

# Summary

Audio can add background music or sound effects to a game. Audio can also give feedback such as when players get die or pick up a treasure. The next time you play a video game, turn off the sound, and then play it with the sound turned on. You should notice that even if you're not conscious of the sound, you suddenly notice it when it's missing.

The AudioStreamPlayer node can play sound, while the AudioStreamPlayer2D node is useful for attaching sound to a game object such as a player or enemy. You can play, pause, and stop audio as well as change the volume and pitch of audio. By controlling sound through the Inspector dock and through GDScript code, you can control how audio works within your game.

# CHAPTER 19

# Creating and Using Scenes

Every video game consists of objects such as a player, enemies, and fixed obstacles such as walls, floors, or ceilings. To create anything in Godot, you use nodes that work together to create a scene. A scene can represent a single object. However, you can also place scenes inside of another scene where a scene can represent a single object or an entire playing field. The scene then displays all your objects in the graphic interface.

In previous projects, we learned how to create a scene out of nodes where each node serves a specific purpose. For example, a Sprite2D node defines an image to display, while a CollisionShape2D node defines the physical boundaries of an object that can collide with other objects. The combination of nodes working together can create a scene. By using existing scenes, you can create complex games one step at a time.

## Automatically Adding Objects in Scenes

In a video game, you'll typically need to add a player object along with enemies or obstacles. While you could drag and drop game objects into a scene, it's often more convenient to let GDScript code place enemies and obstacles in random locations on the screen.

To do this, you must first create scenes that define the enemies or obstacles you want to place inside a bigger scene. Once you've created an enemy or obstacle, you need to follow several steps:

- Create a .tscn scene to hold the objects (such as enemies or obstacles) that you want to add.

- Create a variable to hold the .tscn scene that you want to add.

- Create a variable that holds a copy (instantiation) of the .tscn scene.

- Use the randi_range function to randomly define an x and y position to place the object within the scene.

To see how to use GDScript code to add objects to a scene, we'll first need to create two .tscn scenes. One .tscn scene will represent the objects to add, and the second .tscn scene will display the different objects on the screen.

To create these two .tscn scenes, follow these steps:

1. Create a new Godot project.

2. Click Other Node in the Scene dock. A Create New Node dialog box appears.

3. Click the Search text field, type Area2D, and then click Create. Godot creates an Area2D node as parent node in the Scene dock.

4. Double-click Area2D in the Scene dock and change the name to Obstacle.

5. Click the Add Child Node (+) icon. A Create New Node window appears.

6.  Click the Search text field, type Sprite2D, and then click Create. Godot creates a Sprite2D node as a child of Obstacle (Area2D).

7.  Drag and drop the icon.svg image into the Texture property in the Inspector dock.

8.  Click Obstacle in the Scene dock and then click the Add Child Node (+) icon. A Create New Node window appears.

9.  Click the Search text field, type CollisionShape2D, and then click Create. Godot creates a CollisionShape2D node as a child of Obstacle (Area2D).

10. Click the Shape property in the Inspector dock. A pull-down menu appears.

11. Choose New RectangleShape2D.

12. Resize the collision boundaries to cover the icon. svg image.

13. Press Ctrl/Command+S to save the scene as an obstacle.tscn file.

The preceding steps have created a simple scene that we can randomly place within a video game playing field. Now the next step is to create that playing field by following these steps:

1.  Make sure you have created and loaded the Godot project from the previous section.

2.  Choose Scene ➤ New Scene.

3.  Click Other Node in the Scene dock. A Create New Node dialog box appears.

4.  Click the Search text field, type Node, and then click Create. Godot creates a generic Node as the parent node in the Scene dock.

5.  Double-click Node in the Scene dock and rename it **Main**.

6.  Press Ctrl/Command+S to save your scene as main.tscn.

7.  Choose Project ➤ Project Settings. A Project Settings dialog box appears.

8.  Click Run under the Application category.

9.  Click the folder icon that appears to the right of Main Scene. An Open a File dialog box appears.

10. Click main.tscn and click Open.

11. Click Close to make the Project Settings dialog box disappear.

12. Click the Attach a Script icon (+). An Attach Node Script dialog box appears that will create a main. gd file.

13. Click Create.

14. Edit the main.gd file as follows:

```
extends Node

@export var obstacle_scene: PackedScene
```

The @export part of the code creates a property in the Inspector dock. In this case, the property is the arbitrarily named "obstacle_scene," but you can use any name you wish.

The more important part is PackedScene, which
creates a property in the Inspector dock as shown
in Figure 19-1. This Inspector property will let us
drag and drop a .tscn file, so our GDScript code can
access it.

***Figure 19-1.*** *The @export keyword creates a property in the*
*Inspector dock*

15.  Click 2D at the top of the screen.

16.  Drag and drop the obstacle.tscn from the FileSystem
     dock into the Obstacle Scene property in the
     Inspector dock as shown in Figure 19-2. Now we can
     access the obstacle.tscn scene through the
     obstacle_scene variable name.

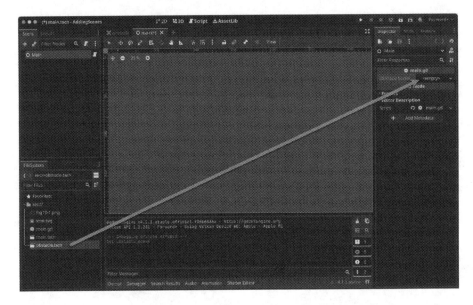

*Figure 19-2.*  *Dragging a .tscn file from the FileSystem dock into the Inspector dock*

17.   Edit the main.gd file as follows:

```
extends Node

@export var obstacle_scene: PackedScene
var screensize

func _ready():
    const total_number = 10
    screensize = get_viewport().get_visible_rect().size
    for x in total_number:
        var new_obstacle = obstacle_scene.instantiate()
        add_child(new_obstacle)
        new_obstacle.position = Vector2(randi_range(0,
        screensize.x), randi_range(0, screensize.y))
```

The screensize variable first gets declared and then retrieves the total game window size that's returned by the get_viewport().get_visible_rect(). size property. Inside a for loop that repeats ten times (defined by a constant called total_number), the GDScript code does three tasks:

- Creates or instantiates a new object based on the .tscn scene stored in the Obstacle Scene property defined by the @export var obstacle_scene: PackedScene line

- Adds the newly instantiated object to the main.tscn scene using the add_child command

- Randomly places this new object using the randi_ range functions that create a random number between 0 and the screensize in the x and y direction

18. Click the Run icon. The (DEBUG) window appears and displays ten (10) objects randomly scattered around the game window.

19. Click the close icon of the (DEBUG) window to make it go away.

20. Repeat steps 11 and 12. Notice that each time you run the project, the exact location of each of the ten objects changes because the randi_range function calculates a different random number each time for both the x and y positions.

# Modifying Instances of a Scene

When you add a scene into another scene, that's called instancing a scene by essentially making a copy of a scene. In the previous project, you wrote GDScript code to randomly place ten objects within a scene where every object is defined by the same .tscn file. Instantiating a scene is another way to load one scene into another without dragging a sprite or node into the scene.

One advantage of instancing a scene is that you can define it once and have Godot create as many exact duplicates as you need. However, there may be times when you want to customize one or more instances of a scene without changing all of those scenes.

So in this part, you'll learn how to change a .tscn scene once to change it everywhere and how to customize specific instances of a scene.

To see how changing a single .tscn scene can change the appearance of multiple objects, follow these steps:

1. Make sure you have created and loaded the Godot project from the previous section that randomly places ten objects within a scene.

2. Double-click the obstacle.tscn file in the FileSystem dock. Godot displays all the nodes that make up the obstacle.tscn scene in the Scene dock as shown in Figure 19-3.

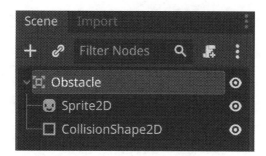

*Figure 19-3.* *The nodes that make up the obstacle.tscn scene*

3. Click the Sprite2D child node under Obstacle.

4. Click the Modulate property under the Visibility category in the Inspector dock. A color dialog box appears.

5. Choose a color to change the appearance of the icon.svg image.

6. Click the Run icon. The (DEBUG) window appears and displays ten (10) objects randomly scattered around the game window. Notice that all ten objects now appear in the color you chose in step 5.

7. Click the close icon of the (DEBUG) window to make it go away.

By changing a single .tscn file, you can automatically change all instances of that scene. However, sometimes you may create a scene and want to customize one or more copies differently than the settings defined by its .tscn file. In that case, you'll need to modify each instance of that scene individually.

To see how to modify individual copies of a .tscn file, follow these steps:

1. Create a new Godot project.

2. Click 2D Scene in the Scene dock. Godot creates a Node2D as the parent node in the Scene dock.

3. Double-click Node2D and change its name to **Enemy**.

4. Click the Add Child Node (+) icon. A Create New Node window appears.

5. Click the Search text field, type Sprite2D, and then click Create. Godot creates a Sprite2D node as a child of Node2D.

6. Drag and drop the icon.svg image file from the FileSystem dock into the Texture property in the Inspector dock.

7. Click the Modulate property under the Visibility category in the Inspector dock. A color dialog box appears.

8. Pick a color to change the appearance of the icon. svg image.

9. Press Ctrl/Command+S to save your scene. A Save Scene As dialog box appears.

10. Click Save to save it as enemy.tscn.

At this point, we've created an enemy.tscn that we can duplicate within another scene. Now we need to create a main scene where we place multiple copies of the enemy.tscn:

1.  Choose Scene ➤ New Scene.

2.  Click Other Node in the Scene dock. A Create New Node dialog box appears.

3.  Click the Search text field, type Node, and then click Create. Godot creates a Node as the parent.

4.  Double-click Node and rename it **Main.**

5.  Press Ctrl/Command+S and click Create to save the scene as main.tscn.

6.  Choose Project ➤ Project Settings. A Project Settings window appears.

7.  Click Run under the Application category and click the folder icon that appears to the right of Main Scene. An Open a File dialog box appears.

8.  Click main.tscn and click Open.

9.  Click Close.

We've now created an enemy.tscn scene and a main.tscn. Now we just need to add the enemy.tscn scene into the main.tscn:

1.  Double-click the main.tscn file in the FileSystem dock to make sure Main appears in the Scene dock.

2.  Drag and drop the enemy.tscn three times from the FileSystem dock into the viewport as shown in Figure 19-4.

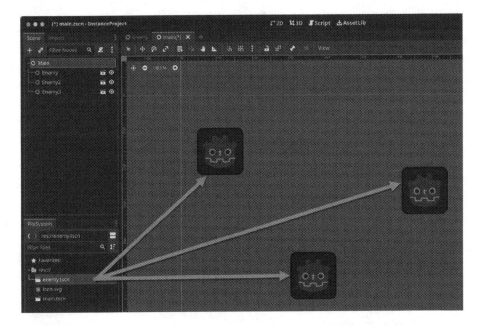

***Figure 19-4.*** *Placing three enemy.tscn objects into the main.
tscn scene*

3.  Press Ctrl/Command+S to save the scene with the
    three objects added.

4.  Double-click the enemy.tscn file in the FileSystem
    dock to make its nodes appear in the Scene dock.

5.  Click Sprite2D to select it.

6.  Click Modulate under the Visibility category in the
    Inspector dock. A color dialog box appears.

7.  Click a different color.

8.  Press Ctrl/Command+S to save the new colors.

9.  Double-click the main.tscn file in the FileSystem dock.
    All three instances of the enemy.tscn file should now
    display the new color you selected in step 7.

Any time you change the .tscn file, all instances of that file also change. However, now we only want to change one instance of the enemy.tscn file. To change just one instance without changing all of them, we need to follow several steps:

- Select the instance of the enemy.tscn file that we want to modify.

- Expand that enemy.tscn's nodes so we can edit them.

- Edit the node that we want to change.

The main.tscn Scene dock should contain three instances of the enemy.tscn file (named Enemy, Enemy2, and Enemy3) as shown in Figure 19-5.

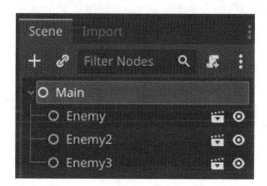

***Figure 19-5.*** *Three instances of the enemy.tscn file stored in the main.tscn file*

To see how to edit just a single instance, follow these steps:

1. Make sure the Godot project is loaded, which displays the three enemy.tscn scenes in the main. tscn (see Figure 19-5).

2. Right-click Enemy. A pop-up menu appears as shown in Figure 19-6.

445

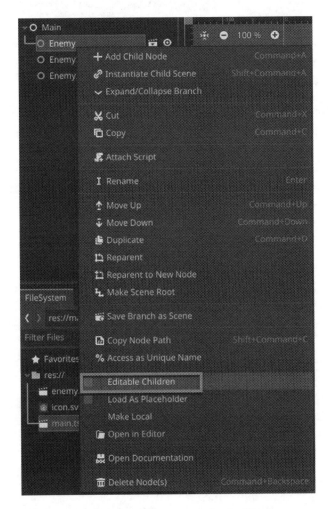

***Figure 19-6.*** *Right-clicking in the Scene dock displays a pop-up menu*

3.  Choose Editable Children. Godot now expands the
    Enemy instance to display its nodes as shown in
    Figure 19-7.

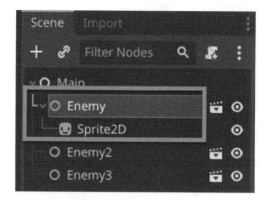

***Figure 19-7.*** *Editable Children expands an instance to view its node tree*

4.  Click Sprite2D underneath Enemy. The Sprite2D properties appear in the Inspector dock.

5.  Click the Modulate property under the Visibility category in the Inspector dock. A color dialog box appears.

6.  Choose a different color.

7.  Click the Run icon. Notice that the changes you made to that one enemy.tscn object does not affect the appearance of the other two enemy.tscn objects.

8.  Click the close icon of the (DEBUG) window to make it go away.

# Automatically Moving and Rotating a Scene

In many games, you may need objects to constantly move on their own such as asteroids flying around or spiked traps rotating in circles. To move or rotate an object, Godot offers two functions:

- apply_force(Vector2(x, y))

- apply_torque_impulse(value)

The apply_force function lets you define an x and y direction to move an object using a Vector2 to define the force in both the x and y directions. A positive x value moves an object to the right. A positive y value moves an object down.

The apply_torque_impulse function rotates an object where a positive value rotates it clockwise and a negative value rotates it counterclockwise. The higher the value, the faster the object rotates.

To see how to use both the apply_force and apply_torque_impulse functions, follow these steps:

1. Create a new Godot project.

2. Click Other Node in the Scene dock. A Create New Node dialog box appears.

3. Click in the Search text field, type Node, and then click Create. Godot creates a Node as the parent.

4. Double-click Node in the Scene dock and rename it to **Main**.

5. Press Ctrl/Command+S to save the scene as main.tscn.

6. Click the Run icon. When a dialog box appears asking to select a scene, click Select Current.

7. Click the close icon in the (DEBUG) window to make it go away.

At this point, we've just created a main scene and set it as the default scene to run. Now we need to create two scenes. We'll use the apply_force function on one scene to make it move across the screen. Then we'll use the apply_torque_impulse function on the second scene to make it rotate in place:

1. Choose Scene ➤ New Scene. Godot creates a new scene.

2. Click Other Node in the Scene dock. A Create New Node dialog box appears.

3. Click the Search text field, type RigidBody2D, and then click Create. Godot creates a RigidBody2D as the parent node.

4. Double-click RigidBody2D and change the name to **MoveMe**.

5. Click the Gravity Scale property in the Inspector dock and set its value to 0 to turn off gravity.

6. Click the Add Child Node (+) icon. A Create New Node window appears.

7. Click the Search text field, type Sprite2D, and then click Create. Godot creates a Sprite2D node as a child of Node2D.

8. Drag and drop the icon.svg image file from the FileSystem dock into the Texture property in the Inspector dock.

9. Click MoveMe (parent node) to select it.

10. Click the Add Child Node (+) icon. A Create New Node window appears.

11. Click the Search text field, type CollisionShape2D, and then click Create. Godot creates a CollisionShape2D node as a child of MoveMe (RigidBody2D).

12. Click the Shape property in the Inspector dock. A pull-down menu appears.

13. Choose New RectangleShape2D.

14. Resize the collision boundaries to cover the icon. svg image.

15. Press Ctrl/Command+S to save the scene as a move_me.tscn file.

16. Click MoveMe in the Scene dock to select it.

17. Click the Attach a Script icon. An Attach Node Script dialog box appears.

18. Click Create. Godot creates a move_me.gd file.

19. Edit the move_me.gd file as follows:

```
extends RigidBody2D

var x_speed = 100
var y_speed = 45

func _physics_process(delta):
        apply_force(Vector2(x_speed, y_speed))
```

20. Press Ctrl/Command+S to save the move_me.gd file.

21. Double-click the main.tscn file in the FileSystem dock and click 2D at the top of the screen to display the main.tscn scene.

22.   Drag and drop the move_me.tscn file from the
       FileSystem dock to the upper left corner of the main.
       tscn scene as shown in Figure 19-8.

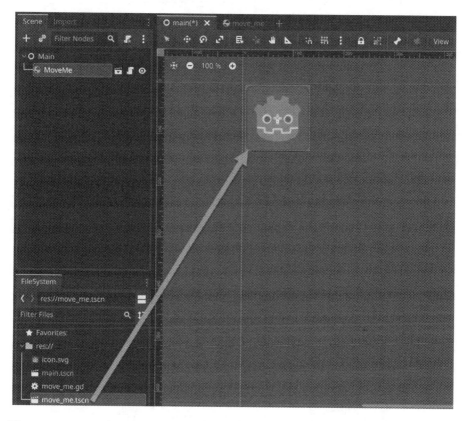

*Figure 19-8.* *Placing the move_me.tscn scene inside the main.*
*tscn scene*

23.   Press Ctrl/Command+S to save the modified main.
       tscn scene.

24.   Click the Run icon. Notice that the icon.svg image
       moves diagonally down to the right.

25.   Click the close icon in the (DEBUG) window to
       make it go away.

Now let's create a scene that will use the apply_torque_impulse function to rotate another copy of the icon.svg image in place:

1.  Choose Scene ➤ New Scene. Godot creates a new scene.

2.  Click Other Node in the Scene dock. A Create New Node dialog box appears.

3.  Click the Search text field, type RigidBody2D, and then click Create. Godot creates a RigidBody2D as the parent node.

4.  Double-click RigidBody2D and change the name to **RotateMe**.

5.  Click the Gravity Scale property in the Inspector dock and set its value to 0 to turn off gravity.

6.  Click the Add Child Node (+) icon. A Create New Node window appears.

7.  Click the Search text field, type Sprite2D, and then click Create. Godot creates a Sprite2D node as a child of Node2D.

8.  Drag and drop the icon.svg image file from the FileSystem dock into the Texture property in the Inspector dock.

9.  Click RotateMe (the parent node) in the Scene dock to select it.

10. Click the Add Child Node (+) icon. A Create New Node window appears.

11.   Click the Search text field, type CollisionShape2D, and then click Create. Godot creates a CollisionShape2D node as a child of RotateMe (RigidBody2D).

12.   Click the Shape property in the Inspector dock. A pull-down menu appears.

13.   Choose New RectangleShape2D.

14.   Resize the collision boundaries to cover the icon. svg image.

15.   Press Ctrl/Command+S to save the scene as a rotate_me.tscn file.

16.   Click RotateMe in the Scene dock to select it.

17.   Click the Attach a Script icon. An Attach Node Script dialog box appears.

18.   Click Create. Godot creates a rotate_me.gd file.

19.   Edit the rotate_me.gd file as follows:

```
extends RigidBody2D

var rotation_speed = 100

func _physics_process(delta):
        apply_torque_impulse(rotation_speed)
```

20.   Press Ctrl/Command+S to save the rotate_ me.gd file.

21.   Double-click the main.tscn file in the FileSystem dock and click 2D at the top of the screen to display the main.tscn scene.

22. Drag and drop the rotate_me.tscn file from the FileSystem dock to the lower left corner of the main.tscn scene.

23. Press Ctrl/Command+S to save the modified main.tscn scene.

24. Click the Run icon. Notice that this newly added icon.svg image rotates clockwise while the other icon.svg image moves diagonally down to the right.

25. Click the close icon in the (DEBUG) window to make it go away.

# Following the Player with a Camera

In many video games, the game boundary is not limited to the size of the game window. That means the player can move across the boundaries of the game window to explore more of the game world. To do this, the game must follow the player's movement and that involves using a Camera node.

Without a Camera node (such as Camera2D), the player can move beyond the game window boundaries and disappear. By using a Camera node, the player always remains visible, allowing the player to explore multiple areas of the game world.

To see how to use the camera to follow a player's movement, follow these steps:

1. Create a new Godot project.

2. Click 2D Scene in the Scene dock. Godot creates a Node2D as the parent node.

3. Click the Add Child Node (+) icon. A Create New Node window appears.

4. Click the Search text field, type Polygon2D, and then click Create. Godot creates a Polygon2D node as a child of Node2D.

5. Click the Create Points icon that appears at the top middle of the screen as shown in Figure 19-9.

*Figure 19-9. The Create Points icon*

6. Click the upper left corner of the game window boundary.

7. Click the lower left corner of the game window boundary.

8. Click the lower right corner of the game window boundary as shown in Figure 19-10.

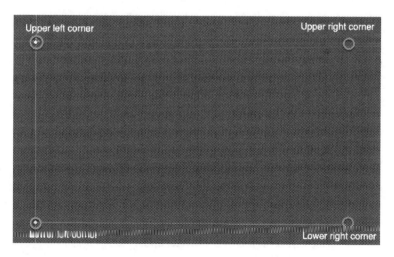

*Figure 19-10. Clicking the four corners of the game window boundary to define a polygon*

455

9. Click the upper right corner of the game window boundary.

10. Click the upper left corner of the game window boundary. Godot fills the polygon with a white color.

11. Click the Color property in the Inspector dock. A color dialog box appears.

12. Click a color. Godot displays your chosen color inside the polygon you just created. This colored polygon defines the background of the game playing field.

13. Click Node2D in the Scene dock to select it.

14. Click the Add Child Node (+) icon. A Create New Node window appears.

15. Click the Search text field, type Area2D, and then click Create. Godot creates an Area2D node as a child of Node2D.

16. Click Area2D to select it and then click the Add Child Node (+) icon. A Create New Node window appears.

17. Click the Search text field, type Sprite2D, and then click Create. Godot creates a Sprite2D node as a child of Area2D.

18. Drag and drop the icon.svg from the FileSystem dock into the Texture property in the Inspector dock.

19. Click Area2D to select it and then click the Add Child Node (+) icon. A Create New Node window appears.

20. Click the Search text field, type CollisionShape2D, and then click Create. Godot creates a CollisionShape2D node as a child of Area2D.

21. Click the Shape property in the Inspector dock. A pull-down menu appears.

22. Choose New RectangleShape2D.

23. Resize the collision boundaries to cover the icon. svg image.

24. Press Ctrl/Command+S to save the scene as a node2d.tscn file.

25. Click Area2D in the Scene dock to select it.

26. Click the Attach Script icon. Godot creates an Area2D.gd file.

27. Edit the Area2D.gd file as follows:

```
extends Area2D

func _process(delta):
        var velocity = Vector2.ZERO
        var speed = 500

        if Input.is_key_pressed(KEY_RIGHT):
                velocity.x += speed

        if Input.is_key_pressed(KEY_LEFT):
                velocity.x -= speed

        if Input.is_key_pressed(KEY_DOWN):
                velocity.y += speed

        if Input.is_key_pressed(KEY_UP):
                velocity.y -= speed

        position += velocity * delta
```

28.  Click the Run icon and choose Select Current
     to make the current scene the main scene. The
     (DEBUG) window appears.

29.  Press the up/down, left/right keys to move the icon.
     svg image around. Notice that if you move off the
     game window boundary (top, bottom, left, or right),
     the icon.svg image disappears.

30.  Click the close icon in the (DEBUG) window to
     make it go away.

The icon.svg image disappears from off the game window boundary
because we don't have a camera to follow the player. With a camera, we
can follow the player wherever it moves.

To add a camera, follow these steps:

1.  Make sure the previous Godot project is loaded,
    which lets you move an icon.svg image against a
    colored background.

2.  Click Area2D in the Scene dock to select it.

3.  Click the Add Child Node (+) icon. A Create New
    Node window appears.

4.  Click the Search text field, type Camera2D, and then
    click Create. Godot creates a Camera2D node as a
    child of Area2D.

5.  Click the Run icon. The (DEBUG) window appears.

6.  Press the up/down, left/right keys to move the icon.
    svg image around. Notice that no matter where you
    move, the icon.svg image always appears in the
    center of the game window, even if you move past
    the original game window boundary, defined by the
    colored polygon.

7.   Click the close icon in the (DEBUG) window to
     make it go away.

The Camera2D node offers several properties you can modify to
change the way the camera works. The two most useful camera properties
are Enabled (selected by default) and Anchor mode (Drag Center by
default) as shown in Figure 19-11.

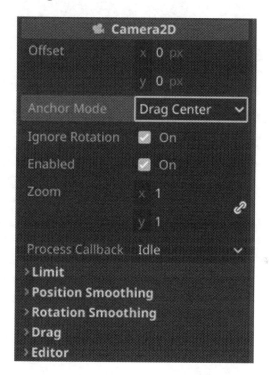

***Figure 19-11.***  *The properties of the Camera2D node*

Turning Enabled off simply turns the camera off. The Drag Center
option in the Anchor Mode property keeps the player object in the center
of the game window at all times. The other option for the Anchor Mode
property is Top Left, which keeps the player object in the upper left corner
of the game window at all times. In most cases, you won't need to change
either the Enabled or Anchor Mode properties.

One particularly useful property is the Zoom property, which is set to 1 for both the x and y properties. A higher Zoom property x and y value zooms in, showing less of the game playing field. A smaller Zoom property x and y value zooms out, letting you see more of the game playing field as shown in Figure 19-12.

*Figure 19-12.* *A lower Zoom property value shows more of the game playing field*

# Summary

Nodes represent building blocks, and a hierarchy of nodes defines a scene. When creating a game, you'll likely create separate scenes to represent different parts of the game such as a player, enemies, obstacles, and the user interface. By using GDScript code, you can make various objects move or rotate.

A scene can define a single object such as a player or an obstacle, but you can combine multiple scenes together to create larger items such as the main game playing field along with enemies and obstacles. The main idea behind Godot is that nodes offer specific features such as the Sprite2D node used to define an image and the CollisionShape2D node used to define the boundaries.

By combining nodes, you can create a scene to define a single object. Then you can combine multiple scenes to create more complex scenes such as a game playing field. By dividing a large project into multiple smaller objects, Godot makes it easy to create a game one piece at a time.

# CHAPTER 20

# Using Signals

No matter what programming language you use, the main goal is to break a large program into smaller parts known as functions. If the project is not broken down, then the program will be difficult to follow. At the simplest level, you can attach a GDScript to a node and divide that code into one or more functions. Some functions can run automatically when certain events occur, such as when the game starts. Other functions will only run when specifically called from other GDScript codes stored in the same file.

Calling functions within the same file is easy since you just have to specify the function name to run. However, one file may need to call a function stored in a different file. To call functions stored in another file, there are two possibilities as shown in Figure 20-1:

- A parent node calls down to a function stored in a child node.

- A child node signals up to a function stored in a parent node.

© Wallace Wang, Tonnetta Walcott 2024
W. Wang and T. Walcott, *Programming for Game Design*,
https://doi.org/10.1007/979-8-8688-0190-7_20

Calling down to a
function stored lower
in a node hierarchy.

Signaling up to a
function stored higher
in a node hierarchy.

*Figure 20-1.* *Two ways to call a function attached to a different node*

To call down to a function stored lower in a node hierarchy, you must specify the node that contains the function you want followed by the function name.

To signal up to a function stored higher in a node hierarchy, you must use signals. First, you must specify the function name you want to call. Then you must connect that function into a GDScript file attached to a node higher in the node hierarchy.

# Calling Down to a Function

Since Godot lets you create scenes in isolation from other scenes, any GDScript code you attach to a node won't know of the existence of any other GDScript code. So before you can call down to a function stored in a node lower in a hierarchy, you must first add a scene to a bigger scene where each node represents a complete scene.

In the following project, we'll create two separate scenes. One scene will define a simple user interface to display a number. The second scene will contain this user interface and display a Button that lets us increment the number on the user interface.

To see how to call down to a function, follow these steps:

1. Create a new Godot project.

2. Click Other Node in the Scene dock. A Create New Node dialog box appears.

3. Click the Search text field, type Control, and then click Create. Godot creates a Control node as the parent node in the Scene dock.

4. Double-click Control in the Scene dock and change the name to HUD.

5. Click the Add Child Node (+) icon. A Create New Node window appears.

6. Click the Search text field, type Label, and then click Create. Godot creates a Label node as a child of HUD (Control).

7. Resize the Label to make it larger.

8. Click the Text property in the Inspector dock and type 0. A 0 appears in the Label. Notice that the 0 appears small.

9. Click the Label Settings property in the Inspector dock. A pull-down menu appears as shown in Figure 20-2.

***Figure 20-2.*** *The Label Settings menu in the Inspector dock*

10. Choose New LabelSettings. The Label Settings property now displays LabelSettings.

11. Click LabelSettings in the Label Settings property. Godot displays a list of additional properties as shown in Figure 20-3.

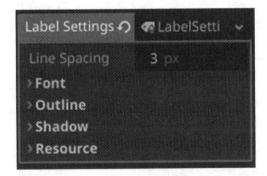

***Figure 20-3.*** *The additional properties displayed in Label Settings*

12.  Click the arrow to the left of Font. A list of Font properties appears as shown in Figure 20-4.

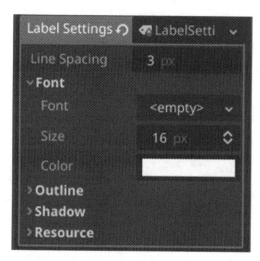

***Figure 20-4.*** *The additional Font properties*

13.  Click the Size property and change it to a larger value such as 32. Notice that the 0 in the Label now looks bigger.

14.  Press Ctrl/Command+S to save the hud.tscn file.

15.  Click HUD in the Scene dock to select it.

16.  Click the Attach Script icon to create a hud.gd file.

17.  Edit this hud.gd file as follows:

```
extends Control

func update_score(score):
    $Label.text = str(score)
```

The hud.gd file receives a number (score) and converts it into a string (str) to display it in the text property of the Label node.

18.  Press Ctrl/Command+S to save the hud.gd file.

This completes the hud.tscn scene that displays a simple user interface. Now let's create another scene to display a Button that will increment the number displayed in the hud.tscn scene.

To create another scene, follow these steps:

1.  Make sure the previous Godot project is loaded, which contains a hud.tscn file.

2.  Choose Scene ➤ New Scene.

3.  Click Other Node in the Scene dock. A Create New Node dialog box appears.

4.  Click the Search text field, type Node, and then click Create. Godot creates Node as the parent node in the Scene dock.

5.  Double-click Node in the Scene dock and change the name to Main.

6.  Click the Add Child Node (+) icon. A Create New Node window appears.

7.  Click the Search text field, type Button, and then click Create. Godot creates a Button node as a child of Main (Node).

8.  Resize the Button and move it away from the upper left corner of the game window.

9.  Click the Text property in the Inspector dock and type Increment.

10.   Press Ctrl/Command+S to save the main.tscn file.

11.   Click the Main parent node in the Scene dock to select it.

12.   Click the Attach Script icon to create a main.gd file.

13.   Click the Button in the Scene dock to select it.

14.   Click the Node tab in the Inspector dock.

15.   Double-clicked **pressed()**. A Connect a Signal to a Method dialog box appears as shown in Figure 20-5.

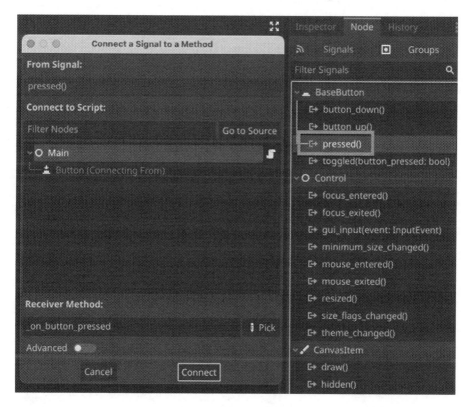

***Figure 20-5.*** *Connecting the pressed() function to the Main node*

16.   Make sure Main is selected and click Connect. Godot adds an _on_button_pressed() function in the main.gd file.

17.   Press Ctrl/Command+S to save the main.gd file.

At this point, we've created two separate scenes. Now it's time to combine the hud.tscn into the main.tscn and call the update_score function stored in the hud.gd file:

1.   Make sure the previous Godot project is loaded, which consists of two scenes: hud.tscn and main.tscn.

2.   Click 2D near the top middle of the screen.

3.   Double-click the main.tscn file in the FileSystem dock. Godot displays the main.tscn scene in the Scene dock.

4.   Drag and drop the hud.tscn from the FileSystem dock on to Main in the Scene dock. This makes the hud.tscn scene a child of the Main node as shown in Figure 20-6. Notice that since HUD is a child of Main, the main.gd file (attached to the Main node) can call down to the function stored in the hud.gd file (attached to the HUD node).

***Figure 20-6.*** *The node hierarchy of the main.tscn scene after adding the hud.tscn scene*

5. Double-click the main.gd file in the FileSystem dock. Godot displays the main.gd file.

6. Edit the main.gd file as follows:

```
extends Node

var score: int = 0

func _on_button_pressed():
        score += 1
        $HUD.update_score(score)
```

This code creates a variable called "score," which is defined as an integer with an initial value of 0. Within the _on_Button_pressed() function, the code increments the value of score by 1 (score += 1). Then it calls down to the $HUD node to call the update_score function, which is stored in the hud.gd file that's attached to the HUD parent node.

7. Click the Run icon and choose Select Current when Godot asks which scene to set as the main scene. A (DEBUG) window appears.

8. Click the Increment Button. Notice that each time you click the Increment Button, the number increments in the upper left corner where the Label node appears.

9. Click the close icon of the (DEBUG) window to make it go away.

# Signaling Up

In the previous example, we saw how to call down to run a function stored in a node lower in the hierarchy. However, sometimes you may need to call a function stored in a node higher in the hierarchy. You can't simply specify the node name and function name such as $HUD.update_score(score) because nodes lower in a hierarchy can't directly access nodes that are higher in the hierarchy.

Instead, we have to use signals. First, we need to define the function name we want to access using the Signal keyword. Second, we need to call that function by using the emit_signal command. Third, we need to connect the signal from one .gd file to another higher up in the hierarchy. Signals are sometimes needed to track certain events within a game.

To see how to use signals, we'll create a simple game that keeps track of collisions. If a player collides with treasure, they get a point. Then the game displays the number of collisions on the screen.

Tracking collisions involves several steps:

- Detecting the collision

- Counting the collision

- Displaying the results on the user interface

Detecting collisions can occur by assigning objects to a group name and then detecting whether the player collided with any item in a specific group. Each time a collision with a specific object occurs, the GDScript code needs to increment a variable. Finally, the user interface must update to display the latest results. In many games, collisions can be used to detect enemies or other objects so that if the player collides, there will be different interactions.

Our project will consist of the following scenes:

- Main.tscn that will hold all other scenes as children

- HUD.tscn that will display a Label on the user interface

- Player.tscn that will define a player object that can move

- Treasure.tscn that will act as treasures for the player to hit and get points that will appear in the Label of the HUD.tscn file

To see how to use signals, follow these steps:

1. Create a new Godot project.

2. Click Other Node in the Scene dock. A Create New Node dialog box appears.

3. Click in the Search text field, type Node, and then click Create. Godot creates a Node as the parent node in the Scene dock.

4. Double-click Node in the Scene dock and change the name to HUD.

5. Click the Add Child Node (+) icon. A Create New Node window appears.

6. Click the Search text field, type Control, and then click Create. Godot creates a Control node as a child of HUD (Control).

7. Click the Add Child Node (+) icon. A Create New Node window appears.

8. Click the Search text field, type Label, and then click Create. Godot creates a Label node as a child of Control as shown in Figure 20-7.

*Figure 20-7.*  *The node hierarchy of the HUD.tscn scene*

9.  Click the Text property and type 0.

10. Click the Label Settings property in the Inspector
    dock. A pull-down menu appears.

11. Choose New LabelSettings. Godot displays
    LabelSettings in the Label Settings property.

12. Click LabelSettings. Godot displays a list of
    additional properties such as Font, Outline, Shadow,
    and Resource.

13. Click the arrow that appears to the left of Font. A
    new list of additional Font properties appears.

14. Click the Size property and type a large number
    such as 32.

15. Press Ctrl/Command+S to save your scene as
    hud.tscn.

16. Click HUD in the Scene dock to select it.

17. Click the Attach Script icon. Godot creates a hud.
    gd file.

18.   Edit the hud.gd file as follows:

```
extends Node

func update_score(score):
        $Control/Label.text = str(score)
```

19.   Press Ctrl/Command+S to save the hud.gd file.

We created a simple scene to display a user interface along with a function called update_score(score). Now the next step is to create a treasure scene by following these steps:

1.   Make sure you have created and loaded the previous Godot project that contains a single hud.tscn scene.

2.   Choose Scene ➤ New Scene.

3.   Click Other Node in the Scene dock. A Create New Node dialog box appears.

4.   Click the Search text field, type Area2D, and then click Create. Godot creates an Area2D node as parent node in the Scene dock.

5.   Double-click Area2D in the Scene dock and change the name to Treasure.

6.   Click the Add Child Node (+) icon. A Create New Node window appears.

7.   Click the Search text field, type Sprite2D, and then click Create. Godot creates a Sprite2D node as a child of Treasure (Area2D).

8.   Drag and drop the icon.svg image into the Texture property in the Inspector dock.

9.  Click the arrow that appears to the left of Visibility in the Inspector dock. A list of visibility properties appears.

10. Click the Modulate property. A color dialog box appears.

11. Choose a color.

12. Click Treasure in the Scene dock and then click the Add Child Node (+) icon. A Create New Node window appears.

13. Click the Search text field, type CollisionShape2D, and then click Create. Godot creates a CollisionShape2D node as a child of Treasure (Area2D).

14. Click the Shape property in the Inspector dock. A pull-down menu appears.

15. Choose New RectangleShape2D.

16. Resize the collision boundaries to cover the icon. svg image.

17. Click Treasure in the Scene dock to select it and then click the Node tab and Groups in the Inspector dock.

18. Click the text field, type **treasure**, and press Enter.

19. Press Ctrl/Command+S to save the scene as a treasure.tscn file.

The preceding steps have created a simple scene that we can randomly place within a video game playing field. Now the next step is to create a player scene that we can move around. To create a player scene, follow these steps:

1.  Make sure you have created and loaded the previous Godot project that contains a hud.tscn scene and a treasure.tscn scene.

2.  Choose Scene ➤ New Scene.

3.  Click Other Node in the Scene dock. A Create New Node dialog box appears.

4.  Click the Search text field, type Area2D, and then click Create. Godot creates an Area2D node as parent node in the Scene dock.

5.  Double-click Area2D in the Scene dock and change the name to Player.

6.  Click the Add Child Node (+) icon. A Create New Node window appears.

7.  Click the Search text field, type Sprite2D, and then click Create. Godot creates a Sprite2D node as a child of Player (Area2D).

8.  Drag and drop the icon.svg image into the Texture property in the Inspector dock.

9.  Click Player in the Scene dock and then click the Add Child Node (+) icon. A Create New Node window appears.

10. Click the Search text field, type CollisionShape2D, and then click Create. Godot creates a CollisionShape2D node as a child of Player (Area2D).

11. Click the Shape property in the Inspector dock. A pull-down menu appears.

12. Choose New RectangleShape2D.

13. Resize the collision boundaries to cover the icon. svg image.

14. Press Ctrl/Command+S to save the scene as a player. tscn file.

At this point, we have three scenes: hud.tscn to create the user interface, treasure.tscn to create a treasure, and player.tscn to create a player we can move around. Now it's time to create a main scene that contains one player object and three treasure objects.

To create a main scene, follow these steps:

1. Make sure you have created and loaded the Godot project from the previous section.

2. Choose Scene ➤ New Scene.

3. Click Other Node in the Scene dock. A Create New Node dialog box appears.

4. Click the Search text field, type Node, and then click Create. Godot creates a generic Node as parent node in the Scene dock.

5. Double-click Node in the Scene dock and rename it **Main**.

6. Press Ctrl/Command+S to save your scene as main.tscn.

7. Click the Attach a Script icon (+). An Attach Node Script dialog box appears that will create a main.gd file.

8. Click Create.

9. Edit the main.gd file as follows:

```
extends Node

var score: int = 0
```

10. Press Ctrl/Command+S to save the main.gd file.

11. Click 2D near the top middle of the screen to display the contents of the main.tscn scene.

12. Drag and drop the player.tscn file from the FileSystem dock into the main.tscn scene.

13. Drag and drop the hud.tscn file from the FileSystem dock on to Main in the Scene dock.

14. Drag and drop the treasure.tscn file from the FileSystem dock into the main.tscn scene. Do this three times, so there should be one player object and three treasure objects in the main.tscn scene as shown in Figure 20-8.

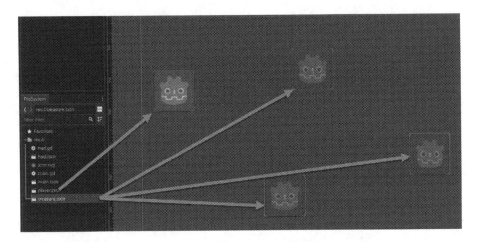

***Figure 20-8.*** *Adding a player and three treasures into the main.*
*tscn scene*

At this point, we have a hud.gd file and a main.gd file. We need to
create a player.gd file to move the player around. Plus within this player.gd
file, we need to create a signal to run a function that we'll store in the main.
gd file.

To create a player.gd file, follow these steps:

1. Make sure you have created and loaded the Godot
   project from the previous section.

2. Double-click the player.tscn file in the FileSystem
   dock to display it in the Scene dock.

3. Click Player in the Scene dock to select it.

4. Click the Attach Script icon to create a player.gd file.

5. Edit the player.gd file as follows:

   ```
   extends Area2D

   func _process(delta):
           var velocity = Vector2.ZERO
           var speed = 500
   ```

```
if Input.is_key_pressed(KEY_RIGHT):
    velocity.x += speed

if Input.is_key_pressed(KEY_LEFT):
    velocity.x -= speed

if Input.is_key_pressed(KEY_DOWN):
    velocity.y += speed

if Input.is_key_pressed(KEY_UP):
    velocity.y -= speed

position += velocity * delta
```

6. Click Player in the Scene dock to select it and then click the Node tab in the Inspector dock.

7. Double-click area_entered(area: Area2D). A Connect a Signal to a Method dialog box appears as shown in Figure 20-9.

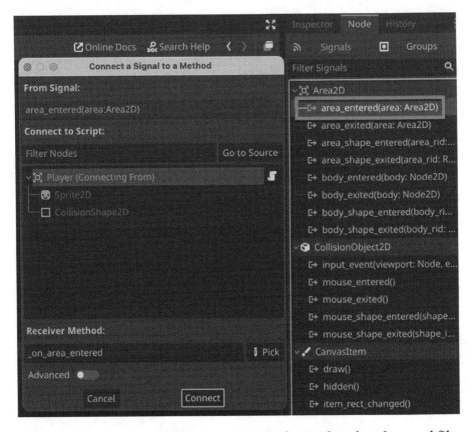

***Figure 20-9.*** *Connecting the area_entered signal to the player.gd file*

8.  Make sure Player is selected in the Connect a Signal
    to a Method dialog box and click Connect. Godot
    creates an _on_area_entered(area) function.

9.  Edit this _on_area_entered(area) function as follows:

```
func _on_area_entered(area):
    if area.is_in_group("treasure"):
        area.hide()
        emit_signal("update_display")
```

10.  Add the following underneath "extends Area2D":

```
signal update_display
```

The entire player.gd file should look like this:

```
extends Area2D
signal update_display

func _process(delta):
     var velocity = Vector2.ZERO
     var speed = 500

     if Input.is_key_pressed(KEY_RIGHT):
         velocity.x += speed

     if Input.is_key_pressed(KEY_LEFT):
         velocity.x -= speed

     if Input.is_key_pressed(KEY_DOWN):
         velocity.y += speed

     if Input.is_key_pressed(KEY_UP):
         velocity.y -= speed

     position += velocity * delta

func _on_area_entered(area):
     if area.is_in_group("treasure"):
         area.hide()
         emit_signal("update_display")
```

11.  Press Ctrl/Command+S to save the player.gd file.
     Notice that by adding the "signal update_display"
     line near the top of the player.gd file, the update_
     display function now appears in the Signals group in
     the Inspector dock as shown in Figure 20-10.

***Figure 20-10.*** *The update_displays function appears in Signals*

We've created a separate main.gd, hud.gd, and player.gd file. Within the player.gd file, we defined a signal called update_display. Now we need to connect this update_display signal to the main.gd file.

To connect a signal from the player.gd file to the main.gd file, follow these steps:

1. Make sure you have created and loaded the Godot project from the previous section.

2. Double-click the main.tscn file in the FileSystem dock to display it in the Scene dock.

3. Click Player in the Scene dock to select it. The Player scene, three Treasure scenes, and the HUD scene should all be children of the Main scene as shown in Figure 20-11.

***Figure 20-11.*** *The hierarchy of the main.tscn scene*

4. Click the Node tab in the Inspector dock and then click Signals.

5. Double-click update_display(). A Connect a Signal to a Method dialog box appears as shown in Figure 20-12.

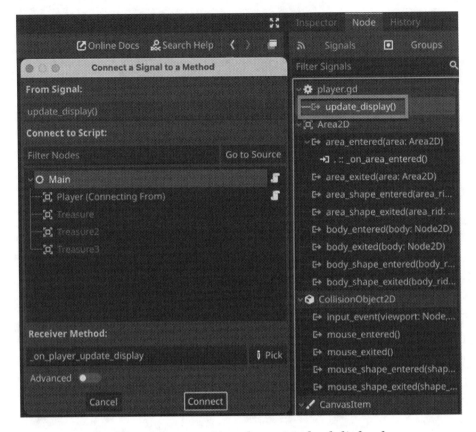

*Figure 20-12.* *The Connect a Signal to a Method dialog box*

6.  Make sure Main is selected in the Connect a Signal
    to a Method dialog box and click Connect. Godot
    adds an _on_player_update_display() function
    inside the main.gd file.

7.  Edit the main.gd file as follows:

```
extends Node

var score: int = 0
```

```
func _on_player_update_display():
    score += 1
    $HUD.update_score(score)
```

This _on_player_update_display() function connects to the signal defined in the player.gd file. This function increments the score variable by one and sends the result to the update_score(score) function stored in the hud.gd file.

8. Click the Run icon and choose Select Current when Godot asks which scene to set as the main scene. A (DEBUG) window appears.

9. Press the up/down, left/right arrow keys to move the player object around the screen. Notice that each time the player collides with a treasure object, the treasure object disappears, and the score gets updated by 1 in the Label displayed in the upper left corner of the screen.

10. Click the close icon of the (DEBUG) window to make it go away.

# Summary

Functions can be stored in separate files. When calling a function within the same .gd file, you just need to use the function name. When you want to call a function stored in a separate file, you have two options:

- Call down – If the function is stored in a .tscn scene file that's a child of the node doing the calling, call the scene file by name and then the function name such as $HUD.update_score().

- Signal up – If the function is stored in a .tscn scene file
  that's a parent of the node doing the calling, use signals.
  Define the function name in the child node, and
  connect it to the parent node.

By keeping functions separated in different files, you can keep related code together and isolate them from other code. By calling functions stored in other files, you can reuse code.

# CHAPTER 21

# Creating a Simple Tic-Tac-Toe Game

So far, you've learned some of the important elements used to make a basic video game such as shooting projectiles and writing GDScript to make those projectiles possible. With Godot, making any game is possible, even the game Tic-Tac-Toe.

Tic-Tac-Toe is a classic game that was created in 1884. Traditionally, the game is played on paper with a 3x3 grid for two players. One player is an "X," while the other is an "O." The goal of Tic-Tac-Toe is for one of players to either get three Xs or three Os in a row, in a column, or diagonally. Tic-Tac-Toe plays quick, yet it's simple and fun at the same time. Though it is usually played on paper, it can also be played online by computer. In this chapter, you'll learn how to make a Tic-Tac-Toe game using Godot.

To make the Tic-Toe-Game through Godot, you'll need three images as shown in Figure 21-1:

- An image of a Tic-Tac-Toe 3 by 3 grid

- An image of an "X" Tic-Tac-Toe symbol

- An image of an "O" Tic-Tac-Toe symbol

© Wallace Wang, Tonnetta Walcott 2024
W. Wang and T. Walcott, *Programming for Game Design*,
https://doi.org/10.1007/979-8-8688-0190-7_21

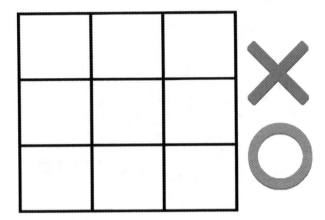

***Figure 21-1.***   *The three images needed to make a Tic-Tac-Toe game*

You can create these three images using a graphics editor such as Photoshop, or simply search the Internet for a 3 by 3 grid, an X and an O or any other images you want to use.

To see how to display the Tic-Tac-Toe grid, follow these steps:

1.  Create a new Godot project.

2.  Drag and drop the three images (grid, X, and O) that you created or downloaded from the Internet into the FileSystem dock.

3.  Click 2D Scene in the Scene dock. Godot creates a Node2D node as the parent node in the Scene dock.

4.  Double-click Node2D and change its name to Board.

5.  Click the Add Child Node (+) icon. A Create New Node window appears.

6.  Click the Search text field, type Sprite2D, and then click Create. Godot creates a Sprite2D node as a child of Board (Node2D).

7.  Drag your grid image into the Texture property in
    the Inspector dock. Godot displays the grid in the
    upper left corner of the game window as shown in
    Figure 21-2.

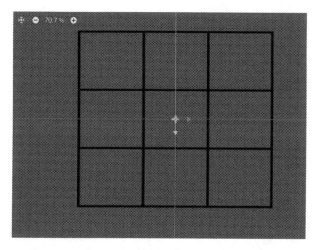

***Figure 21-2.*** *The default location of the playing board in the*
*game window*

8.  Press Ctrl/Command+S to save your scene as a
    board.tscn file.

# Detecting Clicks on the Board

Since this version of Tic-Tac-Toe runs on a computer, we'll need to make
the board functional by making the positions on the board clickable. Once
we can click around on the board, we can place the X and O symbols in
specific locations.

To see how to detect the position of a mouse click, follow these steps:

1.  Make sure the previous Godot project is loaded, which displays the Tic-Tac-Toe board.

2.  Click Board (Node2D) in the Scene dock to select it.

3.  Click the Attach a Script icon. Godot creates a board. gd file.

4.  Edit the board.gd file as follows:

```
extends Node2D

func _input(event):
    if event is InputEventMouseButton:
        if event.button_index == MOUSE_BUTTON_LEFT and
        event.pressed:
            print(event.position)
```

5.  Press Ctrl/Command+S to save the board.gd file.

6.  Click the Run icon and choose Select Current when Godot asks which scene to set as the main scene. A (DEBUG) window appears.

7.  Click anywhere inside the game window. Notice that Godot prints the x and y coordinates in the Output dock as shown in Figure 21-3.

*Figure 21-3. Displaying the location of mouse clicks*

8. Click the close icon of the (DEBUG) window to make it go away.

Functions do something specific within a program. For example, the ready() function runs automatically every time the node loads. So "func _ready():" generally runs certain commands to initialize variables or set up a game before it starts running.

Godot provides many functions that respond to certain events. This project uses "func _input(event) to respond to the user's input and trigger a certain event. Because we want players to click the board, the code checks to see if the event is using a mouse with the phrase:

```
if event is InputEventMouseButton
```

Then "func _input(event)" checks if the left mouse button has been pressed or clicked:

```
if event.button_index == MOUSE_BUTTON_LEFT and event.pressed
```

This line specifically makes the board clickable. The "print(event. position)" command simply prints the position where you clicked on the board that consists of an x and y value.

# Displaying Player Moves

In the previous example, we were able to click around on the board. Now it's time to display the "X" and "O" symbols on the board. To display the symbols, we'll create a function to place a symbol on the board whenever it is clicked.

In previous projects, we created scenes separately, but Godot also lets you create nodes and turn them into separate scenes. We'll use this technique as just another way to create separate scenes in a project.

To see how to create symbols for our game, follow these steps:

1.  Make sure you have loaded the previous Godot project that displays a game grid on the screen and prints the location of where the user clicked the mouse. You should also have a graphic image for the X and O symbols stored in the FileSystem dock.

2.  Click Board as the parent node in the Scene dock.

3.  Click the Add Child Node (+) icon. A Create New Node window appears.

4.  Click in the Search text field, type Sprite2D, and then click Create. Godot creates a second Sprite2D node as a child of Board.

5.  Drag and drop the image for the X symbol into the Texture property. Godot displays the X symbol image on the screen.

6.  Double-click Sprite2D node that displays the X symbol image and rename it as x.

7.  Right-click the x (Sprite2D) node. A pop-up menu appears as shown in Figure 21-4.

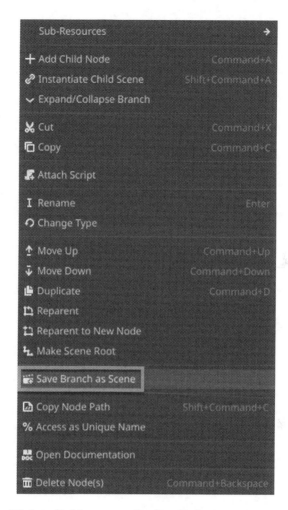

*Figure 21-4. Right-clicking a node displays a pop-up menu*

8.  Choose Save Branch as Scene. A Save New Scene As dialog box appears.

9.  Click Save to save the node as a scene called x.tscn.

10. Right-click the x (Sprite2D) node, and when a pop-up menu appears, choose Delete node(s). A dialog box appears to confirm deleting the node.

11. Click OK.

12. Repeat steps 2–11 except use the O image and rename the Sprite2D node as o to save it as an o.tscn file. You should now have an o.tscn and an x.tscn file stored in the FileSystem dock as shown in Figure 21-5.

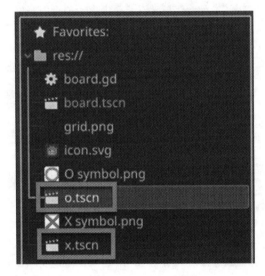

***Figure 21-5.***  *An o.tscn and an x.tscn file in the FileSystem dock*

We created two separate scenes (x.tscn and o.tscn). The Scene dock should contain nothing but Board as the parent node and Sprite2D that displays the playing board. Now we need to make the X and O symbols appear when we click the board.

To see how to display symbols on our game board by writing GDScript code, follow these steps:

1. Make sure you have loaded the previous Godot project that displays a game grid on the screen and prints the location of where the user clicked the mouse. You should also have an x.tscn and o.tscn file stored in the FileSystem dock.

2. Click the script icon that appears to the right of Board as the parent node in the Scene dock. (Or double-click board.gd in the FileSystem dock). Godot displays the contents of the board.gd file.

3. Add the following function in the board.gd file as follows:

```
func createSymbol(next_player, new_position):
    if next_player == 1:
        var createX = preload("res://x.tscn")
        var getX = createX.instantiate()
        add_child(getX)
        getX.position = new_position
    else:
        var createCircle = preload("res://o.tscn")
        var getCircle = createCircle.instantiate()
        add_child(getCircle)
        getCircle.position = new_position
```

This code loads the X or U symbol and places it on the game board. The createSymbol function passes the values of "player" and "position." Notice that we can load a .tscn scene by using the preload command. Once we load a .tscn file, we instantiate that file, which makes a copy of that .tscn scene.

The add_child() method takes the .tscn file, and then the position property places it on the screen. Right now the createSymbol function never gets called, so we need to call it within the _input(event) function.

4.  Edit the board.gd file as follows:

```
func _input(event):
        if event is InputEventMouseButton:
                if event.button_index == MOUSE_BUTTON_LEFT
                and event.pressed:
                        # print(event.position)
                        createSymbol(player, event.position)
                        updatePlayer()
```

This code calls the createSymbol function along with another function called updatePlayer(0, which we'll need to create.

5.  Edit the board.gd file to add the updatePlayer() function as follows:

```
func updatePlayer():
        if player == 1:
                player = 2
        else:
                player = 1
```

This code simply alternates between player 1 and player 2. Notice that this updatePlayer() function uses a variable called "player," which doesn't exist yet. So we need to declare a "player" variable in the next step.

6.  Edit the board.gd file to add the following underneath the "extends Node2D" line:

```
var player: int = 1
```

This code defines a "player" variable as an integer data type and sets its initial value to 1.

7.  Click the Run icon. Notice that the game board still appears in the upper left corner of the game window. We could manually move it, but it's more accurate to move it to the center of the game window using GDScript code.

8.  Click the close icon of the (DEBUG) window to make it go away.

First, we need to move the board to the center of the game window. We can do that by simply placing the board in the center.

9.  Edit the board.gd file as follows:

```
extends Node2D

var player: int = 1
var screensize: Vector2
var offset: Vector2

func _ready():
        screensize = get_viewport().get_visible_rect().size
        position = screensize/2
        offset = position
```

10.  Edit the createSymbol function in the board.gd file
as follows:

```
func createSymbol(next_player, new_position):
    if next_player == 1:
        var createX = preload("res://x.tscn")
        var getX = createX.instantiate()
        add_child(getX)
        getX.position = new_position - offset
    else:
        var createCircle = preload("res://o.tscn")
        var getCircle = createCircle.instantiate()
        add_child(getCircle)
        getCircle.position = new_position - offset
```

Notice that we need to subtract the value of "offset"
for the X or O symbol's position. That's because the
board has been moved to the center of the game
window, and without subtracting the offset variable,
the placement of the X and O symbols wouldn't
appear in the grid where the user clicked.

The entire board.gd file should look like this:

```
extends Node2D

var player: int = 1
var screensize: Vector2
var offset: Vector2

func _ready():
    screensize = get_viewport().get_visible_rect().size
    position = screensize/2
    offset = position
```

```
func _input(event):
    if event is InputEventMouseButton:
        if event.button_index == MOUSE_BUTTON_LEFT and
        event.pressed:
            print(event.position)
            createSymbol(player, event.position)
            updatePlayer()

func updatePlayer():
    if player == 1:
        player = 2
    else:
        player = 1

func createSymbol(next_player, new_position):
    if next_player == 1:
        var createX = preload("res://x.tscn")
        var getX = createX.instantiate()
        add_child(getX)
        getX.position = new_position - offset
    else:
        var createCircle = preload("res://o.tscn")
        var getCircle = createCircle.instantiate()
        add_child(getCircle)
        getCircle.position = new_position - offset
```

11.  Click the Run icon.

12.  Click the board. Notice that each time you click,
     the game alternates between displaying an X and
     O image.

13.  Click the close icon of the (DEBUG) window to
     make it go away.

# Summary

Godot lets you make any game that you like from RPG, shooter, and fighting games to card games like UNO and Go Fish! This chapter showed how to create a simple Tic-Tac-Toe game with Godot and demonstrated several features of Godot:

- Right-clicking a node in the Scene dock lets you choose the "Save Branch as Scene" command, which lets you save a node as a separate scene.

- The input(event) function can detect a left mouse click.

- The preload command can load a .tscn file.

As a beginner, learning to code can seem difficult. However, by combining your interest in video games with programming, this book can help you learn the basics to programming that will apply to any programming language. Since programming and creating video games in particular can seem like massive projects, it's important to take small baby steps at a time. If you ever become stuck on a project, take breaks in between. Better yet, take a deep breath, and think of all the simple projects you've already created such as Tic-Tac-Toe.

The more you program and complete projects similar to Tic-Tac-Toe, the more you will learn about programming in general and Godot in particular. Tic-Tac-Toe is only the beginning of your game development journey. If you want to make games, go for it! The only limitations are your own imagination.

# Index

© Wallace Wang, Tonnetta Walcott 2024
W. Wang and T. Walcott, *Programming for Game Design*,
https://doi.org/10.1007/979-8-8688-0190-7

Printed in the United States
by Baker & Taylor Publisher Services